CW01083954

Grounding Concepts

Grounding Concepts

An Empirical Basis for Arithmetical Knowledge

C. S. Jenkins

OXFORD
UNIVERSITY PRESS

OXFORD
UNIVERSITY PRESS

Great Clarendon Street, Oxford OX2 6DP

Oxford University Press is a department of the University of Oxford.
It furthers the University's objective of excellence in research, scholarship,
and education by publishing worldwide in

Oxford New York

Auckland Cape Town Dar es Salaam Hong Kong Karachi
Kuala Lumpur Madrid Melbourne Mexico City Nairobi
New Delhi Shanghai Taipei Toronto

With offices in

Argentina Austria Brazil Chile Czech Republic France Greece
Guatemala Hungary Italy Japan Poland Portugal Singapore
South Korea Switzerland Thailand Turkey Ukraine Vietnam

Oxford is a registered trade mark of Oxford University Press
in the UK and in certain other countries

Published in the United States
by Oxford University Press Inc., New York

British Library Cataloguing in Publication Data

Data available

Library of Congress Cataloging in Publication Data

Jenkins, C. S. (Carrie S.)
    Grounding concepts: an empirical basis for arithmetical knowledge / C. S. Jenkins.
        p. cm.
    Includes bibliographical references and index.
    ISBN-13: 978-0-19-923157-7 (alk. paper) 1. Arithmetic—Philosophy. I. Title.
    QA248.J46 2008
    513.01—dc22   2008015452

Typeset by Laserwords Private Limited, Chennai, India
Printed in Great Britain
on acid-free paper by
Biddles Ltd., King's Lynn, Norfolk

ISBN 978-0-19-923157-7

10 9 8 7 6 5 4 3 2 1

Contents

Preface

This book is a philosophical discussion of arithmetical knowledge. This is a topic that has attracted philosophers in the western tradition for as long as the tradition itself has existed, and for good reasons. A heady philosophical mix is obtained when one considers arithmetic's richness of content, its apparent objectivity, its applicability to all aspects of the world, its seeming necessity, and the special certainty with which we think we know about it. Moreover there exists, to date, nothing which could be called a philosophical consensus concerning arithmetical knowledge, except in so far as it is fairly widely agreed that no extant account is fully satisfactory.

How do we come by arithmetical knowledge, and what sort of knowledge is it? It doesn't really seem like our everyday and scientific knowledge of the physical world; we do not learn arithmetical truths by looking, listening, or doing experiments, but by *thinking*. How, then, can it be knowledge of objective truths? Perhaps arithmetic is somehow created by, or dependant upon, the operations of our own minds? But why, if that is so, are we so convinced that the truths of arithmetic obtain independently of how things happen to stand with us? Might we, perhaps, have some special faculty which enables us to access an independent mathematical realm just by thinking? If so, why do we have no scientific understanding of the workings of this faculty, to compare with our understanding of our other knowledge-gathering mechanisms (vision, hearing, etc.)?

If we turn to the philosophical corpus for help, we are confronted with a dazzling proliferation of radically different proposals.[1] Traditional 'Platonists' tell us arithmetical knowledge is obtained through using a special faculty to intuit facts about arithmetical objects, which are independent of us but are not located in space or time. 'Intuitionists' tell us we are responsible for arithmetical truth; that arithmetical knowledge is knowledge

---

[1] The positions described in this paragraph are simplistically sketched and no doubt somewhat caricatured; my intention here is not accurately to represent any particular philosopher's view but to recreate the impression formed on first encountering the range of options available to an epistemologist of arithmetic.

of our own mental constructions. 'Structuralists' tell us it is knowledge of structures; 'logicists' tell us it is logical knowledge; 'empiricists' tell us that (contrary to appearances) it is a species of empirical knowledge like any other. 'Kantians' tell us that our sensibility imposes arithmetical structure on the world we experience, so that arithmetic can be known by reading off that structure from our experience. 'Formalists' tell us there is actually nothing to know, since arithmetic is merely a game played with symbols. 'Error-theoretic nominalists' tell us that, although there may be *something* to know, it is not the literal truth of arithmetical claims, since arithmetical claims (at least in so far as they imply that there are numbers) are literally false. 'Set-theoretic foundationalists' tell us knowledge of arithmetic is grounded in knowledge of set theory. The list goes on.

But each of these programmes, even if promising in some respects, raises philosophical questions as troubling as those it answers. Not one, or so it seems to me, is able to respect simultaneously these three strong pretheoretic intuitions:

(a) that arithmetic is an a priori discipline;
(b) that arithmetical realism is correct, i.e. that arithmetical claims are true independently of us;
(c) that empiricism is correct, i.e. that all knowledge of the independent world is obtained through the senses.

In this book I shall be investigating the possibility of a new kind of epistemology for arithmetic, one which is specifically designed to respect all of (a)–(c). I propose that we could develop such an epistemology if we were prepared to accept three claims:

(1) that arithmetical truths are known through an examination of our arithmetical concepts;
(2) that (at least our basic) arithmetical concepts map the arithmetical structure of the independent world;
(3) that this mapping relationship obtains in virtue of the normal functioning of our sensory apparatus.

Roughly speaking, the first of these claims protects apriorism, the second realism, and the third empiricism. Whether they might be made to add up to (the basis for) a promising account of arithmetical knowledge will, of course, be for the reader to decide.

Although my target is the epistemology of arithmetic, I think that the theory I propose may well be generalizable to other kinds of a priori knowledge—perhaps all of them. In effect, I am using arithmetic as an interesting test case for a new theory of the a priori. Because I hope the theory developed has application not only to arithmetic but to other kinds of a priori knowledge as well, this book is not aimed only at philosophers of mathematics, but at epistemologists of all stripes.

A word is thus in order here to reassure any readers who may be concerned that a discussion on the philosophy of arithmetic will abound with complex formulae and proofs, and be inaccessible to all but the illuminati of mathematical philosophy. My approach is not of this kind. Everyone who knows some basic arithmetic has first-hand experience of the kind of knowledge which presents the philosophical problems I am interested in, and in my opinion this suffices for a good deal more philosophical progress in this area than one might imagine when surveying the contemporary literature on the philosophy of mathematics.

Of course, the more mathematics one is familiar with, the more complex and detailed the questions one can consider, and the philosophy arising from consideration of such questions may be of great interest. But serious pursuit of various fundamental questions in the epistemology of mathematics demands no more of the reader than philosophical literacy and curiosity about her own knowledge that $7 + 5 = 12$.

In my opinion, one of the most important tasks currently facing a philosopher of arithmetic is that of securing a proper philosophical understanding of how the epistemology of arithmetic relates to the rest of epistemology, and to our understanding of the world in general. Global philosophical issues and issues in the philosophy of mathematics are intimately related, and philosophers of mathematics ignore this at their peril. Even when it is not explicitly related to mathematics, philosophical discourse on many topics may be highly relevant. For instance, almost any philosophical discussion of what knowledge is can offer something to anyone seriously interested in how we know that $7 + 5 = 12$.

Work on the Quinean 'indispensability' project and the 'neo-Fregean' programme associated with Wright and Hale are two traditions in the contemporary epistemology of mathematics which exemplify the kind of emphasis I wish to endorse on the consideration of fundamental questions within their broader philosophical context. In these cases, intense technical work[2] can proceed alongside discussion of the central philosophical underpinnings (which, of course, remain hotly disputed).

Another important influence behind the current work is that of the 'British empiricist' John Locke. Locke is not generally accounted an important philosopher of mathematics, and perhaps rightly so: his explicit concern with the subject is fleeting, and indeed he seems to have considered a priori knowledge in general unproblematic (resting content with the metaphorical claim that we can 'perceive' relations between our ideas). His philosophy more generally, however—in particular as concerns the relationship between ideas and experience—contains insights which I think the epistemology of mathematics would do well to revisit, even if Locke himself did not apply these insights to the philosophy of mathematics (or epistemology in general) in the most productive way.

Between first thinking about the central idea of this book about six years ago and completing the final version I have received help from numerous sources. Many people have contributed to the work and several of them gave me more suggestions, corrections, and comments than I have been able to do justice to in the final version, for which I apologize.

I would like to express sincere thanks to Simon Blackburn, Edward Craig, and Jane Heal for supporting my doctoral studies at Cambridge. Simon in particular is responsible for pointing me in the direction of swathes of relevant literature, and several passages in this book owe their existence to his suggestions and guidance. Thanks also to Bob Hale and Edward Craig for examining the doctoral thesis out of which this book developed, and for their many helpful comments thereupon.

I have benefited enormously in my thinking about these topics from philosophical interaction of various kinds with the following people: Arif Ahmed, Elizabeth Barnes, Ross Cameron, Dave Chalmers, Alix Cohen, Ben Colburn, Nick Denyer, Philip Ebert, Daniel Elstein, Hartry Field, Dominic Gregory, Katherine Harloe, Katherine Hawley, Aviv Hoffmann, Jeff Ketland, Brian King, Mary Leng, David Liggins, Aidan McGlynn, Hugh Mellor, Alex Oliver, Alexander Paseau, Michael Potter, Denis

---

[2] Feferman (1993), for instance, goes to great lengths to ascertain exactly how much mathematics is really indispensable. And technical developments of neo-Fregean ideas abound (see e.g. Hale 2000; Cook 2001; Ketland 2002).

Robinson, Gideon Rosen, Stewart Shapiro, Anna Sherratt, Neil Sinclair, Peter Smith, Daniel Stoljar, Neil Tennant, Ralph Wedgwood, Jan Westerhoff, Robbie Williams, Timothy Williamson, and Crispin Wright. Special thanks are due to Dave Chalmers, Aidan McGlynn, and Daniel Nolan, who gave me detailed written comments on late drafts of this book which helped me to improve many sections and, in some cases, to avoid silly errors.

Further insights have been gleaned from discussions with audiences in Cambridge, Oxford, Belfast, St Andrews, Stirling, Canberra, and Wellington to whom I've presented versions of parts of this work, and from anonymous referees for various journals. I would also like to thank Patricia Blanchette and a second (anonymous) OUP reader for their constructive comments on the manuscript as originally submitted. Many improvements were made at this stage as a result of their careful scrutiny.

The later stages of the work were completed at the Arché Research Centre at the University of St Andrews, and at the Philosophy Program in the Research School of Social Sciences at the Australian National University. I am very grateful for having had the opportunity to participate in the lively philosophical culture of these departments. My doctoral work and part of my time at St Andrews were funded by the Arts and Humanities Research Council, and my stint at the Australian National University was funded by the Australian Research Council. Many thanks are also due to Ole Koksvik, who helped prepare the index and spotted many typos, and to Peter Momtchiloff for his help and guidance during the publishing process.

I am especially grateful to Sue and Nick Jenkins, and to my friends, particularly Simon Betts, for all their support and kindness to me during the time I've spent working on this material.

Last, but not least, I want to thank my partner Daniel Nolan for everything in the fridge. I owe him far too many philosophical debts for me to acknowledge them all separately in the text; I have merely tried to record some of the more significant ones. On an aprofessional level he has also been one of my most significant sources of help and happiness whilst preparing this book.

Material related to some parts of this book (including earlier versions of some of the sections) has appeared in print in various places:

Jenkins (2005*a*) contains material related to Chapter 1;
Jenkins (2005*b*) contains material related to Chapter 4;
Jenkins (2006) contains material related to Chapter 3;
and Jenkins (2008*a*) contains material related to Section 2.4.

I am grateful to the editors of the *British Journal for the Philosophy of Science*, *American Philosophical Quarterly*, *Canadian Journal of Philosophy*, and *Croatian Journal of Philosophy* respectively for their permission to reproduce this material here. I would also like to repeat my thanks to everyone acknowledged in these papers.

There is a glossary of key terms at the end of the book to which readers may find it helpful to refer during the course of the book. I introduce a lot of new terminology for talking about the relationship between concepts and experience, and it will also help to be clear about the senses I am attaching to certain familiar terms like 'a priori'.

Introduction

The project

My goal in this book is to locate, as an attractive option in philosophical space, a new kind of arithmetical epistemology: one which respects certain important intuitions, hitherto considered to be in tension and impossible to satisfy simultaneously. These intuitions are apriorism, realism, and empiricism. Although I am very sympathetic to this kind of epistemology, I should make clear from the outset that I will not be attempting here to argue conclusively that it is the best approach, but only presenting and defending it as a live option worthy of serious consideration. One reason for this is that the approach differs sufficiently from its rivals to make it necessary to spend a good deal of time explaining exactly what it is, before taking on the task of arguing that it is correct. Another is that there are so many rivals out there as to make a thoroughgoing comparison another book-length task.

The kind of epistemology I shall develop here could, as far as I can tell, be extended to many—perhaps all—other kinds of a priori knowledge. Little is said about arithmetic that I would not also wish to say about (for instance) set theory and logic. However, arithmetic's accessibility to non-specialists and its obvious applicability to the physical world make it, in certain respects, particularly suitable as a starting point and, in certain respects, particularly challenging as a test case.

Mathematics in general presents itself as a difficult test case for accounts of a priori knowledge. For one thing, mathematics is a subject of serious study, the results of which are applicable to the world in ways crucial to the success of our scientific enterprises. These features make it difficult for philosophers to dismiss mathematical knowledge as, say, trivial (in the way that knowledge that all bachelors are unmarried might be thought to be trivial), or as any straightforward kind of self-knowledge. Arithmetic is especially challenging in so far as most people, mathematicians or not, have some arithmetical knowledge, and this renders inadequate (or at least incomplete) epistemological accounts which are only applicable to specialists or to those who have spent time reflecting on their sources of arithmetical justification.

I have restricted myself to discussing arithmetic for two main reasons. First, the application of the proposal to the whole corpus of mathematical knowledge (never mind the a priori in general) would require me to write much more than will fit into one book. Second, I want to write a book that is accessible to philosophers without a mathematical background. The current work is intended as a philosophical foundation upon which a more mathematically sophisticated edifice could later be built by those with the inclination and the ability. This is what I think the philosophy of mathematics stands most in need of at the present time.

A few words are in order here to explicate the three intuitions I shall be focussing on. The arithmetical *realist*, as I define her, is someone who believes that how things are with arithmetic is independent of how things are with us and in particular our mental lives. Realism in this sense is widely regarded as a natural and intuitive position, which should be rejected only if it turns out to be unsustainable. I share that view. I do not, however, plan to offer any substantial positive argument for arithmetical realism in this work. I am interested rather in examining whether realism can be *defended* against the objection that it is epistemologically implausible.

But I shall only be satisfied with an epistemological story which would be acceptable to an *empiricist*. An empiricist is someone who insists that all our knowledge of the world as it is independently of us must either be, or else ultimately rest upon, knowledge obtained through the senses.[1] She is motivated by the thought that there seems to be nothing, beyond sensory input, which connects us epistemically with the world as it exists independently of ourselves. In particular, she will brook no appeal to an unexplained faculty of rational or mathematical 'intuition' which supposedly enables us to access a mind-independent realm of logical and/or mathematical truth. For we have no scientifically respectable evidence

---

[1] The empiricist traditionally allows that knowledge of ourselves or of mind-dependent subject matters, such as knowledge of truths which are consequences of our linguistic conventions, need not depend upon any use of the senses.

that any such faculty exists. We know how the mind–independent world affects the brain via our sensory mechanisms, and hence we know at least something of how the senses can supply us with knowledge of that world. Surely, if there were another faculty, enabling us to access such truths in another way, we should have some similar evidence of its existence and some similar scientific understanding (however limited) of the way it was functioning.

To be an empiricist, in the sense I intend, is not (in Kantian terms) to attempt to reduce all understanding to sensibility, or (translating into lay terms) to attempt to reduce all thought to feeling. Of course, one might attempt such things and call oneself an 'empiricist' for so doing. And there are many other uses of the term 'empiricist'; for instance, it can be used to refer to people who merely emphasize the *importance* of experience as a basis for knowledge, and/or its importance to some other aspect(s) of our mental lives. Or it can be used to refer to those who believe (following Hume[2]) that every (bona fide) idea or concept is derived from some corresponding source impression(s),[3] or else the weaker claim that all our (bona fide) concepts are acquired in response to experience. (See Section 5.3 for some discussion of this last view and its relationship to empiricism in my sense.)

As with realism, I shall not offer any substantial positive argument for empiricism in this book. Rather, I shall attempt to face up to a key challenge faced by those who find empiricism attractive: that of accommodating arithmetical knowledge without either rejecting realism or diminishing the special epistemic status which arithmetic has relative to what are ordinarily called the 'empirical sciences' (physics, chemistry, etc.). An epistemological proposal will be philosophically unsatisfying if it fails to account for the fact that there is a difference in kind, not just some difference in degree, between our way of knowing that gravity draws massive objects towards the centre of the earth and our way of knowing that $7 + 5 = 12$.

This is the difference philosophers allude to by saying that arithmetic is knowable a priori and physics and chemistry are knowable only a posteriori. *Apriorism* is the third of the three intuitions which I try to respect in this

---

[2] See Hume (1748: sect. 2).

[3] Although I shall suggest that there are epistemically important relationships between arithmetical concepts and experience, I do not assume any simplistic one–one correlation between concepts and kinds of sensation (see Section 5.3).

book. However, the task of accommodating the difference between a priori and a posteriori knowledge is made more complex than it should be by a degree of terminological disarray in this area of philosophy. Terms like 'conceptual truth', 'analytic', 'synthetic', 'a priori', 'a posteriori', and so on have been defined in multifarious and incompatible ways. Faced with such a situation, the best one can do, I think, is to fix upon meanings for our key terms which, without departing from the spirit of the kinds of definition which are widely accepted, will allow us to make the important points as straightforwardly as possible. This will be my strategy.

In one strand of ordinary philosophical usage, 'a priori' knowledge is knowledge secured without epistemic reliance on any empirical evidence.[4] I shall follow this tradition. It is often further assumed (generally without acknowledgement that this *is* a further assumption) that a priori knowledge is knowledge which does not depend epistemically on the senses *at all*. Indeed, a priori knowledge is often *defined* as knowledge which does not depend epistemically on the senses at all (i.e. knowledge which is not empirical).[5] As far as I can ascertain, this sort of definition is usually no more nor less than an attempt to capture what is intended when we say that a priori knowledge is independent of empirical *evidence*. But, I shall argue, there is a significant difference between epistemic independence of empirical evidence and epistemic independence of the senses altogether.

The reason is that there is a possibility which has been overlooked: the possibility of a kind of empirical epistemic grounding which is not equivalent to grounding in empirical evidence. I shall suggest in this book that it is possible that arithmetical knowledge is epistemically independent of empirical evidence but not altogether epistemically independent of the senses. That is to say, it is possible that there is a non–evidential empirical source of epistemic grounding for our arithmetical beliefs. To anticipate, the idea will be that experience grounds our concepts (which is not the same as supplying evidence for any proposition), and then mere conceptual examination enables us to learn arithmetical truths.

This, I shall argue, makes it reasonable to describe our means of acquiring such knowledge as both a priori (in the sense of independent of empirical

---

[4] See Section 9.5 for discussion of this tradition in defining the a priori.

[5] To get a flavour of this see e.g. Kant (1781: A2/B2−3), C. I. Lewis (1923: 231), Kripke (1980: 34−5), and Casullo's 'most familiar negative analysis' of the a priori (Casullo 2003: 29). (The rest of Casullo's sect. 1.6 is also relevant, as is his ch. 2.)

evidence) and empirical. Many philosophers will initially consider this to be a contradiction in terms. I shall argue, however, that careful reflection on the core accepted meanings of 'a priori' and 'empirical' reveals that this *is* in fact a genuine possibility, one whose oversight has allowed philosophers to define 'a priori' carelessly as 'non-empirical'.

It is important to stress that I am not going to try and show that arithmetical knowledge is both a priori and empirical by appealing to definitions of 'a priori' and 'empirical' which make them *obviously* compatible. This sort of project has been attempted: Fisher (2002), for instance, argues that logic is 'modestly' empirical because it can be revised using a method conservative over the empirical evidence, but a priori because it cannot be revised using 'our best empirical methods (e.g. Bayesianism, hypothetico–deductivism)' (pp. 80–1). Alternatively one might propose that for knowledge to be empirical is for it to be rationally revisable in the light of experience, and for it to be a priori is for it to be known (however defeasibly) without reliance on experience. These also seem to be compatible properties (see e.g. BonJour 1998: 120–4 for discussion).

But 'a priori' and 'empirical' are not here defined in these ways. For one thing, I do not define either property in terms of revisability.[6] What I propose here is much more radical than the two suggestions of the previous paragraph. (Note that this is also different from the far less radical project of showing that there are both empirical and a priori ways of knowing the truths of arithmetic.)

Because of the possibility that our definitions are concealing important assumptions, we should, when pressed, be prepared to question what seem to be matters of definition. And realist philosophers of arithmetic *should* feel themselves pressed at the present time, because the single philosophical problem with which I intend to concern myself threatens to undermine all extant realist accounts of arithmetical knowledge. This is the problem of reconciling, on the one hand, the fact that our knowledge of arithmetic does

---

[6] I do not think aprioricity requires empirical unrevisability, and many (though not all) philosophers agree. For instance, Boghossian (1997: 333) writes:

On a minimalist reading, to say that the warrant for a given belief is a priori is to say that it is justified, with a strength sufficient for knowledge, without appeal to empirical evidence. On a stronger reading, it is to say that, and to say in addition that the justification in question is not defeasible by any future empirical evidence ... My own view is that the minimal notion forms the core of the idea of apriority.

For some discussion of the arguments for and against including an unrevisability condition see Jenkins (2008b: sect. 1).

not depend on empirical testing with, on the other, naturalistic pressure to regard the senses as our only source of knowledge about the world beyond ourselves.[7] Anti-realists can accommodate both pressures by arguing that arithmetical knowledge is not knowledge of the mind-independent world. But for those who share my view that realism has a strong pretheoretic appeal, anti-realism is a retreat position, enforced by the absence of a realist alternative. We should always be trying to do better. And if the realist is to respect both apriorism and empiricism, radical thinking of one kind or another will be unavoidable. There will be no conservative option. Moreover, it isn't only the realists who should feel pressure to re-examine what appear to be matters of definition in this area. As I will argue in Section 9.5 it is actually impossible for *anyone* to hold on to all the platitudes about a priori knowledge, if my suggestion of Chapter 4 is right.

Nothing much hangs on how we decide to use the term 'a priori' after appreciating this problem. I am happy to give up the term 'a priori' to those who are attached to the idea that being a priori is incompatible with being empirical. What matters is that the kind of arithmetical epistemology I propose makes arithmetical knowledge different in kind from ordinary empirical knowledge (of the physical world, of the laws of nature, etc.) whether or not it is well described as making arithmetical knowledge 'a priori'. I do think the best fit with extant usage demands that we call arithmetical knowledge both empirical and a priori on this view. But the real action is elsewhere.

The plan

Part I of the book deals with a couple of preliminaries to the central project: it attempts to set out first what I think realism amounts to, and second what I think counts as knowledge.

Chapter 1 aims to determine in exactly what sense we should be 'realists' about arithmetic; that is, exactly what kind of arithmetical 'independence' from the mind we should be interested in defending. This is no easy matter. One prevailing conception of independence is modal. Something

---

[7] Naturalism may also be consistent with there being innate knowledge, provided a naturalistic—perhaps evolutionary—story can be told to accommodate this. But see Section 8.3 for an explanation of why I do not think innate beliefs can count as knowledgeable.

is modally independent of us just in case it is possible for that thing to be the case without our being appropriately related to it (e.g without its being knowable by us). I argue in Chapter 1 that taking modal independence as characteristic of realism is a mistake, and we should instead characterize realism in terms of what I call 'essential independence'. Something is essentially independent of us just in case it is no part of *what it is* for that thing to be the case that anything about us is the case.

Chapter 2 has two aims. First, it discusses my commitment to epistem-ological externalism. Although this is important to the project, I shall not have much to say about it beyond exposition of my own definitions and views, as the relevant arguments have already been well exposed by others. Second, it discusses empiricism, about which I have more to say. It has often been claimed that empiricism cannot deal properly with the a priori. I describe the most common worries, and express sympathy with them; but I argue that, since the account of a priori arithmetical knowledge that I envisage is very different from the existing (and admittedly problematic) empiricist accounts of the a priori, the existing critiques do not apply. In this context I discuss problems for Boghossian's 'analytic' theory of the a priori in some depth, as it is a well-developed candidate for the sort of theory one traditional kind of empiricist might be attracted to. Later in this chapter, I also consider two alternatives to empiricism about the a priori, one developed by Peacocke and Bealer, the other due to Field. These seem to be two of the most attractive alternatives currently on the market, because they eschew traditional rationalist appeals to a faculty of 'rational intuition'. But ultimately neither offers a satisfying solution to the puzzles surrounding a priori knowledge. Empiricism thus seems to be motivated both by naturalistic concerns and by the impoverishment of alternatives.

I next attempt to sketch a general account of what counts as knowledge, against which background my discussion of arithmetical knowledge will (I hope) seem particularly plausible. This occupies Chapter 3. I propose that a subject A knows that p just in case p would be a good explanation of A's believing p to someone not acquainted with A's specific situation (an 'outsider'). I include this discussion in the hope of heading off at the pass any possible concerns as to whether the arithmetical epistemology to be developed later can be made to cohere with a plausible account of what knowledge is in general, and also to make clear what I think is really needed from an account of arithmetical knowledge. Mathematical epistemology can seem more difficult than it really is if we assume some theory of knowledge which cannot be made to not work in the mathematical case. (The classic case is Benacerraf's dilemma as originally conceived—see Benacerraf (1973)—which depends upon the assumption of a causal theory of knowledge.)

Part II forms the heart of this work: in this part, I attempt to show how we might go about developing the new approach to arithmetical knowledge mentioned earlier. In Chapter 4, I first argue that there is no objection to the claim that arithmetical truths can explain our arithmetical beliefs. Therefore, I suggest, there is no reason to doubt *that* we can have knowledge of arithmetical truths, according to the account of knowledge proposed in Part I. The way is therefore clear to consider *how* we could have knowledge of arithmetical truths; that is, to consider what the explanatory link between arithmetical truths and our arithmetical beliefs might look like.

This task occupies the remainder of Chapter 4. I assume that arithmetical truths are conceptual truths; that is, that we can tell that they are true just by examining our concepts (i.e. certain of our mental representations). But, I say, the epistemological story cannot end there. In order for an examination of our concepts to supply us with knowledge of an independent reality, it must be that those concepts are appropriately sensitive to the nature of that reality, or what I call *grounded*. A concept's being grounded in my sense requires that it (or, perhaps, the constituent concepts from which it is built) should accurately represent some feature of the independent world.[8] That is, groundedness requires that the concept be what I call *fitting*. But more is also required: just as knowledge requires more than truth, groundedness requires more than fittingness. In fact, I suggest that there is a very tight analogy between the two cases.

The core idea here—and indeed the core idea of this book—is that grounded concepts are like trustworthy on-board maps of the independent world.[9] By examining them, we can learn what the independent world is like. Although conceptual examination can be done in the armchair, it secures us knowledge of mind-independent subject matters such as arithmetic because information about the mind-independent world is

---

[8] In fact, there is a little more subtlety involved in the precise formulation of this notion. But this sketch will do to convey the general idea.

[9] Using map analogies to explain one's view is part of the realist tradition (see e.g. Wright 1986: 1–2). Thanks to Aidan McGlynn for reminding me of this.

encoded in our grounded concepts, and conceptual examination is nothing more or less than a way of recovering this information.

I then suggest that it is through the normal functioning of our senses that our arithmetical concepts come to be grounded. And I argue that, if this is so, then the ultimate source of our arithmetical knowledge is empirical. But because arithmetical truths are conceptual truths, there is no need to gather any empirical evidence for them, or conduct any empirical tests to confirm them. Thus they remain a priori by many traditional definitions. Sensory input plays a non-evidential role in underwriting our arithmetical knowledge: it grounds our arithmetical concepts, examination of which in turn grounds our arithmetical beliefs. This, I argue, is not the same thing as what happens when the senses supply us with evidence which confirms an arithmetical proposition.

Later in Chapter 4, I appeal to the indispensability of arithmetical concepts as evidence that they do in fact accurately represent features of the independent world. Chapter 5 then consists in development of some of the key ideas of the previous section. I begin by showing how an arithmetical epistemology along the lines suggested in Chapter 4 sits well with a structuralist conception of arithmetic and arithmetical concepts (although it is also compatible with other views). Then I caution against a simplistic understanding of the envisaged grounding relationship between concepts and sensory input. I go on to show how the proposed account would allow us to say that arithmetical truths explain our arithmetical beliefs in the right sort of way for those beliefs to count as knowledge by the lights of Chapter 3 and that it is consistent with realism as characterized in Chapter 1. Next, since I shall have appealed to the notion of unconceptualized sensory input in explaining concept grounding, I spend some time discussing this notion. I also offer some comments on ungrounded and unfitting concepts, which I hope will help to elucidate the notions of groundedness and fittingness of concepts.

In Chapter 6, I distinguish my project from other philosophical enterprises which bear some prima facie similarities to it. These range from linguistic conventionalism, through pragmatism, to Lockean empiricism. Finally, I offer some tentative explanations for the absence from the extant philosophical literature of the kind of epistemological proposal discussed in this book.

Part III is a discussion of objections to the project. Initially, I focus on objections to the claim that arithmetical concepts are empirically grounded.

In Chapter 7, I argue that the most common form of objection to projects of this type is based upon a failure to appreciate that it is even *possible* that empirical input grounds our arithmetical concepts. I trace this view through an illustrative selection of influential philosophers: Kant, C. I. Lewis, Ayer, Quine, and Fodor.

Chapter 8 is taken up with discussion of other, subtler, objections to the idea that arithmetical concepts have empirical grounding. These include some objections derived from McDowell, and some arguments to the effect that arithmetical concepts are too rich to be grounded in sensory input. One such argument appeals to certain results in empirical psychology which purport to show that arithmetical concepts (or even knowledge) are innate. But I argue that the question of innateness is at best tangential to my project (since the *origin* of a concept and its *epistemic status* are distinct issues).

In Chapter 9, I consider other objections to the proposal of Part II—ones which are not simply objections to the claim that our arithmetical concepts are empirically grounded. These include some objections that might be generated by a broadly Quinean outlook; a circularity worry (which I relate to the Wittgensteinian notion of 'deep nonsense'); and a number of issues concerning the epistemic step from possession of concepts to belief in conceptually true propositions. In this chapter, I also discuss in some detail the objection that, by definition, arithmetical knowledge cannot be a priori if it is empirical.

In my Final Remarks, I consider the relevance of the current project to other areas of philosophy, and some ways in which the ideas discussed warrant further research. Among other things, I argue that the notion of empirical grounding for concepts could have significant applications in many other areas. For instance, it suggests a new way to defend the position known as empirical foundationalism, and points to an empiricist theory of meaningfulness which (unlike the logical positivists' version) considers the relation between sensory input and concepts (rather than that between experience and propositions) to be of primary importance. The possibility of a novel defence of the correspondence intuition in the theory of truth is also raised, before I conclude with some larger-scale reflections on the significance of the book's main thesis.

PART I

Realism and Knowledge

1

Realism

1.1 Introduction

I want to defend arithmetical realism in this book, by showing that there is a convincing epistemology compatible with it. In order to do this, I must first make clear exactly what sort of realism I am interested in defending. Mathematical realism has been defined in multifarious, and at best loosely connected, ways. The term 'realism' might, with precedent, be applied to any of the following views (and others besides):

(1) Mathematics is independent of our mental lives.
(2) Distinctively mathematical objects exist.
(3) Mathematics is a process of discovery rather than creation.
(4) There could be recognition-transcendent mathematical truths.
(5) Classical bivalent logic is appropriate when reasoning about mathematics.
(6) Mathematical truths do not reduce to truths about provability.
(7) A mathematical proposition is true just in case it corresponds to the mathematical facts.
(8) It is possible that everyone is wrong about mathematics.
(9) Mathematical truth is conceptually prior to mathematical proof.
(10) Mathematics as currently practised is, by and large, correct.

Certain combinations of these views are also sometimes taken as definitive of 'realism'; (1) and (2) make a popular combination for this purpose.

When I say 'realism' I am only talking about view (1), and by 'anti-realism' I mean the view that mathematics is dependent upon our mental lives. This is a contrary view but not a contradictory view. Rejection of (1) could arise *either* out of the thought that mathematics is mind-dependent (anti-realism), or out of the thought that it is a mistake to say that mathematics is either mind-dependent or mind-independent. The latter might, for example, be the view of someone who thought that there were no mathematical facts or truths, and hence that mathematical truths and facts neither depend nor fail to depend on minds. Talk of mathematical 'objectivity' (at least when it arises in connection with realism) I take to amount to talk of mind-independence, and this I take to include independence of our language and our concepts.

One of the reasons that (1) is particularly interesting is that it has some unifying power: (3)–(9) can all be reasonably interpreted as consequences of, or ways of spelling out, what is intended by (1). I do not say that all of them *are* consequences of, or ways of spelling out, what I think is intended by (1). ((1) does not commit us to (5), for instance.) It's merely that all of (3)–(9) could be, and/or have been, thought of as such.

Views (2) and (10) are slightly different, however. Proposition (10) follows a common use of the term 'realism' in the philosophy of science to express the view that science as currently practised is by and large getting things right. This issue is orthogonal to the issue of whether (1) is true, and I won't be talking about it here.

More importantly for current purposes, the issue of whether (2) is true is also orthogonal to the issue of whether (1) is true. Realists in my sense may or may not believe in mathematical objects; the independent facts/truths of mathematics might be taken to be facts/truths about objects or they might not. The same goes for anti-realists in my sense. They may accept that there are mathematical objects; for instance, they might believe that there are mathematical objects which are constructed by us. Or they might think that we somehow construct mathematical facts/truths which are not about objects.

The most famous epistemological objection to mathematical 'realism' is pressing only if one decides to develop the realist intuition in a particular way. The objection in question is that knowledge of mind-independent mathematical objects is perplexing given that such objects are abstract and causally isolated. Benacerraf's dilemma challenges us to choose between denying that there is a causal condition on knowledge and denying that there are acausal mathematical objects to which our mathematical language refers and about which we are learning when we learn mathematical truths (Benacerraf 1973). In response it can be argued that the choice is not troublesome, because it is not too counter-intuitive either to refuse to accept causal conditions on knowledge, or to claim that the surface grammar of mathematical sentences is misleading. However, Field's attempt (1988) to reinstate something like Benacerraf's dilemma as a going concern poses a serious challenge: that of saying how we can be reliable concerning mathematics if we are causally isolated from its objects.[1]

Interesting though this challenge is, this sort of thing is only a problem if one decides to develop the realist intuition into the claim that causally isolated mathematical objects exist independently of our minds. This claim is, to my mind, far less intuitive and far less compelling than (1) alone.

By contrast, the difficulties which arise when we try to reconcile aprioricity with independence and empiricism arise through a clash of deeply intuitive views, none of which is easily set aside. There have been famous attempts to deny that mathematics is a priori (e.g. by Mill and Quine), attempts to deny that it is mind-independent (e.g. by Kant), and attempts to deny that empiricism is correct (e.g. by Peacocke and Bealer). But, as will become clear over the course of this book, I find all three manoeuvres deeply philosophically unsatisfying. And, more importantly, I do not think we have to choose one of them.

It might be suggested that the Benacerraf challenge and the one I am addressing are not really so different. After all, knowledge obtained through the senses is presumably knowledge obtained through some causal process. Hence, my attempt to reconcile empiricism about arithmetic with its other features bears some resemblance to the attempt to reconcile a causal constraint on arithmetical knowledge with certain other features of arithmetic.[2] However, the way causation is involved is importantly different. Causal conditions on knowledge typically require causation of belief by the facts, events, or objects known about. That is what is so problematic for knowledge of arithmetical objects, which do not seem to be the right kind of thing to enter into causal relations—whereas sense perception, while a causal process, can lead to knowledge without our beliefs being caused by the facts, events, or objects known about. Take ordinary cases of enumerative induction: I have seen and/or been told that

---

[1] It turns out that although addressing this challenge is not one of my aims here, the proposal of this book does suggest a possible response to it—see the second section of my Final Remarks. My reason for focusing on (1) rather than (2) is not that I think (2) is false or that it raises insuperable epistemological challenges. It is merely that these challenges are less central and less pressing than the one I aim to address.

[2] Thanks to an anonymous OUP reader here.

every chicken egg to have hatched so far has hatched into a chick, so I know that the next chicken egg to hatch will hatch into a chick. I have knowledge about this future event and the so-far-unobserved chick which is not caused by either. Yet it is obtained through the senses, via a causal process.

1.2 Essential independence and modal independence

Let me now specify in more detail the sense I attach to 'realism', by explaining what I take the 'independence' of arithmetical truth to consist in. In the literature on mathematical realism there is not often any detailed discussion of what exactly mathematical independence amounts to. This is significant because, as I shall argue, at least two importantly different readings are available. Their conflation generates confusion as to the nature and commitments of realism, and might even have been partly responsible for the emergence of scepticism as to whether realism is a well-defined position.

Realism about a subject matter is often defined as the view that truths or facts or states of affairs relating to that subject matter are mind-independent—that is, that they obtain independently of their being known, knowable, conceivable, or related in some other way to our mental lives. One question this raises is whether it is really (or primarily) truths, or facts, or states of affairs, or something else altogether, that the realist should take to be mind-independent. But I would like to try and sidestep this question here. In order to avoid taking a stand on such issues, let us (at least while we are being cautious) avoid talk of mind-independent truth, facts, and states of affairs, and simply talk neutrally about *something's being mind-independently the case*.[3]

Another consideration is that there are various mundane ways in which something's being the case can depend upon our mental lives without this automatically engendering anti-realism. I can be a realist about states of the physical world (e.g. states concerning the position of my desk) whilst acknowledging that there being a desk in my office depends in *some* sense

---

[3] At times it will be much less cumbersome to talk about mathematical truth or mathematical facts; readers may supply their own translation into this neutral vocabulary if desired.

upon the mental states of the people who designed that desk, manufactured it, and put it where it is in my office. Similarly, it seems, one can be a moral realist whilst acknowledging that the wrongness of kicking innocent passers-by depends in a mundane way upon the fact that it causes them pain. These mundane kinds of dependence on the mental are not supposed to entail anti-realism, even when realism is characterized as a commitment to mind-independence.

We should, however, acknowledge that it is not an entirely straightforward matter to say which kinds of dependence are mundane. Although we have clear intuitions in many cases, subtle issues are raised by consideration of (e.g.) realism about the mental, and realism about social matters such as the position of legal borders. Be that as it may, here it will be assumed that mundane kinds of mind-dependence can be identified and set aside. This should be easier in the philosophy of mathematics than elsewhere, since there seem to be fewer kinds of mundane mind-dependence here. (It would be far from mundane, for instance, to claim that someone designed and manufactured the number 4, and put it where it is between 3 and 5; or that what is the right answer to a mathematical question depends on how much human suffering is caused by each available answer.)

We should also note that in many cases the relevant debates concern independence not just from our mental lives as they actually are, but from the mental lives of any being with some finite extension of our cognitive powers. For instance, a certain kind of anti-realist would claim that something's being the case in mathematics is a matter of that thing's being provable by some finite being, albeit one who is far smarter than we are. For current purposes, I suggest we understand 'our mental lives' as including the mental lives of such beings, wherever appropriate.

Even with these points settled (or postponed), at least two significantly different readings of the mind-independence claim are available. On one reading, p's being the case[4] is independent of our mental lives iff it is no part of *what it is* for p to be the case that our mental lives be a certain way.[5]

---

[4] This 'p' is just a place-holder for things which are the case.

[5] Note that I do not intend the negation to have widest scope in the right-hand side of this biconditional. I intend the reading on which it is equivalent to: what it is for p to be the case has nothing to do with our mental lives. If the negation had widest scope, essential independence claims would be consistent with thinking that *nothing* is what it is for p to be the case, which I do not want to allow.

I call this sort of independence *essential independence* from our mental lives. Note that different species of essential independence claim may emphasize p's independence from different aspects of our mental lives (independence from provability, independence from knowledge, etc.), according to which aspect thereof is taken to be the best candidate for the aspect on which p's being the case depends. A typical essential independence claim about arithmetic is that it is no part of what it is for every even number to be the sum of two primes that this result be provable.

I take the notion of essential independence to capture the sense in which truths about trees, quarks, and planets are independent of our mental lives but truths about humour, love, and legality are not. I take it that, on an ordinary understanding, it is no part of what it is for trees to have roots that they can be known to have roots (or that this fact is in any other way related to the mental life of any intelligent being). But it *is* part of what it is for a joke to be funny that it would be found funny by at least some of us. Arithmetical realists, in my sense, are those who believe that nothing to do with our mental lives is any part of what it is for something to be the case in arithmetic.

On another reading, independence amounts to what may be called *modal independence*.[6] Something is modally independently the case iff, for all[7] aspects *x* of our mental lives, there is a possible world where that thing is the case although our mental lives are different with respect to *x*. Different kinds of modal independence claim may emphasize different aspects of our mental lives, as with essential independence, depending on what is taken to be the best candidate for the aspect on which p's being the case depends. A typical kind of modal independence claim about arithmetic is that it is possible that every even number greater than 2 is the sum of two primes although this is not provable.

Neither modal nor essential independence is assumed here to have any implications for whether or not one accepts bivalence for propositions about the subject matter under consideration. Those who are tempted by

---

[6] Fine (1994) provides a helpful analogue of my distinction between essential and modal independence. Fine argues that modal notions come apart from the notion of a thing's essence or *what that thing is*, much as it is argued here that modal notions come apart from the notion of *what it is* for something to be the case.

[7] Restrictions must be made here, as usual, to avoid interference from mundane kinds of mind-dependence.

certain modal or essential *dependence* claims may tend to find bivalence *un*attractive. For instance, if one thinks that, in mathematics, something's being the case amounts to, or is modally inseparable from, its being the case that that thing is provable, then one might consider it unlikely that every mathematical proposition is either true or false. For one might doubt that every mathematical proposition is either provable or disprovable; and, with the relevant dependence claim in place,[8] this doubt gives rise to a corresponding doubt as to whether every mathematical proposition is true or false. Those who reject such dependence claims will not have this sort of reason to be suspicious of bivalence. But that is not to say that they must accept bivalence, or that they will have no other reasons to reject it. To that extent, I eschew Dummett's characterizations of realism and mind–independence (e.g. 1963, 1982).

I should note that essential and modal dependence are merely two members of a larger family of interrelated notions of dependence which often are not clearly separated from each other. I take members of this family to include explanatory dependence, conceptual dependence (p is conceptually dependent upon q iff q's being the case is conceptually prior to p's being the case), metaphysical dependence (p is metaphys-ically dependent upon q iff q's being the case is metaphysically prior to p's being the case), and constitutive dependence (p is constitutively dependent upon q if q's being the case is what constitutes p's being the case).[9] The essential independence claim which I think characterizes realism is distinct from each of these other notions, as well as from the notion of modal independence with which it seems most often to be conflated.

Some philosophers, when they talk about 'what a truth is constituted by', might intend to talk about essential dependence rather than constitutive dependence as characterized here. I am not sure whether Peacocke (2004: sect. 7.4) or Wright (1997: 277), for instance, might intend this sort of reading. But it seems best to be clear at the outset about the difference between constitutive and essential dependence (though one may later choose to *argue* that they come to the same thing). In the same way that you might think a statue can be constituted by some clay but not essentially

---

[8] Together with certain views about the connection between the truth of not-p and the falsity of p.

[9] The convenient and ubiquitous phrase 'in virtue of' generally serves to indicate the presence of some member of this family, but often without much indication as to which.

made of that clay, you might think p's being the case could be constituted by q's being the case although q's being the case isn't part of *what it is* (in the essence sense) for p to be the case.[10]

A word is in order at this stage concerning the notion of essence which underlies essential independence. Essence raises deep and difficult philosophical questions which I cannot address thoroughly in this context. I am here attempting to argue that questions about essence are relevant to debates about realism, rather than to answer those questions. However, a few comments may help to avert misunderstanding.

First, it is not the essence of *objects* that is under consideration here. Rather, it is the essence of *something's being the case*. But although this is a non-standard use of the notion of essence, it does not seem particularly problematic. It is natural to understand, say, talk of *what it is for lying to be wrong* as akin to, say, talk of *what a person is*. Saying that it is of the essence of lying's being wrong that we have a certain emotive response to lying seems, at least until we have reason to think otherwise, recognizably similar to saying that it is of the essence of a person that she be a human animal.

Second, 'essentially', as I'm using the term, is obviously not supposed to mean the same thing as 'necessarily'. Essence claims in the sense I intend might be thought to explain certain corresponding modal claims, but I doubt whether essence is fully explicable in purely modal terms. For instance, suppose that what it is for a sunset to be beautiful is for somebody to find it beautiful. This might be taken to explain why it is not possible for there to be a beautiful sunset which nobody ever finds beautiful (more on this suggestion below, however). But I think this explanatory relationship would be asymmetric: the modal claim cannot be taken to explain the essence claim. This asymmetry is designed to respect a certain pretheoretic understanding of essence, which demands that we do not tie essence to modality in too simplistic a way. Intuitively, for instance, it is no part of

---

[10] There is an interesting question to be addressed here; namely, whether constitutive independence can be used to characterize a(nother) kind of realism. One feature of such a notion of realism is that the requisite constitution relation is somewhat hard to make sense of unless it is a constitution relation between facts. This makes it unsuitable for the purposes of the more neutral project I am trying to engage in; namely, a characterization of the mind-independence/mind-dependence debate which foists as few metaphysical assumptions as possible on the two parties. It may, nonetheless, be of interest for other purposes; I hope to address this question in further work.

what I am that I be such that $7 + 5 = 12$, although it is impossible for me to exist and not be such that $7 + 5 = 12$.[11] (See Fine 1994 for some more detailed considerations of this nature.)

Third, and finally, it is not obvious that essence in the relevant sense need be an a priori matter. In the same way in which one might think that being H_2O is a posteriori essential to water, so one might (for all that is said here) think that a joke's being found funny is a posteriori essential to its being funny. It could be that we need to do a lot of a posteriori empirical psychology to discover what is essential to something's being funny. At any rate, that is a possibility which I want to leave open.

The two notions of independence, essential and modal, are often not as clearly separated in the literature on realism and anti-realism as would be desirable. Sometimes it can appear as if anti-realism is being characterized as essential dependence and realism is being characterized as modal independence in the same breath. Dummett (1963: 147), for instance, says that 'for the anti-realist, the truth of the statement can only *consist in* the satisfaction of [evidential] criteria, whereas, for the realist, the statement *can be* true though we have no means of recognising it as true' (emphases added). This is not to say that Dummett is necessarily conflating modal and essential independence claims. He may not even be intending to characterize realism in modal terms. He may, for instance, be taking the realist's modal claim as a consequence of her characterizing view as to what the truth of the statement in question consists in. But it is far from ideal to mix modal and essential independence talk at the outset and without discussion.[12]

It is quite common to see mind-independence defined in modal terms and matters left there, particularly by those who are less than sympathetic to

---

[11] One might wonder whether the essential properties of an object could be characterized as the properties which are necessary and intrinsic to it. (Since I do not think they can, I leave open the question of whether and how this proposal might be extended to the case at hand, where what is at issue is the essence of something's being the case as opposed to the essence of an object.) I think the identification can be counter-exampled in both directions. Someone could reasonably believe, for instance, that I am not essentially a physical thing although I am necessarily and intrinsically a physical thing. Or one might believe that the extrinsic property of being born of my parents is essential to me.

[12] Although it is unusual to see modal and other kinds of independence clearly separated, an honourable exception to the rule is Peacocke, who defines the 'subjectivist fallacy' as the move 'from a premiss stating that certain mental states are sufficient, or stating that certain mental states are necessary, for a given content to be true to the conclusion that the truth of the content consists, at least in part, in something subjective or mental' (2004: 226; the remainder of his sect. 7.4 is also interestingly related to the present discussion).

realism. Wright (1986: 5), for instance, claims that to say truth is 'objective' or 'not of our making' is just to say that there could be truths which we could not know:

> To hold that a class of statements may be fully intelligible to us although resolving their truth-values may defeat our cognitive powers (even when idealized) may naturally be described as believing in the *objectivity of truth*. For such statements, truth is not 'of our making' precisely because it may defy our powers of rational appraisal.

This is not a statement of some idiosyncratic view as to what objectivity amounts to: it accurately captures a commonplace conception of objectivity or independence. But I don't think independence should be cashed out as modal independence, in the context of a discussion of realism. Essential independence is a view about the very nature of something's being the case: a view about *what it is* for that thing to be the case. Modal independence, on the other hand, merely concerns the possibility of that thing's being the case while something else is *not* the case. So modal independence appears to be, at the very least, less fundamental than essential independence. I shall argue in this section that it is also less suited to serve as definitive of realism. But first it is important to get clear as to how exactly the two notions of independence differ and how they are related to each other.

One noteworthy difference between the two conceptions of independence is that they yield different ways of spelling out the claim, often taken as characteristic of realism, that realism allows for reality (or the facts, or the truths, ...) to be 'recognition-transcendent'. Essential independence yields the claim that certain aspects of reality *would not cease to be what they are* if they were recognition-transcendent, whereas modal independence yields the claim that *it is a genuine possibility* that these aspects of reality be recognition-transcendent. There is scope for confusion here, so, just as it will not do simply to say that realists are those who are committed to 'mind-independence', it will not do simply to say that realists are those who allow for 'recognition-transcendence'. But this point is often not remarked upon. (To get a flavour of this, one could refer to Dummett 1963: 146, 1982: 230; Resnik 1997: 11; Blanchette 1998: sect. 1; Craig 1998: sect. 3; or Shapiro 2000: 29.)

Wright (1986: 3) proposes that

[w]hat seems essential [to realism] is the conception of truth as constituted by fit between our beliefs, or statements, and an independent, determinate reality. One way of making this conception more concrete is indeed to hold that the world may be determinate in … unascertainable ways. But it is very far from obvious that such is the only way …

This seems right in that it suggests that being a realist may not amount to admitting that recognition-transcendence is a genuine possibility.[13] But Wright still relies on the unexplicated notion of beliefs or statements fitting an 'independent' reality. Unless it is explicitly stated that *essential* independence is intended, slippage between essential and modal independence is liable to result.

Modal independence claims seem prima facie to be strictly stronger than the corresponding essential independence claims. If there are worlds where p is the case but our mental lives are not such that q, then it seems to follow that it is not part of *what it is* for p to be the case that our mental lives be such that q. In other words, modal independence implies essential independence. But the converse surely does not hold: it may not be part of what it is for p to be the case that our mental lives are such that q, yet there might for some other reason be no possible world where p is the case and our mental lives are not such that q (for instance, there might be no possible world where our mental lives are not such that q). In other words, essential independence does not imply modal independence.

If modal independence implies essential independence, then establishing modal independence is one way of establishing essential independence. Perhaps this would excuse the lack of separation between the two notions in discussions where the aim is to establish realism. But it would *not* excuse the conflation in discussions where the aim is to discredit realism. To discredit modal independence is to discredit something strictly stronger than essential independence; essential independence claims may therefore

---

[13] Two small reservations should be mentioned, however. The first is that Dummett's influence may be responsible for Wright's describing the realist's 'independent' reality as being also 'determinate'. Dummett certainly suggests in many places that realists are committed to determinacy in the sense that they are committed to bivalence for statements about the subject matter under consideration (see e.g. Dummett 1959: 175; 1975: 228). But I do not see why we need include anything of this kind in a definition of realism. The second reservation is due to the fact that, as will be argued shortly, there is a perspective from which it seems wrong to describe modal independence claims as a way of making essential independence claims 'more concrete'. (This is the perspective, to be discussed shortly, on which a modal claim and its corresponding essence claim are two-way independent.)

survive criticisms levelled at modal independence. (This point merits serious consideration if it is even plausible that essential independence is the distinctive commitment of realism, since it will not do to reject realism by arguing against only the stronger of two plausible interpretations of the realist's thesis.)

Before proceeding, it is worth noting that some philosophers seem to think of modality in a way that would falsify the claim that modal independence implies essential independence (and would therefore render the conflation of the two kinds of independence even less excusable, whichever side of the realism/anti-realism debate one is on). From this perspective, modal and essential independence appear to be two-way independent: neither implies the other.

Consider an constructionist philosopher of mathematics who is asked to imagine a possible world w with no people in it, and say whether $2 + 2 = 4$ at w. She may argue that she is at liberty to answer 'yes', provided she maintains that its being the case at w that $2 + 2 = 4$ amounts to nothing more than the fact that *she*, in assessing w, subjects it to the mathematical structure which she has constructed. She would then appear to be consistently accepting a kind of modal independence (whereby it is possible for $2 + 2 = 4$ to be the case at a world although mathematics is not constructed by us at that world) but rejecting the corresponding form of essential independence (by maintaining that what it is for $2 + 2 = 4$ to be the case is for us to construct mathematical structures of a certain kind). If this consistency is genuine, then modal independence claims do not imply the corresponding essential independence claims.

Whether or not it is genuine depends upon whether it is permissible for $2 + 2 = 4$ to be the case at w where this depends not upon intrinsic facts about w, but upon whether (and how) w is assessed by an actual being. A consequence of the line of thought ascribed to our constructivist is that one must believe that $2 + 2 = 4$ is the case at w although something which is essential to its being the case that $2 + 2 = 4$ is not the case at w. Some constructivists might find this too counter-intuitive, and prefer to say that $2 + 2 = 4$ is *not* in fact the case at w because nobody exists at w to perform the requisite mathematical construction. Saying that $2 + 2 = 4$ is the case at w because *we* are imposing our own mathematical constructions on w was intended to maintain the intuition that $2 + 2 = 4$ at uninhabited worlds, but perhaps our intuitions in this area can be sufficiently respected by claiming that *if* we inhabited worlds like w, *then* $2 + 2 = 4$ would be the case at these worlds.

The issue need not be decided here[14] (indeed, it may be that both perspectives have something going for them[15]); but it is worth noting that the perspective which gives rise to the claim of two-way independence also suggests an objection to characterizing realism as a commitment to modal independence. The objection in question is that, to assess the modal independence of p from q, we imagine possible worlds where p, and consider whether, at those worlds, q. But (according to this perspective) our thinking about possible worlds is done through the lens of our actual understanding. So arguments for modal independence obviously do not speak to the anti-realist's concerns. Her interest is not in what we can see *through* the lens of our own ways of understanding; what she claims is that, in the relevant respects, *the lens itself* is not created to fit with the structure of the world but rather imposes a structure upon it. Hence, our constructivist does not feel that her anti-realism (the view that mathematics is the study of a structure we create) is threatened by arguments for modal independence, which can be made without ever considering whether mathematics is the study of a structure we create. And if modal independence is compatible with so extreme an anti-realist view as the view that mathematics is the study of a structure we create, then modal independence is surely not the defining commitment of realism.

The train of thought which gives rise to this sort of objection is not uncommon. We can imagine a possible world where there are no people but where the sunsets are still beautiful. Does this mean we should be realists about beauty? It is often thought that it does not: the anti-realist can argue that the possible world we imagine only counts as beautiful because

---

[14] One possible response to the argument for two-way independence would be to claim that the interesting dependence relations are those involving rigidification. For instance, we might postulate a modal dependence relation between *x is beautiful* and *x is actually considered beautiful*. If that's right, then in cases where essential independence fails, so that e.g. what it is for Bres to be beautiful is for him actually to be considered beautiful, modal independence fails too, because it's not possible that [Bres is beautiful but he is not actually considered beautiful]. But if we take this route, then provided that Bres is actually considered beautiful, the failure of modal independence is *trivial*. Modal independence claims of this sort would not be very interesting. They are unlikely to be what people had in mind when trying to characterize realism in terms of modal independence.

[15] This view might go hand in hand with the application of a two-dimensional semantics to modal claims. More on two-dimensional semantics in nn. 16 and 19.

we, in assessing it, see beauty in it (Moore 1903: ch. 6 invokes this sort of point). Likewise, we cannot easily refute Kant's transcendental idealism by arguing that, since there were mountains before there were people, it must be possible for there to be mountains but not people, so that mountains cannot be part of the phenomenal world (which is a joint product of us and our surroundings). For Kantians can reply that when we consider whether or not there were mountains before there were people, we are imposing our sensibility on the prehistoric world.

If one finds this perspective appealing, then one has reason to think both that modal independence and essential independence are two-way independent and that there is a serious objection to the identification of realism with modal independence.[16] But, whatever our verdict on this point, there are other ways of arguing that realism and anti-realism should not be defined in modal terms. These will occupy the remainder of this section.

Failures of modal independence often seem to be insufficient to determine whether or not anti-realism is true. Must we be anti-realists about arithmetic just because, for any arithmetical p, there is no possible world where p is the case but where p cannot be proved? This is not clear. For the non-existence of such a world may simply be due to the fact that, at *every* world, every arithmetical p *is* provable. Whether or not we *agree* that at every world every arithmetical p is provable, it does not seem that realism should follow from this alone.

This point will stand to be spelled out a little more. Surely it is consistent with arithmetical realism to think that, although arithmetical reality is essentially mind-independent, it is also by nature the kind of thing which is epistemically tractable, so that there could not be an arithmetical truth which could not possibly be proved. Let's call this combination of views 'optimistic realism'. If realism is defined as a modal independence claim, then optimistic realism about arithmetic is not coherent.

Suppose we take realism to imply that, for any arithmetical p, there is a possible world where p is the case but p is not provable. Then the optimistic thought that arithmetic is bound to be epistemically tractable

---

[16] For the two-dimensionalist, this objection becomes a cautionary note: it shows that realism can at best be defined as a commitment to one dimension of the modal independence claim.

rules out realism in a decisive and straightforward way. Assuming that optimism of this kind ought *not* to rule out realism (at least, not without substantial further argument), realists are not committed to modal independence. Hence, an argument for the modal dependence of arithmetic upon provability is not sufficient to refute realism.[17]

By contrast, optimism about the epistemic tractability of arithmetic is perfectly compatible with a commitment to the *essential* independence of arithmetic. It makes sense to say that, for any arithmetical p, there is no possible world where p is the case but p is unprovable, while maintaining that p's being provable is no part of *what it is* for p to be the case. In just the same way, there is no possible world where I exist and $7 + 5 = 12$ is not the case, and yet its being the case that $7 + 5 = 12$ is not, on any reasonable understanding, part of *what it is* for me to exist.

We can lend further support to the claim that essential independence is the key commitment of realism by noting that *anti*-realist views generally consist in views about the nature of reality, and not in the rejection of any modal claim. For instance, Kantians argue that phenomenal reality *is* (in part) a product of our sensibility (see e.g. Yablo 2002: 237: 'Numbers and sets are "there" because they are inscribed on the spectacles through which we see things'). Berkelian idealists believe that the physical world *consists of* ideas in the mind of God (Berkeley 1710, 1713). Craig (1998) characterizes anti-realism about humour as the view that 'something's being funny is very much *a matter of* whether we find it funny' (emphasis added). The slogan *esse est percipi* asserts that to exist *is* to be perceived. And Wright says that truth is *essentially* a goal of enquiry (1986: 24–6). These are the kinds of grounds on which anti-realists claim that truth is not 'independent' of us, and they all appear to be claims of essential, rather than modal, dependence.

Insofar as anti-realists are committed to modal dependence claims (or to rejecting the modal independence claims they associate with realism), such commitments tend to be presented only as a consequence of their commitment to essential dependence. Craig (1998) summarizes a common train of anti-realist thought with this rhetorical question: '[I]f [something's] whole nature is due to the way we "construct" it through our style of

---

[17] Note that the argument here is structurally similar to that found in Tennant (1997: sects. 6.3–6.4), except that Tennant's 'Gödelian optimist' will be accounted a 'realist' (if at all) because he accepts bivalence for mathematical statements, whereas bivalence is not here taken to be a commitment of optimistic realism.

experience and investigation, how could there be anything about it that our cognitive faculties cannot recover?'.

It is, perhaps, surprising that realism should be often defined in modal terms, when many anti-realists clearly consider some kind of essential-dependence claim to be the core of their position. We could, of course, resolve the discrepancy either by characterizing both realism and anti-realism in terms of essence, or by characterizing both in modal terms. But our choice on this matter should be informed by the fact that the question of essential independence is, as mentioned earlier, more philosophically fundamental than the question of modal independence. For that reason, if we understand the realism/anti-realism debate as a deep debate about the nature of reality, characterization in terms of essential independence looks more promising. While modal independence claims may turn out to be interestingly related to realism, they do not constitute the core of the realist position, and the relationship is not straightforward enough for anything to be assumed about it without careful discussion.

1.3 Essential independence and the quasi-realist

Blackburn has argued that any attempt to characterize realism in terms of a commitment to 'objectivity' or 'mind-independence' can tend to under-mine our grasp on what realism is. It is important to note, therefore, that being clear about the difference between essential and modal independence may help us to address this claim in a novel way.

Blackburn's 'quasi-realist' is a character designed to illustrate the diffi-culties of giving a proper account of the debate between the realists and their opponents. The quasi-realist is supposed to begin life as a non-realist, but ends up 'progressively able to mimic the intellectual practices sup-posedly definitive of realism' (1980: 15). He is eventually able to assert various mind-independence and other claims which have been taken as distinctively realist. We thus seem to be left without a handle on what is at issue between the quasi-realist and the realist.

Blackburn has claimed that, for any realist-sounding assertion, the quasi-realist can understand that assertion in a way which makes it acceptable to him. So, for instance, when the realist says something like *It's really a fact that p*, the quasi-realist applies a minimalist interpretation and hears only something akin to *p to you with brass knobs on*. And, taking the brass knobs to be merely decorative, he consequently assents to the realist's claim, all the while maintaining (for example) that assertions like p are nothing but expressions of attitude (see e.g. Blackburn 1988).

Similarly, when the realist says that lying would have been wrong however things had been with us and our attitudes, the quasi-realist can hear this as the claim that, since our standards for moral disapprobation of lying do not involve reference to us or our attitudes, those standards would be met in a situation where we and our attitudes were different. Rejecting the claim that lying would have been morally acceptable had we but approved of it amounts to rejecting the claim that our moral standards tie approbation of lying to our attitudes about lying (see e.g. Blackburn 1984: 219). For all that she rejects this, the quasi-realist can maintain that the standards in question are standards *for the adoption of a certain kind of moral attitude* (or standards for an emotive rather than a cognitive response, or whatever). It's just that respecting those standards makes us *responsive* not to our attitudes, but to other salient features of lying (its capacity to cause people distress, for instance).

The quasi-realist's strategy, when dealing with realist-sounding mind-independence claims, is to try to make them 'internal' to the subject matter under consideration. An 'internal' claim about (e.g.) ethics is one which is internal to ethical discourse; that is, one which is itself an ethical claim. One way of explicating Blackburn's underlying thought would seem to be as follows. The quasi-realist can understand the claim that lying would have been wrong however things had been with us as the claim that all (close) possible worlds where things go differently with us are worlds where lying is still wrong. Accepting this does not undermine his anti-realism, he argues, since in accepting it he is simply adopting an attitude towards the possible worlds in question; he can hear assertions like 'Lying is wrong at world w' as internal to ethical discourse by hearing them as expressions of ethical attitudes towards acts of lying that take place at w. The quasi-realist thus understands 'Lying would have been wrong however things were with us and our attitudes' in such a way that asserting it makes clear that our standards for disapprobation of lying do not simply track the attitudes we happen to have towards lying in various situations. But he does this while leaving room for the (external, meta-ethical) claim that our standards for disapprobation of lying are standards for the adoption of a negative attitude towards lying.[18]

Notice that in adopting this line the quasi-realist takes a stance as to which of the two perspectives on modality described in the preceding section is correct. I remain neutral for present purposes, but will grant for the sake of argument that his response to counterfactual mind-independence claims is fair.[19]

The realist who defines her position in terms of essential independence is free to acknowledge Blackburn's insights. She can allow that *It's really a fact that p* has a minimalist reading whereby it is merely a stylistic variant of p, and even that it has no other reading. And she can allow that counterfactual independence claims do not adequately characterize realism because they are indeed to be understood in the way Blackburn requires. (This should not be surprising, given the modal nature of counterfactuals: I have acknowledged above that prima facie realist-sounding statements of modal independence may be susceptible to interpretation in such a way as to make them acceptable to the anti-realist.) The question is: What can the quasi-realist say about the essential independence claim: *It is no part of what it is for lying to be wrong that we have a negative attitude to lying*? Once we take care to define realism in terms of essential independence, can he continue with his customary mimicry?

Blackburn shows how the ethical quasi-realist might accept certain claims that might initially sound like claims of essential independence. For

---

[18] Blackburn suggests that rejecting the claim that lying would have been acceptable had we but approved of it is a matter of expressing *moral disapprobation* of the kind of ethical standard which links the acceptability of lying to our attitude towards it in this manner (see e.g. 1981: 179, 1988: 173). But the expression of disapprobation of these standards would seem to be inessential to the quasi-realist's story (although of course such disapprobation may often also be present). As long as the quasi-realist can hear the claim that lying would have been acceptable had we but approved of it as indicating that our standards for disapproving of lying make us responsive to our attitudes about lying rather than to lying's other salient features, he can reject it as *false*, regardless of whether or not he thinks it is morally reprehensible.

[19] Peacocke (2004: 210–17) thinks that the possibility of a two-dimensional semantics for evaluating the relevant counterfactual claims is problematic for Blackburn. But this is not straightforward. If Blackburn can establish that the 'vertical' reading, not the 'diagonal' one, is the *only* interesting and/or natural reading of the counterfactual claims, the existence of another merely possible reading might be argued to be irrelevant to the question of whether these counterfactuals can be appropriated by the quasi-realist. A separate question is whether the other reading provides us with an *alternative* place to look for something that the realist will assert that the quasi-realist cannot. But for all that has been said so far, it may be that Blackburn (or a Blackburnian) can address this issue, for instance by arguing that the diagonal reading simply is *not* one of the mind-independence claims that characterize realism.

instance, the quasi-realist can accept that '[w]hat makes cruelty abhorrent is not that it offends us, but all those hideous things that make it do so' (1988: 172). For he can say that the standards according to which we apply moral censure are concerned solely with the relevant features of actions (causing pain, causing distress, etc.), and make no mention of us or our attitudes to those actions. For all that, he is at liberty to regard moral censure as the expression of an attitude. So the quasi-realist can imitate the realist when it comes to saying what *makes it the case that p*.

But that is not the same thing as imitating her when it comes to saying *what it is for p to be the case*. In asking what makes it the case that p, we are asking what standards have to be met in order for p to be correctly asserted. We are asking after sufficient conditions: what it *takes* for p to be the case. That is not the same thing as asking what it *is* for p to be the case.

An example may help to elucidate this point. What it *takes* for Blackadder to be funny is for him to refer to Baldrick's cunning plan in a particular tone of voice, or get drunk and start singing that song about a goblin, or do any of a number of other things. But what it *is* for Blackadder to be funny is for him to do the kinds of things which make people laugh. When we are asked for a (non-trivial) account of what it is for X to be funny, our anti-realism about humour will out, even though it can be concealed if we ask only what it *takes* for X to be funny, what *makes* X funny, or even what it is *in virtue of which* X is funny.[20]

Questions about what it *takes* for p to be the case can be made internal (in Blackburn's sense) to the target discourse by making them questions about the standards for accepting that p is the case—either questions about what those standards are, or questions about whether they are met in particular cases. This is what is happening when the quasi-realist interprets the claim that lying would have been wrong however things had been with us as the indicating that our standards for disapproving of lying are responsive to other factors than our own attitudes. The reason the quasi-realist can adopt the 'realist-sounding' answers to these questions is that answering them tells us nothing about what the standards are standards *for*, and it is precisely on this point that the realist and Blackburn's quasi-realist disagree. That is why

---

[20] Note that realists about a subject matter may find it hard to give any non-trivial account at all of what it is for something to be the case with regard to that subject matter. But they can still specify that nothing to do with our mental lives is part of what it is for such things to be the case (with the mundane exceptions noted in Section 1.2).

the quasi–realist need not retract any of the realist-sounding internal claims he has made as soon as the external perspective is adopted.

Can we make assertions of essential independence internal? In asking *what it is* for p to be the case, can we be taken as asking a question on the same level as the question of *whether* p is the case or *what it takes* (i.e. what are some sufficient conditions) for p to be the case? The usual quasi-realist strategy does not deal easily with this challenge: in asking what it *is* for p to be the case, it does not seem that we can be understood as asking what it takes for the standards for accepting p to be met, or as asking whether these standards are met in any particular (actual or possible) situation.

How might the quasi-realist understand, in a way which makes it acceptable to him, the essential independence claim that it is no part of what it is for lying to be wrong that we have a negative attitude to it? Perhaps a quasi-realist can say in good faith that what it is for lying to be wrong is for it to be dishonest, and there's no more to it than that. After all, he might argue, if dishonesty is the feature of lying that we are responding to when we say it is wrong, there is in a sense nothing more to lying's being wrong than its being dishonest.

But this seems like a false start. If dishonesty is the feature we are responding to when we disapprove of lying, all that means is that lying's being dishonest is *sufficient* for lying to count as wrong. It shows that lying's being dishonest is what it *takes* for lying to be wrong, not what it *is* for lying to be wrong.

A point of clarification: quasi-realists are non-realists by my lights not because they must accept some essential dependence claim, but merely because they cannot accept the relevant essential independence claim. The quasi-realist's non-realism could (and Blackburn's does) amount simply to non-cognitivism, and this might plausibly be thought to be antithetical to either a claim of essential independence or one of essential dependence. For both these claims are claims about what it is for (e.g.) murder to be wrong, but the non-cognitivist could say that, in the relevant sense, *nothing* is 'what it is' for murder to be wrong, because to say that murder is wrong is not to say that something is the case but to express an attitude. If he does say this, however, he must reject the distinctively realist essential independence claim that it is no part of what it is for murder to be wrong that our mental lives be a certain way. For it is a presupposition of that claim (on the reading I intend) that *something* is what it is for murder to be wrong (see n. 4 above).[21]

Blackburn is right to note that many of the usual ways of spelling out what mind-independence amounts to are susceptible to quasi-realist reinterpretation and hence may not help us distinguish the realist from the non-realist. But this, I think, is because they do not adequately capture the notion of mind-independence which best characterizes realism. The conflation of essential and modal independence leaves the realist open to quasi-realist reinterpretation. But by being clear that it is an essential independence claim the realist intends to assert, we can, at the very least, present the quasi-realist with a significantly new interpretative challenge. At best, we can hope that we might have put our finger on what is lacking in the characterizations of realism that Blackburn takes issue with.[22]

1.4 Summary

My aim in Chapter 1 has been to make clear what I mean by 'realism', and hence what it is I take myself to be defending in showing that arithmetical realism, when taken together with apriorism and empiricism, is not epistemologically implausible. I have distinguished essential from modal independence, and explained why I think realism is best characterized in terms of the former. I have also argued that Blackburn's quasi-realist cannot easily mimic the realist's essential independence claims.

---

[21] I am indebted to Gideon Rosen for pressing me on this point and to Neil Sinclair for helpful discussions.

[22] Sinclair (forthcoming) takes issue with some of the claims of this chapter. Sinclair is responding to Jenkins (2005a), and his discussion has enabled me to make a number of improvements here to my views as expressed in that paper. Sinclair also raises other interesting points which are not discussed here as they are less relevant to the aims of this book. I plan to respond to these in future work.

2

Externalism and Empiricism

2.1 Introduction

The first part of this chapter consists in a brief discussion of epistemological externalism. I then move on to discuss empiricism. On the face of it, empiricism seems unable properly to account for the aprioricity of arithmetical knowledge. I shall outline below the arguments purporting to establish this, and I shall note that these are targeted on traditional empiricist views which are quite different from the view to be described in Part II. I shall pay particular attention to Boghossian's developed version of the traditional empiricist view that aprioricity can be accommodated by appealing to the analyticity of the propositions known.

I shall then consider and reject two of the most plausible-sounding contemporary *alternatives* to empiricist accounts of the a priori: the 'moderate rationalism' of Peacocke and Bealer, and Field's evaluativism.

2.2 Why externalism?

It would take me too far afield to engage seriously here with the debate over whether we should be externalists and/or internalists about justification and knowledge. My primary intention is simply to flag the fact that I shall be assuming a certain—fairly weak—kind of externalism about both in this book, and to cite a few brief reasons (some of which will be relevant later) for my doing so.

Internalists about justification, for current purposes, are those who believe that in order to be justified in believing a proposition p, one must be aware (or at least capable of becoming aware) of what one's justification for p is. Similarly, internalists about knowledge are those who believe that in order to know p, one must be aware (or at least capable of becoming aware) of what one's grounds for p are.[1]

Externalists reject these constraints on justification and knowledge. However, externalism per se implies no particular positive views about justification or knowledge. For instance, not all externalists about knowledge are reliabilists. (Reliabilists about knowledge are those who hold that S knows that p iff S has a true belief that p which is produced by some mechanism or procedure which is, in some significant sense, reliable.)

In this book I shall be assuming that there is a good sense of 'knowledge' and a good sense of 'justification' on which externalism is correct. It may be, for all I say here, that there is another good sense of each term on which internalism is correct. (This seems to me particularly plausible for 'justification'.) This does not interfere with the central claims of this book, which should be understood as having to do *only* with arithmetical knowledge and justification in the externalist senses. In order to defend the intuition that we have a priori knowledge of arithmetic, I shall be defending the claim that we have such a priori knowledge in the externalist sense of 'knowledge'. It might turn out that no similar defence is available for the internalist sense (if there is one). So much the worse, I should say, for those who think that the internalist sense is the only one (and do not want to be sceptics about arithmetic).

It is a difficult question when an apparent disagreement—such as that between an internalist and a corresponding externalist—should be taken as a genuine disagreement about a single notion of justification or knowledge, and when it is best diagnosed by pointing out that each party is on to something, that there are two notions in the vicinity, and that the parties need not disagree about either notion. That question—the question of what the actual internalists and externalists are up to—does not need to be resolved here. Nor does the question of whether there is really one notion of justification and one notion of knowledge, which the internalists are

---

[1] Another kind of 'internalism' requires only (potential) awareness *of* one's justification or grounds, where this need not include awareness *that* they are one's justification or grounds. The argument of this book requires one to understand 'knowledge' and 'justification', on at least one of their readings, in a way which demands at least the rejection of internalism in the sense described in the main text, and will probably be more plausible to those who reject this weaker kind of internalism as well. Yet another view labelled 'internalism' (or, rather, range of views, some of which overlap with kinds of internalism already mentioned) holds that 'internal factors' wholly determine whether or not one is justified or possesses knowledge, for some interesting sense of 'internal'. This will not be discussed here.

wrong about in each case, or whether in each case there are really two notions that happen to be associated with the same word, one of which is as the internalist says. All I assume is that there is an externalist notion in each case.

A common objection to internalism is that it launches infinite regresses. Suppose, for instance, that I must be (capable of becoming) aware of what my justification for p is in order to be justified in believing p. Such 'awareness' presumably consists in possession of a belief to the effect that my justification for believing p is blah. It is unlikely that the internalist will be satisfied with *any* old belief to that effect, however. The fact that I possess a completely irrational belief that my justification is blah cannot be relevant to the question of whether I am justified in believing p or not. 'Awareness' of one's justification for p really amounts to possession of a *justified* belief that one's justification for believing p is blah.

And now the regress is obvious: by the internalist's lights, in order for my belief that my justification for believing p is blah to be justified (or for me to be capable of having a justified belief of this kind), it must be the case that I have (or am capable of having) a further belief to the effect that *that* belief is justified by blahblah. And so on, ad infinitum. In other words, the chain of justifying beliefs required to support my initial belief that p has no beginning. It seems therefore that no belief can ever be justified.

It won't help to reply that the internalist need only claim that for each justified belief in the chain I am *capable* of having that justified belief, which is not the same as claiming that I have it, and doesn't imply that I am capable of having all of the (infinitely many) justified beliefs in the chain simultaneously. Problems remain. For one thing, the propositions I am required to be capable of believing will soon become so complex that I will be unable even to entertain them. For another, the problem is not that I need to have, or be capable of having, infinitely many beliefs. It is rather that the internalist places a condition on knowledge which is incompatible with a foundationalist intuition—the intuition that justification for a belief must 'ground out' somewhere. If internalism is true, the grounding-out point is never reached. My having justification for p rests on the fact that I am capable of coming to have a justified belief regarding my justification for p, which in turn rests on the fact that I am capable of coming to have a justified belief regarding my justification for that belief, and so on. At every stage there is dependence on the next stage.

The internalist might reply that the problem highlighted by the regress is a real sceptical problem, which cannot be swept under the carpet by simply rejecting internalism. (This sort of point is made by Dancy in his 1985: 47–8.) No more can one deny that atheism is true simply because it removes a powerful source of moral motivation in which one previously believed. Internalists might then shore up their position by claiming that internalism has intuitive force: surely one cannot know—or justifiedly believe—a proposition p if one has no inkling of how one knows—or justifiedly believes—p?

Externalists do not find this convincing, however. For one thing, the claim that internalism is intuitive is undermined by the fact that it tends to launch regresses which lead to an extremely *counter*-intuitive sceptical position. Externalists can also note that it is intuitively acceptable to ascribe knowledge to creatures to whom it is difficult to ascribe the potential for awareness of what their epistemic grounds are. For instance, I find it appropriate to say that my cat knows where the cat food is kept, although it seems inappropriately anthropomorphic to say that she could come to be aware of what her grounds for that belief are. It can, of course, be objected against this that the seeming 'appropriateness' of ascribing knowledge of where the food is kept to my cat is *not* due to the fact that she knows where the food is kept, since animals like cats cannot have beliefs with propositional content (or, at least, not propositional contents as sophisticated as this one).

But the burden of proof is with the objector here, in my opinion, to find a plausible alternative account of our everyday practice of ascribing knowledge to animals. As with all error theories, we are owed an explanation of our mistake if we are to accept that it is indeed a mistake.

I do not imagine that any internalist will be persuaded by these thoughts. Maybe weak forms of internalism, which do not demand that awareness should amount to justified belief, can avoid regress problems of the kind I have described. Or maybe there is something to the thought that the internalist regress highlights a genuine sceptical problem. It is for these reasons that I allow that there may be internalist senses of 'knowledge' and 'justification' which sit alongside the externalist senses. My impression is that if this is right, then even if the internalist regress does raise sceptical problems, these are not too troubling provided we also acknowledge the externalist senses and their important role in everyday knowledge attributions.[2] Acknowledging these enables us to respect our everyday intuitions to the effect that people often have justified beliefs and knowledge despite being incapable of becoming aware of what their justifications or grounds are.[3]

2.3 'Empiricism cannot account for the a priori'

It is often claimed that empiricists cannot deal with the (apparent) phenomenon of a priori knowledge. To assess this sort of objection, we will now need a working definition of 'a priori' to hand. Let us say that a priori knowledge of a proposition p is knowledge which does not rest epistemically upon empirical evidence, either immediately or via a chain of inference. (A more precise definition follows in Section 4.3.)

I would be the first to admit that existing empiricist approaches to the a priori in general—and arithmetic in particular—are unpromising. Nonetheless, we must do more justice to the extant empiricist philosophies of arithmetic than is done by Potter (2000: 6–9; see also 1998: sect. 2), who, in surveying objections to empiricism in arithmetic, considers only one empiricist strategy, and not a particularly promising one. Mill's claim that apparently a priori arithmetical statements are simply empirical generalizations is rejected by Potter on the grounds that the senses supply no confirmation for statements involving very large numbers or the principle of mathematical induction. In fact, this is far from being as obvious as Potter assumes. If inference to the best explanation of observed phenomena, for example, counts as a kind of empirical confirmation for the explanans, then the fact that we cannot directly observe very large numbers of things supplies no obvious bar to supposing that there can be (indirect) empirical confirmation for statements about very large numbers. Maybe a Millian will have more trouble accounting for the special *certainty* of our beliefs about very large numbers if all our empirical confirmation for them is of this indirect kind. But he might also appeal to deduction from extremely well-confirmed statements involving small numbers to help with this problem.

---

[2] This kind of claim is in some (but not all) ways similar to Lewis's contextualism. (See Lewis 1979: 247, and esp. Lewis 1996.)

[3] For more on internalism and externalism I refer the interested reader to a collection of papers edited by Kornblith (2001), to BonJour and Sosa's extended discussion in their (2003), and to Plantinga (1993), where externalism is defended through a substantial critique of internalist alternatives.

But, in any case, no empiricist other than Mill need be concerned by Potter's objection. To mention just a couple of famous examples, Quine's holistic approach to empirical confirmation (see e.g. Quine 1960: ch. 7) enables him to claim that sense experience can confirm arithmetical propositions whenever they appear as parts of our best theory of the world; Ayer (1936) avoids Potter's objection by claiming that arithmetical statements are non-factual and known through our grasp of linguistic conventions. And Ayer's approach is just one instance of a classic empiricist strategy, whereby a priori knowable statements are said to be epistemologically unproblematic because they are analytic.[4]

BonJour (1998: ch. 2) offers a helpful summary of the difficulties empiricism faces in trying to account for the a priori. He finds fault with both the 'moderate' empiricist strategy of arguing that all a priori knowledge is knowledge of 'analytic' truths and that it is therefore unproblematic, and the Quinean ('radical') empiricist strategy of denying that what we think of as a priori knowledge has any peculiar epistemic status.

To undermine the moderate strategy BonJour argues that, even if it is correct to say that all a priori knowledge is in some sense knowledge of 'analytic' truths, the claim that this by itself makes a priori knowledge unproblematic is indefensible (Casullo 2003: ch. 8 and Williamson 2008: ch. 3 make similar points). He considers various ways of spelling out what analyticity amounts to, in terms of logical truth, linguistic convention, stipulation, lack of factual content, and so on, and argues that whichever one we plump for, the empiricists still owe (and have failed to provide) an account of how analytic truths are known.

BonJour considers two groups of conceptions of analyticity, 'reductive' and 'obfuscating'. He rightly notes that 'reductive' conceptions, whereby

---

[4] A possible divergence from standard contemporary usage of the term 'empiricism' is suggested when Potter says: 'That arithmetic is directly about the physical world is the claim of empiricism' (p. 7). Neither Quine nor Ayer believed this, yet both are usually regarded as paradigm empiricists. Maybe this terminological issue explains the appearance of oversight. Or maybe it is that Potter intends to offer a historical study, of which Quinean and Ayerian empiricism (and other forms) are properly outside the scope. However, the strength of the conclusions reached at (e.g.) pp. 287–9 casts some doubt on whether either of these exegetical suppositions can be correct. For instance, on p. 287 Potter takes himself to have established that '[a]rithmetic has a content that logic ... cannot supply. It is senseless to look for that content in the world, for we, being finite, are incapable of experiencing the world directly as infinite, whether it is so or not'. This is a very strong conclusion to reach given that most of the extant varieties of empiricism have not been discussed, and that at least one variety (Quine's) purports to address precisely the kind of worry Potter is raising here. If other empiricist views are being properly ignored, a more modest conclusion would seem appropriate.

analytic truth is defined as some other (presumably previously understood) kind of truth, cannot in themselves serve the ends of the moderate empiricist. Suppose, for instance, we define the analytic truths (with Frege in the *Grundlagen*) as those propositions which are either truths of logic or can be transformed into truths of logic by the substitution of synonyms. Then to say a priori knowledge is knowledge of analytic truths does not in the least explain how we can have such knowledge, since we still need an account of how we can know logical truths and truths which can be transformed into logical truths by substitution of synonyms.

BonJour goes on to show that other, 'obfuscating', conceptions of analyticity are by themselves equally incapable of doing all the work required by the moderate empiricist. For instance, the hypothesis that a priori knowledge is knowledge of propositions which are 'true in virtue of meaning' does not, by itself, tell us how a priori knowledge works; we still await an account of how propositions which are 'true in virtue of meaning' are known.

He considers the possibility of saying that a priori knowledge is knowledge of 'implicit definitions'. But he argues that, on the account of 'implicit definition' which he thinks may be the only clear account in the literature (that due to Butcharov 1970: 109–10), this provides no explanation of how we know things a priori. According to Butcharov, saying that a sentence *s* is an implicit definition amounts to stipulating that any previously unknown terms it contains are to be interpreted so as to make *s* come out true (or necessarily true). The trouble is that this process of interpretation requires that we *already know* that *s* is (necessarily) true on the correct interpretation of the terms: we must *first* know that *s* comes out (necessarily) true on a certain interpretation, in order to see that it is the *intended* interpretation. The question then is: How do we explain this apparently prior knowledge of the (necessary) truth of the proposition which *s* expresses on its intended interpretation? (In the next section, I shall argue that this objection is a problem for Boghossian's 'analytic theory of the a priori'.)

Another 'obfuscating' position considered by BonJour is the view that analytic statements are made true by (and hence can be known through a grasp of) our linguistic conventions. But linguistic conventions certainly don't *seem* to be responsible for the truth of analytic statements. To show this, BonJour asks:

What convention might be adopted that would make it possible for something to be red and green all over at the same time? It is, of course, obvious that new conventions could change the meaning ... of the words 'red' and 'green', but there is no plausibility at all to the idea that such changes would result in the *falsity* of ... the proposition that nothing can be red and green all over at the same time, as opposed to merely altering the way in which [that proposition is] expressed.

(p. 53)

But it could be argued that the objection misconstrues (or at least does not focus on the best version of) the view under consideration. Craig (1975) discusses conventionalism as a view about necessary truth rather than a priori knowledge, but the two kinds of conventionalism are closely related, and the points he makes apply, *mutatis mutandis*, to our discussion. He writes that the term 'conventionalism'

carries the implication that the sources of necessary truth are communal decisions made by groups of people who has other alternatives before their minds. But nothing of this sort is to be regarded as belonging to the doctrine which ... I am calling 'Conventionalism'. That doctrine is simply the assertion that the determinants of necessity are facts about our behaviour with respect to certain *whole sentences*, and that these facts ... are not logical consequences of any *other facts* which determine the meanings of their constituent words and the import of their syntax.

(p. 9)

If conventionalism is something like this, then BonJour's objection, relying as it does upon the thought that if we are conventionalists then we must believe the relevant conventions could be different in such a way as to change the facts, might seem to be off-target.

In fact, however, it is not clear that what Craig says defuses BonJour's objection. Suppose we define conventionalism in Craig's way. That does not prevent our *asking the question* whether it is possible for us to adopt different conventions which would make it possible for something to be red and green all over. If the conventionalist allows that it is possible to adopt such conventions, he is committed to the implausible thesis BonJour is objecting to. If not, he seems to be stuck with the view that (if we adopt any conventions at all on this point) we *have* to adopt conventions according to which nothing can be red and green all over. This raises two problems.

First, it is very counter-intuitive to claim that our linguistic conventions have to be the way they are if we are to have any linguistic conventions at all. Second, we are left wondering where the necessity of adopting a particular convention comes from. If it comes from another convention, this convention in turn will presumably be necessary, and this necessity fact will in turn presumably be underwritten by another convention, leading to an uncomfortable infinite regress of dependence on necessary conventions whose necessity depends on necessary conventions whose necessity... But if it does not come from another convention, there must be some ultimate source of necessity which is distinct from convention.

Maybe the conventionalist would seek to argue that the question of whether it is necessary that we should adopt a particular convention is in some way a bad question. The question, he might argue, attempts to apply standards of necessity which are internal to our language to the conventions which govern that language. But these standards simply cannot be applied outside their sphere in this way. They apply only to what can be expressed in our language, not to the conventions governing it.

But this is a weak response, because it is obvious that the conventions governing our language can themselves be expressed in that language. The claim that we have adopted a linguistic convention according to which nothing can be red and green all over is expressible using an English sentence, so why can't we assess that sentence for necessity in the usual way?

Here is another attempt on behalf of the conventionalist. He might try and distinguish two ways of understanding the claim that if our conventions had been different it would have been possible for something to be red and green all over (cf. Section 1.2). On one of these, we use our actual conventions to determine what proposition is expressed by the consequent, then consider the truth-value of that proposition at the relevant counterfactual worlds. We thus deny that these worlds where our conventions are different are worlds and something can be red and green all over (because our actual-world conventions fix that nothing can be red and green all over in any world, including these ones).

On the other approach, we assess whether the consequent is true at a counterfactual world w by assessing whether the proposition which would be expressed by the consequent at w (given the linguistic conventions in play at w) is true at w. On this second approach we get some worlds where it is possible for something to be red and green all over at the same time.

Maybe the conventionalist could argue that our intuition that changing our conventions wouldn't change the facts is well-enough preserved by the result we get on the first approach, while the sense that our adoption of particular conventions is contingent is explained by the result we get on the second. This does not raise the regress worry, since on neither reading must the conventionalist allow that our conventions are necessarily the way they are.

Even if this sort of response succeeds, however, what it shows is that the best objection to conventionalism should not be framed in modal terms (at least, not *these* modal terms). But a non-modal objection analogous to the original can be formulated. The modality appealed to in the original objection, I submit, was not the driving force in making us feel uneasy about conventionalism: it was merely making the objection vivid. (Modal claims are often thought to make realism/anti-realism debates vivid—see Section 1.2—so it is not surprising to see them making an appearance in the debate between conventionalists and their realist opponents.) The non-modal objection I have in mind goes something like this:

What convention makes it the case that nothing is red and green all over at the same time? It is, of course, obvious that conventions determine the meaning ... of the words 'red' and 'green', but there is no plausibility at all to the idea that such conventions determine the truth-value of the proposition that nothing can be red and green all over at the same time, as opposed to merely determining the way in which that proposition is expressed.

This objection is not answered by any considerations about the assessment of modal claims. It might, though, be felt somewhat question-begging: surely it just asserts that 'there is no plausibility' to the conventionalist's main thesis? However, I think it does more than that. It helps show *why* (the opponent feels) this thesis has no plausibility—the indicated reason being that linguistic conventions are things which determine *how a proposition is expressed*, and as such aren't the right sort of thing to determine whether or not that proposition is true.[5] It also may help show why conventionalism could have seemed attractive to some; namely, to those

---

[5] With, perhaps, a very few exceptions; for instance, self-referential propositions that concern their own means of expression.

who have not properly distinguished between a proposition and its means of expression, or more particularly between the facts which govern the truth-value of a proposition and those which govern how that proposition is conventionally expressed. (An attempt to develop a different, realist version of conventionalism is discussed and rejected in Section 6.2.)

2.4 Boghossian's 'analytic theory of the a priori'

It is worth noting here that Boghossian has argued that it is possible to disentangle an inoffensive 'analytic theory of the a priori' from some of the more questionable commitments commonly associated with such views. It is worth investigating whether this pared-down theory can elude BonJour's criticisms, and provide a genuine explanation of a priori knowledge which will be acceptable to empiricists.

Boghossian (1996, 1997) argues that certain truths can be known a priori because of the existence of implicit definitions; that is, because it is stipulated that certain (implicitly definitional) sentences are to be true or that certain (implicitly definitional) inferences are to be valid, and that certain components of those sentences or inferences (their definienda) are to be interpreted in whatever way will make the sentences true or inferences valid. He believes that this can help to 'demystify' a priori knowledge (2003: 17).

Boghossian helpfully distinguishes two notions in the vicinity of analyticity as traditionally conceived. One is metaphysical analyticity: truth purely in virtue of meaning. This notion, he thinks, has been debunked by Quine (see Quine 1951). The other is epistemic analyticity: knowability purely in virtue of understanding. This notion, according to Boghossian, is in good standing and can help us understand a priori knowledge of certain truths.

Boghossian thinks that epistemic analyticity occurs because of the existence of implicit definitions. A priori knowledge (of certain truths) is available to us because we have available to us instances of the following argument schema (Boghossian 1996: 386, 1997: 348; this one appeals to validity but a similar schema is available for truth):

(1) If **C** is to mean what it does, then **A** has to be valid, for **C** means whatever logical object in fact makes **A** valid.

(2) **C** means what it does.

Therefore,

(3) **A** is valid.

In more recent work Boghossian disclaims the obvious view of how appealing to this argument helps explain a priori knowledge (2003). He suggests that the argument is not to be thought of as an inference we can make from known premises which leads to knowledge of its conclusion, but as somehow 'constitutive' of one's justification for the conclusion. I find this claim somewhat confusing, but later in his paper (p. 26) it transpires that it amounts to the idea that one actually has *no* positive warrant for the conclusion reached at line (3), but nonetheless is 'not epistemically blameworthy' in accepting it or in trusting the inference rule it mentions. This lack of epistemic blameworthiness is supposedly due to the fact that one must be disposed to reason according to the rule in order to have the kind of thoughts required to entertain the conclusion.

This proposal looks like a false step. For one thing, it might be that epistemic error is attendant upon having the kind of thoughts in question. Maybe these thoughts involve a defective concept that we cannot employ without falling into error (cf. Field 2006: 85), in which case it is no defence against the charge that one is epistemically blameworthy in accepting the validity of **A** to say that one could not think **C**-thoughts without accepting that **A** is valid.

Perhaps, as some of his discussion of 'defective' concepts suggests (pp. 29–34), Boghossian wishes to make the externalist claim that we are justified in accepting the conclusion in exactly those cases where we are (as a matter of fact) dealing with non-defective concepts **C**. But unless there is some other relevant difference in our epistemic situation between the defective and the non-defective cases, this is deeply unsatisfying. We haven't ruled out the possibility that our possession of non-defective concepts is accidental or lucky in some knowledge-destroying way.[6] We might as well say that beliefs are justified in just those cases where they are, as a matter of fact, true. (This is not, of course, simply to reject epistemic externalism as characterized in Section 2.2 above. The extra factor which makes possession of non-defective concepts non-accidental need not be one that an internalist would approve of.)

---

[6] A very similar objection can be made against Peacocke's view, which Boghossian mentions as an alternative to his own on p. 28. I argue the point against Peacocke in Section 2.5 below.

Perhaps Boghossian has in mind that in some sense we cannot avoid thinking **C**-thoughts, so that it is not merely conditionally impossible but (in some sense) absolutely impossible for us to avoid accepting the validity of **A**, and this explains why the latter is epistemically permissible. But not only is it difficult to see what sort of impossibility might be intended (it is certainly not metaphysical impossibility), this move also suggests reliance on something akin to an '*ought*'-implies-'*can*' principle, and it is far from clear which—if any—'cans' give rise to acceptable '*ought*'-implies-'*can*' principles for the epistemic 'ought'.[7]

Boghossian claims that the 2003 proposal, whereby the argument (1)–(3) is not to be understood as providing our grounds for its conclusion, is what he intended all along in his 1996 and 1997 papers. This is a strange reading of those papers. But, regardless of what Boghossian may or may not have intended, in this section I shall be discussing the 1996/1997 view as it is most naturally read, since as far as I can see the 2003 interpretation is not very promising. In what follows 'Boghossian' refers to a defender of the 1996/1997 view on its natural reading, irrespective of whether the real Boghossian held that view at the time.

According to Boghossian, it is 'intuitively quite clear' that the premises of the type of argument he is interested in are knowable a priori (1996: 386). And he believes he has done enough to defend epistemic analyticity if he has shown the following conditional (which I shall call 'J') is true:

(J) If someone knows the relevant facts about meaning, then that person will be in a position to form a justified belief about the truth of certain propositions.

A few comments about these two things. First, and obviously, if our epistemic access to the meaning facts (the premises of the above argument) is *not* a priori,[8] or if the way we are justified in using the inferential rules for moving from the argument's premises to conclusion is not a priori, then for all Boghossian shows epistemic analyticity bears no relevance to the debate over how to account for aprioricity. Second, and more importantly for current purposes, if the way we know the meaning facts expressed in the premises is *by* knowing the conclusion propositions, then (J) will

---

[7] See Jenkins (2007b: 28–30) for discussion of a similar point in connection with Wright's notion of unearned warrant or 'entitlement'.

[8] Thanks to an audience at the Australian National University for helping me get clear on this point.

presumably be true but it will bear no relevance to the question of how we come to know propositions like (3) in the first place. I shall argue that this is in fact the situation (provided, as I assume for the sake of argument, that there are indeed implicit definitions of the kind Boghossian appeals to).

This is not in itself a new claim. However, in this section I shall do three other things. Drawing on recent work by Philip Ebert, I shall put a new structure on the objection which reveals the different ways that the objection can be pressed (depending on how you read one of the premises of Boghossian's argument schema). Since Boghossian has responded to the objection in his recent work, I shall argue that his response is unconvincing. And I shall develop some new side objections to Boghossian.

Ebert (2005) claims that arguments of the form of (1)–(3) above, far from showing how a priori knowledge can be acquired through implicit definition, have a fatal flaw: they fail to transmit warrant. I discuss Ebert's objection and how it relates to the objection to be presented in this section in Jenkins (2008 *a*); for now, I will draw only on Ebert's helpful observation that Boghossian's argument schema is not quite complete as stated. For it omits to make transparent a 'disquotational step', without which the conclusion is merely metalinguistic. Even though Boghossian claims (2003: 16) that it doesn't matter whether his conclusion concerns linguistic items or propositions, anything like that conclusion will be metalinguistic in the sense that it merely mentions the inference **A** (even if the metalanguage in which it is couched is the same as the object language to which **C** belongs). Hence, a disquotational step will always be needed to take us from something like this to a first-order piece of logical knowledge.

Revising the argument to include the disquotational step, and applying it for concreteness to the connective 'and', yields the following:

(1) If 'and' is to mean what it does, then 'P and Q $\Rightarrow$ P' has to be valid.
(2) 'and' means what it does.
(3) 'P and Q $\Rightarrow$ P' is valid.
(4) P and Q $\models$ P.

Statement (4) is to be read as expressing the schematic claim that P is a consequence of P *and* Q. (While the step from (3) to (4) is not disquotation in any straightforward sense, it is, as far as I can see, the closest alternative available.) All references to numbered propositions in the rest of this section are to the lines of the version of the argument which I have just laid out.

As mentioned in the preceding section, BonJour argues (1998: 49–51) that an appeal to implicit definition provides no explanation of how we know any proposition a priori. Saying that a sentence *s* is an implicit definition amounts to stipulating that any previously unknown terms it contains are to be interpreted so as to make *s* come out true (cf. Boghossian's (1)). But this process of interpretation would seem to require that we *already know* that *s* is true on the intended interpretation of the terms. We must first know that the proposition *s* expresses on a certain interpretation is a true proposition, in order to see that this interpretation is the *intended* interpretation. So how do we explain this apparently prior knowledge of the truth of the proposition which *s* expresses on the intended interpretation?

My central concern is that Boghossian's argument cannot be the source of our knowledge of (4) because (by the lights of someone who thinks 'and' is implicitly defined, in part by the rule that appears in (1)) the argument can only be employed by someone who already knows (4). There is clearly a problem in this area for Boghossian if his premise (2) is to be read *de re*: as asserting that 'and' means the particular thing that we all know it does mean; namely, *and*. Our epistemic ground for premise (1) is supposed to be that 'and' is implicitly defined as whatever makes 'P and Q ⇒ P' (among other things) valid. But if 'and' is so defined, knowing (2)[9] on its *de re* reading raises the BonJour problem. In order to know that 'and' means the thing we all know it does mean, where 'and' is defined as whatever makes such-and-such rules valid, we need prior knowledge of the fact that those rules are valid when 'and' means the thing we all know it does mean. But knowledge of this kind was supposed to be reached at the *conclusion* of the argument, and therefore cannot be relied upon for knowledge of its premises.

Boghossian (2003) has responded to this objection (which, as he says, is also pressed in Glüer 2003: 57–8). Assuming—with the majority, and without presuming to understand the phenomenon fully—that meaning facts are first-person accessible in a privileged way, Boghossian interprets the BonJour objection as an objection to the effect that 'in the *special* case

---

[9] Note that (2) has to be known, not merely true, or truly believed, if Boghossian is to explain our knowledge of (4) as an inference from known premises as envisaged.

where meaning is fixed by implicit definition, there is a problem with the assumption of privileged access'. 'But', he argues, BonJour has 'supplied us with no special reason to think that, if [a term's] meaning is fixed via implicit definition, the usual assumption of privileged access must be suspended'.

This comment seems to me to evince a misunderstanding of the objection. No argument is being offered in favour of the view that we *do not* know the meaning of 'and' in some privileged way of the sort Boghossian has in mind. Rather, Boghossian is being challenged to *account for* that knowledge; and rightly so, since it is one of the pieces of knowledge on which, according to Boghossian, our a priori knowledge that (4) rests, and the objector suspects that (if implicit definition is really going on) it rests on prior knowledge of (4). What is at issue is not whether we know the meaning of 'and' in some privileged way or other, but whether we know it in a way that depends upon prior knowledge of (4). It is reasonable to be concerned that not that much progress is made concerning the epistemology of (4) by claiming that a priori knowledge derives from knowledge of (2), given that it is on the cards that the only way we can have the required kind of knowledge of (2) is by knowing (4). At least, not much progress is made until some alternative account of our knowledge of (2) is forthcoming.

Gesturing to the fact that we have special, privileged access to meaning facts is in any case not very satisfying. It would not be satisfying to point to a special, privileged kind of access as soon as one is asked how a priori knowledge is possible, and it is hardly more satisfying to be forced into doing so a little further down the line. But this is not the main source of my concern.

Before moving on, it is worth noting that Boghossian appears to be making a positive argument against the point of view which would motivate the BonJour objection when he asks:

But do BonJour and Glüer really wish to say that if the meaning of 'and' is fixed by a thinker's being disposed to use it according to its standard introduction and elimination rules that [sic] he cannot be said to know what 'and' means without first knowing that 'A and B' implies A?

(p. 24)

One point to note about this is that how the meaning of 'and' is *fixed* is one question, and how its meaning is *known* is another. The objection under consideration only requires the claim that if the meaning of 'and' is *known* via our implicit definitions in terms of its standard introduction and elimination rules, then one cannot be said to know what 'and' means without first knowing that A *and* $B \models A$. That is the whole point of the BonJour objection. So the answer to (a suitably adjusted version of) Boghossian's rhetorical question is: Yes, those who think the objection works really do wish to say this, for the reasons explained above.

I do not see what sort of worry there is supposed to be about this. Although we cannot know that A *and* $B \models A$ without having a concept of conjunction (as distinct from knowing that 'and' expresses that concept), this fact does not reduce implicit definition to absurdity as a method of learning the meaning of the *expression* 'and'. It is still perfectly possible that the way we understand 'and' is through implicit definition—for example, by knowing that 'and' is to be interpreted so as to make 'A and B $\Rightarrow$ A' (along with any other relevant rules) come out valid. For we would then be able to come to know what 'and' means by seeing that it expresses conjunction, of which we already have a concept, and for which we already know such principles as A *and* $B \models A$ (even though we don't yet express these principles using the word 'and').

All that is strange, once this picture is set up, is Boghossian's further suggestion that our knowledge of the meaning of 'and' somehow underwrites our knowledge of the proposition A *and* $B \models A$. On the contrary, on this picture, it is our prior knowledge that A *and* $B \models A$ that enables us to know that 'and' expresses conjunction. For it is our prior knowledge of this proposition which enables us to see that conjunction is the intended interpretation for 'and'; that is, enables us to see that this is the interpretation which makes 'A and B' imply A and the other makes rules hold.

Conflation between a proposition and its means of expression might explain Boghossian's apparent confusion concerning the BonJour objection, and his neglect of the importance—and indeed the existence—of the disquotational step. A similar kind of conflation is familiar from (for instance) conventionalist accounts of necessity. Conventionalists argue that our conventions concerning linguistic items make it necessary that all bachelors are unmarried. Of course, all our linguistic conventions actually do is make it the case that the sentence 'All bachelors are unmarried' expresses an already necessary proposition. Similarly, Boghossian thinks that implicit definition of 'and' can give us knowledge that A *and* $B \models A$.

Whereas, in fact, all it does is enable us to see that the sentence 'A and B $\models$ A' expresses this already known proposition.

Boghossian claims (2003: 16) that it doesn't much matter whether we think of implicit definitions as definitions of linguistic items or of concepts. I think this matters a great deal, as the two options generate radically different views, but in addition I don't think that any claim of this sort can help him avert the foregoing worries. For it is far from clear that talk of implicit definition makes any sense for anything but representational items. But once it is understood that definitions are merely definitions of representational devices, and the gap between a proposition and its means of representation is appreciated, then we have all the tools we need in place to raise the BonJour objection against the view that implicit definitions can help us secure knowledge of propositions we did not already know.

The reader might wonder if the BonJour objection will disappear if (2) is read *de dicto*: as asserting merely that 'and' means whatever 'and' means. It would be charitable, and most in keeping with the spirit of Boghossian's writings, to assume that this is Boghossian's preferred reading.

However, this version of the argument still runs into difficulties at the disquotational step. This step, as Ebert (2005: sect. IV) notes, cannot be made unless the subject *understands* 'and'. And understanding 'and' requires more than knowing that 'and' means whatever 'and' means—it requires something much closer to knowing that 'and' means that very thing we all know it does mean. (Plausibly, we don't actually need knowledge of this *proposition* in order to understand 'and'. But we do need something pretty substantial.)

If 'and' is implicitly defined and the BonJour point is correct, then it looks as if this substantial understanding of 'and' will rest on prior knowledge of (4). For how could we get this understanding of 'and' just by knowing that 'P and Q $\Rightarrow$ P' and the other rules are to be valid? How could we tell *which* interpretation of 'and' makes these rules valid? Only by already knowing the validity of the rules which are expressed by the definienda on the intended interpretation; that is, by already knowing (among other things) that *P and Q $\models$ P*.

If our understanding of 'and' rests on our knowledge of (4) in this way, then the disquotational step cannot be made except by someone who already knows (4). In short, even on the *de dicto* reading of (2), there are reasons to doubt that a Boghossian-style argument can be the real source of our knowledge of (4), because such an argument can still only be employed by someone who already knows (4). (Note that this problem with the disquotational step is also a problem for the argument when premise (2) is read *de re*.)

There are, moreover, further problems with this alternative reading of the argument. The *de dicto* reading of (2) may make it appear trivial, but that appearance would be misleading. Even if we do read (2) as having this *de dicto* sense, if 'and' is implicitly defined as Boghossian envisages, knowing (2) still requires knowing that 'and' so defined has some meaning or other (a point raised by Horwich in his 1997). In other words, it requires that we solve something pretty close to BonJour's problem; namely, the problem of saying how we know that the inference 'P and Q $\Rightarrow$ P' is valid on *some* interpretation of 'and'. This is the familiar problem of saying how we know that 'and' gets any meaning assigned to it by this attempted definition. Plausibly, the way we know that there is an interpretation of 'and' which makes 'P and Q $\Rightarrow$ P' come out valid is by knowing that $P \text{ and } Q \models P$, but that can't be Boghossian's answer. There is therefore considerable pressure for an alternative answer to be provided if his account of our knowledge of (4) is to get off the ground.

In the appendix to Boghossian (1997: 358−62) he addresses this sort of problem. His response is to claim that 'we are a priori entitled to believe that our basic logical constants are meaningful because we cannot coherently doubt that they are'. His reason for saying we cannot coherently doubt that they are meaningful is that any proposition expressing that doubt will employ the very constants whose meaningfulness it is supposed to be doubting.

However, this again looks very dubious if we pay attention to the difference between propositions and their means of expression. Let's grant for the sake of argument that we cannot *express* the relevant doubt *in* (the English) *language* without using the constant 'and'. Still, why does it follow that we cannot *entertain the concern* that 'and' may not be meaningful? For Boghossian's point to do the required work, it would need to be the case that whenever we think the thought that 'and' may not be not meaningful we will be somehow employing the very same representational device 'and'. That is a very strong assumption that many would reject.

Perhaps Boghossian would resist this objection as resting too heavily on the idea that the relevant implicit definitions are definitions of English expressions. Perhaps he had in mind rather that we think in a language of thought, and that the item in that language which expresses conjunction is implicitly defined in that language in the way required for a version of his (1)–(4) argument to work for it. (I doubt this would be Boghossian's preferred response, since he claims that he is not committed to anything like a language of thought in order for his view to work—see his 2003: 16. But if the relevant implicit definitions are not definitions of English or mentalese words, what are they 'definitions' of? One possibility that remains is that implicit definition doesn't really come into it. This indeed seems to be Boghossian's view in his 2003, as discussed above. But it cannot be a very satisfactory interpretation of the argument of his 1996 and 1997.)

However, if mentalese implicit definition were on the cards, we should need to hear a lot more about what it is, how it is supposed to work, and why we should believe in it. It is far from clear that one has the same kind of control over the language in which one thinks (if indeed there is such a language) as one has over the language in which one expresses one's thoughts. It is far from clear that one is at liberty to stipulate regarding the meaning of mentalese expressions in the kind of way that seems to be required for implicit definition.

Moreover, no hint is given as to why we should not suppose that mentalese logical constants can have synonyms within mentalese. If they do, perhaps we can employ some synonymous expression (perhaps we can even define one for the occasion) in order to entertain a doubt about the mentalese word for conjunction.

It is also worth noting that even if it is incoherent to think that 'and' is not meaningful, it has not been established that it is incoherent to withhold judgement as to whether or not it is meaningful. For withholding judgement is not a matter of accepting some claim which involves 'and' in some objectionable way—it is simply a matter of not accepting that 'and' is meaningful. So even if it has been shown that we cannot coherently *hold that* 'and' is *not* meaningful, it has not been shown that we cannot *doubt whether* it is meaningful—for we could have such doubts in virtue of withholding judgement on the matter.

Furthermore, even if it is right to think that for whatever reason we cannot coherently doubt that 'and' is meaningful, this is an unsatisfactory response to our original worry. The original worry was that the way we know 'and' has a meaning may be by knowing (4). The response that we cannot coherently doubt that 'and' is meaningful, even if true, is unsatisfactory for (at least) two reasons. First, it does not address the worry. On the face of it, to point out that we can't coherently doubt that 'and' is meaningful is not to explain how (or even assert that) we know that it *is* meaningful. (This point is pressed by Laurence and Margolis 2001: 297.) Thus the worry remains that we know this by first knowing (4).

Perhaps our noticing that we cannot doubt that 'and' is meaningful is supposed to provide our warrant for thinking that 'and' is meaningful. If this is what Boghossian has in mind, it is another substantial assumption in need of defence. On the face of it, there is no reason why noticing such an incapacity of ours should provide warrant for beliefs about the relevant linguistic facts.

Boghossian acknowledges that we might interpret the impossibility of coherently doubting that our logical constants have a meaning as a 'merely pragmatic' result, but argues that '[t]o sustain the claim that the result is merely pragmatic, one would have to make sense of the claim that, although we cannot rationally doubt that our constants are meaningful, it is nevertheless possible that they aren't'. He proceeds: 'However, considerations similar to the ones adduced above would tend to show that we cannot make sense of this thought either' (1997: 362). Maybe, but this is to invite the same response over again. Among other things, we can respond that, at best, all the failure to 'make sense of this thought' would show is that we can't coherently doubt that the result is merely pragmatic. It does not amount to providing a reason to think that the result is *not* merely pragmatic.

The second problem with Boghossian's appeal to the impossibility of doubting that 'and' has a meaning, even supposing that this is impossible, is that this appeal undermines the claim that implicit definition is at the root of our a priori knowledge of (4). According to Boghossian's account, knowledge of (2) is one of the things on which our knowledge of (4) rests. But knowing (2) (even on its *de dicto* reading) requires that we at least know that 'and' has a meaning. However, the way Boghossian thinks we are justified in this belief is through our not being able to doubt coherently that it does. This suggests that one of the interesting, ultimate grounds on which a priori knowledge of (4) rests is located not in anything to do with implicit definition, but in the fact that *we cannot doubt* a certain proposition about 'and'.

Even waiving concerns about the reasonableness of claiming that this incapacity of ours is a source of knowledge, if Boghossian's account of how we know (4) makes our incapacity to doubt one of the ultimate grounds of that knowledge, then on that account implicit definition is not the whole story about our epistemic grounds for (4). This being so, it is reasonable to ask whether Boghossian has really succeeded in 'demystifying' a priori knowledge, or indeed whether Boghossian's proposal has significant advantages over an account of our a priori knowledge of (4), which simply says that we are right to trust that (4) is true because we cannot doubt it. After all, according to Boghossian, that seems to be all we need to say about *some* of our a priori knowledge (namely, a priori knowledge that our basic logical constants are meaningful).

In the light of the difficulties with Boghossian's proposal and the other considerations described in the previous section, I am happy to concede to BonJour that moderate empiricism (at least in its existing guises) is unpromising, and not much progress towards an explanation of a priori knowledge is made merely by our saying that a priori knowledge is knowledge of 'analytic' truths. However, the discussion of arithmetical knowledge in Part II does not depend upon the supposition that we can explain a priori arithmetical knowledge by saying it is knowledge of analytic truths. The 'moderate empiricist' strategies considered by BonJour and Boghossian bear only a superficial resemblance to my strategy. I shall, it is true, assume that arithmetical truths are conceptual truths. But this is merely the first step on the road to an epistemological proposal. What BonJour rightly demands of empiricists, and what I shall be trying to offer in Part II, is an account of how it could be that something like conceptual examination can supply knowledge of independent truths.

Besides moderate empiricism, BonJour argues, the only empiricist option on the market is 'radical' empiricism: the position which denies that a priori knowledge exists at all. Mill (1843) was in favour of this view; he claimed that logical and mathematical truths are simply very well-confirmed empirical hypotheses. The near-universal rejection of Mill's views on this point should have been a warning to anyone willing to ride roughshod over the firmly held intuition that there is a difference in kind, not just a difference in degree, between the epistemic grounds we have for the truths of arithmetic and those we have for the laws of physics. Yet Quine tried to do much the same thing as Mill (though with the added sophistication of confirmational holism) over a hundred years later in his (1951). I shall discuss Quine's views in Sections 7.5 and 9.2. Here I just note that it does not worry me that many philosophers find it unacceptable to reject the a priori, because I do not think we *need* to reject it in order to be good empiricists (at least, not in anything like Mill's or Quine's way).

I acknowledge the failure of existing forms of empiricism, both 'moderate' and 'radical', to deal adequately with the a priori. Therefore I suggest that we should examine whether a new kind of empiricism can fare better than its predecessors on the subject of a priori knowledge. One reason not to give up on empiricism just yet is that the positive non-empiricist views on the market are not philosophically appealing. In the remainder of Chapter 2, I shall consider some of the best available alternatives to empiricism about the a priori, and say what I think is wrong with them. Some useful points of comparison with the discussion to follow in Part II will emerge in the course of this discussion.

2.5 Alternatives to empiricism: Peacocke and Bealer

One approach to a priori knowledge—a traditional form of rationalism—appeals to some non-empirical faculty of 'rational intuition', which enables us to know certain truths. Gödel (infamously) is supposed to have believed in such a faculty, claiming that it enabled us to have 'something like a perception of the objects of set theory' (1947: 484). The consensus now, however, is that such appeals are unacceptable: we must respect the fact that there is no scientific evidence for any special faculty of the kind envisaged. We can only postulate one as a last resort, if all other accounts of a priori knowledge demonstrably fail to do what is required of them.

However, Christopher Peacocke (1993, 1994, 2000, 2004, and elsewhere[10]) has defended a different, and intriguing, view which (in recent work) he calls *moderate* rationalism. The moderate rationalist is someone who appreciates that appeals to a quasi-perceptual faculty of rational

---

[10] References in this section are to Peacocke (2000) unless otherwise stated.

intuition are not convincing, yet maintains that, somehow, it is rational thought or understanding that underwrites a priori knowledge.

Peacocke (2000: 260, 262) defines his moderate rationalism as consisting of two claims:

(1) For any a priori way of coming to know that p, there is a substantive explanation of why that way is an a priori way of coming to know, which involves the nature of the concepts in p.[11]
(2) There is no third realm of concepts or meanings, such that understanding is a matter of explanatory relations holding between us and the inhabitants of this realm.

Claim (1) is supposed to preserve rationalism, while claim (2) expresses the rejection of (a particular form of) rational intuition. An interesting feature of this definition of moderate rationalism is the apparent assumption that ways of knowing p which 'involve the nature of the concepts in p' cannot be empirical ways of knowing. If they *can* be empirical, then a certain kind of empiricist might count as a moderate rationalist by Peacocke's lights, which he surely does not intend to be possible.

Relatedly, but more significantly for current purposes, I think there is a lacuna in Peacocke's approach to a priori knowledge. This second point is related to the first because it turns out to be possible to fill this lacuna in such a way that one ends up both an empiricist by my criteria and a moderate rationalist by Peacocke's lights. (Something like this is, I think, what happens if one adopts the proposal to be outlined in Part II of this book.)

A quick way into the problem I want to raise for Peacocke is to point out that satisfying epistemologies of realistically construed subject matters seem to fit a three-step pattern. First, there is worldly input of some kind into our mental processes. Then, at least typically, some kind of mental processing takes place. And finally, we arrive at a belief. Take, for example, the visual story which we tell to account for much of our knowledge of the physical world around us. First, the physical world impacts causally upon our eyes, and the eyes carry signals to the brain. This constitutes

---

[11] It should be noted that by a 'concept' Peacocke does not mean any kind of mental representation, but rather something more like a Fregean sense, a mode of presentation, or a constituent of a proposition (see Peacocke 1992: sect. 1). In this discussion of Peacocke I shall use 'concept' in his way, though much of what I say can be translated into 'concept'-talk in my preferred sense.

the worldly input into our mental processes. Then various sorts of mental processing of that input take place. And the upshot is that we arrive at a belief about what the physical world around us is like which is responsibly based upon the information received. Of course, there is a great deal of detail to be filled in around this bare-bones outline, but (except in sceptical moods) most of us are confident that some story of this general kind can be told to account for visually based knowledge in the good cases.

There is widespread disquiet as to how such apparently non-empirical methods as analysing concepts can lead to knowledge of realistically construed subject matters. In my opinion, the correct diagnosis of (at least much of) this disquiet is that knowledge which can be had merely by these means does not appear to fit the three-step pattern for realist epistemology. The second two steps seem fine (or, rather, although they are not fully worked out, they are at least not obviously problematic): the mental processing in this case is some sort of introspective investigation of concepts one possesses, and at the end of this process a belief is arrived at. But what of the initial step, the input step? It seems to be missing. My complaint against Peacocke is essentially that his account lacks any input step (empirical or otherwise).

According to Peacocke (2000), what the moderate rationalist needs to do to account for a priori knowledge of p is discover some 'key' relation which holds between

  (a) the possession conditions for certain concepts C involved in p;
  (b) the semantic values of these concepts C;
  (c) the way W in which p is known.

The most important aspects of these 'key' relations will be relations of correlation between features of concepts (= a) and features of the aspects of the world which are their semantic values (= b), which correlations enable us to learn truths about the world by examining those concepts (= c). For instance, Peacocke says that '[t]he possession conditions for the concept *red* of the colour red are tied to those very conditions which individuate the colour red' (2000: 267), and argues that for this reason we can learn something about worldly redness by thinking about the concept *red*.

Peacocke says that '[t]he key relation is one which explains why, when a thinker comes to believe [p] in way W, he can know it to be true in the actual world, justificationally independently of perceptual experience'

(p. 264). But let's begin by noting that it is not clear why merely *identifying* a correlation (or, as Peacocke tends to call it, a 'tie') between concepts and the world should do this kind of explanatory work. In order to explain why W is an a priori way of knowing p, it seems that we will need not only to identify a correlation between (a) and (b), but also to say something about *how it is that we have come to possess concepts for which such a correlation obtains*. To see why, suppose that all we can say on that score is that it fortuitously happens to be the case that subject A possesses a concept *red* whose possession conditions are 'tied' in the way Peacocke envisages to the individuation conditions for some property (redness). In this case, we ought to have qualms about saying that A can come to know any truths about redness by examining the concept *red*. He might arrive at true beliefs by doing so, but this will be, in an important sense, a mere stroke of luck. He could easily have possessed and examined some other concept (or pseudo-concept[12]) rather like *red* but lacking this 'tie' to the individuation conditions of any worldly property. Lucky possession of a concept which happens to be appropriately tied to some property seems no more conducive to the acquisition of knowledge through examination of that concept than lucky possession of a belief which happens to be true seems conducive to the acquisition of knowledge through inference from that belief.

A word is in order here to make clear what kind of 'luck' I have in mind. To do this I need to draw a distinction between accidents which prevent our ascribing knowledge and ones which don't, a distinction most easily illustrated by describing some familiar kinds of case. The kind of accidentalness that prevents our ascribing knowledge is the kind that characterizes cases where we accidentally guess correctly the outcome of a die roll. By contrast, the kind of accident which, in Nozick's thought-experiment (1981: 193) leads to a bystander believing that Jesse James committed a certain bank robbery—namely, the accidental slipping of his mask during the raid, enabling the bystander to see his face—does not interfere with our willingness to ascribe knowledge (more on this in Section 3.6.2). I shall now explain how the wrong (knowledge-destroying) kind of accident could occur in the kind of case at issue here, where someone relies on conceptual examination as the ground for certain beliefs.

---

[12] Peacocke suggests in his (1992: 21 ff.) that anything which is not appropriately tied to a semantic value is at best a 'spurious' concept, a mere pseudo-concept.

Begin by considering the concept or pseudo-concept *Boche*; that is, the concept-level analogue of the word 'Boche' as defined by Dummett in his (1973*b*: 454).[13] (For brevity, I shall henceforth omit the words 'or pseudo-concept', but readers who would prefer them to be included should imagine that they are there.) If someone possessed such a concept and trusted an examination of it (along with others, e.g. *German, cruel*) to guide her beliefs about the world, she would end up believing falsehoods (notably *All Germans are cruel*). In Peacocke's terms, this is presumably because the possession conditions for *Boche* are not appropriately correlated with conditions that individuate real semantic values (in this case, a real property of Bochehood out there in the world). If they were, we would be able to learn truths about the world by examining the concept *Boche* in the same way that (according to Peacocke) we can learn such truths by examining the concept *red*. But, in fact, because there is a mismatch between the concept *Boche* and the world, no such knowledge is possible.

There is, then, an epistemically salient difference between the concepts *red* and *Boche* in this respect. Trusting an examination of concepts like *red* leads to true beliefs, and doing the same with concepts like *Boche* leads to falsehood. However, we're not merely interested in the difference between true and false belief here; Peacocke wants to defend the idea that we can obtain *knowledge* through examining concepts like *red*. To do this, I contend, he needs to say *why* we have ended up possessing concepts like *red*, whose possession conditions are correlated with the individuation conditions of their semantic values, rather than concepts like *Boche*. For some ways of ending up with concepts like *red* rather than concepts like *Boche* would not be conducive to our securing knowledge through examining our concepts.

To see why, consider an analogy between trusting to an examination of concepts and trusting to an examination of a map. Trusting an accurate map can sometimes lead to your believing truths without knowing them. For instance, you may be Gettiered. Suppose a trustworthy friend gives you the map in good faith, believing it to be accurate, but that at the time the map-maker drew the map, it was wildly *in*accurate, and he knew this, and had no reason to suppose it would ever become accurate. He just wanted to mislead people. He then palmed his map off on the friend of yours, who,

---

[13] Thanks to an anonymous journal referee for encouraging me to say more about the intended notion of accidentalness, and for suggesting that I discuss this particular concept in doing so.

having no reason to doubt his honesty or to check the map, eventually gave it to you. In this kind of case we have a strong intuition that you do not gain knowledge by examining the map, even though you will end up with true and justified beliefs. Worse still, there could be cases where you don't even have any justification for the true beliefs you end up with. It could be that you have no good reason to assume that the map is accurate—perhaps you even have reason to think it is probably inaccurate—but you trust it blindly and irrationally all the same. Doing this will result in your having true beliefs, since the map is in fact accurate, but they will not count as justified, or knowledgeable, by anyone's standards.

So it is with concepts. A concept could be such that its possession conditions are tied to the very conditions which individuate the referent of that concept (as Peacocke claims is true of *red*), but not in a way that is conducive to our obtaining knowledge by examining the concept. By analogy with the second map scenario just described, there could be no justification at all for our trusting the concept to serve as an accurate guide to truth—there could even be reasons to *dis*trust it. Blindly trusting it may still lead us to true beliefs, but they will not be knowledgeable (or even, perhaps, justified; though things do get a little trickier here). Or, by analogy with the first map scenario, there could be ample justification for trusting the concept to serve as an accurate guide to truth, but there might be something Gettier-like about this justification. (Perhaps a very reliable philosopher has told you, truly, that the concept is a good guide to the truth, but his reasons for thinking so involved a terrible mistake that destroyed her justification for that belief.)

My preferred condition for distinguishing knowledge from other kinds of true belief (one which is designed to be applicable to knowledge of necessary truths as well as others), is an explanationist condition (see Chapter 3). What Peacocke owes us, in my opinion, is some reason to think that there is the right kind of (non-deviant) explanatory link between the facts we learn through conceptual examination and our belief in these facts. Whatever we think knowledge of a necessary truth amounts to, however, it should be common ground that more is required for a belief to count as knowledge than that the belief rest epistemically on our trust in some in-fact-accurate guide. The lacuna in Peacocke's project is that, even assuming everything he says is true, he has offered us no reason to think that concepts are anything better than an in-fact-accurate guide. To do more than that he would need to describe an input step into the process of concept examination—some kind of impact on us by the world, in virtue of which we come, non-accidentally, to possess and be guided by the right sorts of concepts. This is pretty much what Part II of this book attempts to do.

We can fill out the objection to Peacocke a little by turning to some of the details of his discussion. His first and simplest case concerns knowledge that A can be inferred from A&B. This, he says, is a case where 'it is written into, or is a consequence of, the possession conditions for one or more of the concepts in the given principle that to possess those concepts, the thinker must be willing to accept the principle, by reaching it in [a certain] way' (p. 265). He continues:

> The key relation for a special case like this is one abstracted from the following condition: that what makes something the semantic value of conjunction ... is that it makes truth-preserving those inferences, like the inference from A&B to A, which are mentioned in the possession conditions for conjunction, and which are made in the specified way.

I think this is unobjectionable, as far as it goes. But I do not think it can answer the very deep question Peacocke wants it to answer; namely, how is it known a priori that A can be inferred from A&B? For it fails to address the question of how we have come to possess concepts whose possession conditions enshrine a set of genuinely truth-preserving inference types, which, as I have argued, is something we need to know in order to assess the claim that examining these concepts can lead to knowledge. That we do possess such concepts is merely stated. If possession of such concepts enables us to *know* conceptual truths, rather than merely believe them truly, possession of the right concepts cannot be merely accidental in the way that a lucky guess is accidental, or in the way that true belief is accidental in a Gettier case.

Maybe we are supposed to *assume* that our possession of such concepts is non-accidental in the required sense, just as we would normally assume, on being told that a map is accurate, that it was intentionally drawn accurately and so on, so that an examination of it can lead to knowledge about the place it represents. However, to leave matters there would be to leave a lot of epistemological work still to be done, without giving grounds for optimism that it *can* be done. The epistemologist who favours this sort of account of a priori knowledge owes us some grounds for confidence that we can account for our non-accidentally possessing the right kind of concepts. There are certainly no familiar accounts that can be relied upon without comment.

Moreover, the kind of account that I believe we might give (see Part II) finds an essential role for the senses in mediating between the world and our possession of the right kind of concepts. If this is the right approach, it would be at best misleading to describe the resultant view as a kind of 'moderate rationalism'—it would seem, rather, to be a form of empiricism (for reasons which will, I hope, become clear in Part II). If, on the other hand, this sort of mediating role is not played by the senses, what *does* Peacocke think will play it? A rationalist of a more traditional kind might reach for 'rational intuition' here, but the moderate rationalist cannot do this. Yet if there are grounds for confidence that something other than the senses or a faculty of rational intuition will turn the required trick, Peacocke has not yet told us what they are.

Similar points can be made about Peacocke's discussion of numbers and arithmetical relations. He claims that '[j]udgements about the sum of two numbers … will … be correct … because they involve thinking of these relations in ways tied to their very individuation' (p. 270). Similarly, he states that 'to have a canonical concept c of some natural number n is to have a fundamental procedure for determining whether there are c Fs for which *it is immediately obvious* that the procedure respects the condition for there to be n Fs' (p. 271, emphasis added). And again, on p. 277, it is assumed that the concept *natural number* is 'tied to the individuation of the property it picks out'.

In his (2000) and in a later work (2004: ch. 6) Peacocke does appreciate the need to explain why, according to his theory, conceptual examination can generate knowledge and not merely true beliefs. But what he says on this point (2004: 173) is that

[a]ccording to [the] theory, in using an a priori way of coming to judge that p a thinker is using a method which guarantees, as a result of the very nature of p and the way in which its truth-condition is determined, that the thinker judges that p only if it is the case that p. When the soundness of a method is thus internally related to what it is for the content to be true, it is hard to see what more could be required for knowledge. Such a constitutive grounding of the soundness of the method goes far beyond merely reliabilist conditions for knowledge.

This goes a little beyond Peacocke (2000), which also flags what he thinks of as the super-reliability of a priori ways of coming to judgements, but lays less stress on what he is here calling the 'constitutive' or 'internal' nature of the envisaged relationship.

Nonetheless, even the (2004) comments are not, I think, sufficient to address the issue at hand. If it is a mere accident (in the sense outlined above) that we possess concepts which are linked up to the world in the right way, then however 'constitutive' it is of the concepts we actually have that their possession conditions are tied to the individuation conditions of their semantic values, examining our concepts is *not* a very reliable method of securing true beliefs in the relevant sense (never mind whether such reliability would be sufficient for knowledge). For we could so easily have had other, less helpful, concepts.

Admittedly, if we think of the method as examining those very concepts that we actually possess, soundness is assured. But it is *not* assured if we think of the method as examining the concepts we possess whatever they happen to be. Epistemological reliabilism familiarly faces difficult questions about how 'methods' or 'processes' are to be individuated, and it is often possible to cook up 'reliable methods' in cases where knowledge is clearly lacking. There is a risk that this is what is happening when we say that examining our concepts is reliable because it is constitutive of the concepts we actually have that their possession conditions are tied to individuation conditions for their semantic values. By analogy, blindly and irrationally believing what the oracle says is in *some* sense reliable (it won't ever lead us astray) if we happen to live in a world where the oracle only says true things. But (one might well think) this generates no interesting counterfactual reliability of the kind that the epistemological reliabilist should be interested in.

My worry is that, for all Peacocke has told us, the perfect reliability of the envisaged a priori methods of coming to know may be like that of blindly and irrationally trusting the oracle in cases where, fortunately, the oracle speaks only the truth.[14] If we think our method in the oracle case is blindly trusting the things the oracle *actually* says (cf. examining the concepts we actually have), then the method is perfectly sound provided

---

[14] If it would help to make the cases seem even more similar, we could have the oracle utter only necessary truths. Then we can compare the current concern with a concern expressed by O'Leary-Hawthorne (1996: 188–9) about Lewis's claim that one gets modal knowledge 'for free' once one has a true modal belief simply because one could not be mistaken in that belief.

we inhabit a world where the oracle only speaks the truth (cf. a world where we have concepts which are tied to the individuation conditions of real properties). But if we want reliabilism to deliver the right result in the oracle case—that there is no knowledge because of the blind, irrational nature of our trust—then we ought to think of the method involved as being (something at least as general as) blindly trusting the oracle *whatever* she says (cf. examining our concepts whatever they happen to be). And if it's just lucky that the oracle always speaks the truth in the actual world, *this* method doesn't look like a reliable one—at least not in any sense the reliabilist is interested in. More general specifications of the method (e.g. blindly trusting anyone to whom others ascribe authority) are even worse off.

Bealer (2000) also defends a form of what he calls 'moderate rationalism', which is in some ways similar to Peacocke's. However, there are also some important differences, and as a result my objection, although similar to my objection to Peacocke, can profitably be rejigged so that it is explicitly targeted on Bealer's proposal. I shall be brief, however, since the structure of the point is the same.

For Bealer, to be a moderate rationalist is to believe that '[a] person's phenomenal experiences *and intuitions* comprise the person's basic evidence' (p. 7), where to have an 'intuition' that p in Bealer's sense is for it to seem to you in an a priori way as if p (p. 3) and to have evidence is to have a reason (pp. 2–3). So Bealer is effectively saying that if you accept that there are a priori ways for it to seem to you as if p, and these seemings can figure as reasons, then you are a rationalist. This skirts dangerously close to assuming that all apriorism amounts to rationalism, and that strikes me as unwise: there are plenty of (non-Quinean) empiricists who acknowledge and try to make room for some kind of a priori knowledge, and may well want a priori seemings to count as reasons. But presumably Bealer does not intend that an empiricist could be a 'moderate rationalist'.[15]

---

[15] Although I am an empiricist, I am not going to deny that (the things Bealer calls) intuitions can constitute (what he calls) evidence, and therefore am not going to run up against the epistemic self-defeat problems that he presents for empiricists in his (1992). (Only 'radical' empiricists who deny the a priori are targeted by those problems.) Bealer characterizes empiricism as the view that '[a] person's phenomenal experiences and/or observations comprise the person's evidence'. If I am right, it is possible to defend a form of (what I'd call) empiricism whereby a person's reasons can include a priori 'intuitions' which are epistemically underwritten by empirical input. This means that either the

In some ways Bealer sees the problem in a very similar light to Peacocke and myself: he argues that what we need to do is explain how a priori intuitions can constitute what he calls 'evidence'. That is, we need to understand how intuitions can be a good epistemic guide to truth, and he wants to approach this issue by looking to some fact about our concepts as the basis of an explanation of the links between intuitions and truth.

Bealer additionally believes that possession of the relevant concept(s) entails, *by virtue of the definition of concept possession*, a certain kind of modal tie between intuitions involving that concept and truth. One concern this raises is that, to anyone who thinks it is just obvious that we have concepts, Bealer's definition of concept possession, according to which possession entails a modal link between intuitions involving those concepts and the truth, will appear mistaken. For it is far from obvious that, as a matter of definition, our possessing (the things we ordinarily think of as) concepts entails that our intuitions involving them will be modally tied to the truth. This needn't matter too much, however; we can grant Bealer a use of 'concept' whereby the only things that count as 'concepts' meet the condition he specifies.

My primary worry about Bealer's approach is that if Bealer is right about the definition of concept possession, he needs to explain how it comes about that we possess any concepts. By his lights, possessing a concept puts one in a very fortunate position vis-à-vis knowing truths through intuition. So doing the epistemology of intuitions by simply assuming we possess concepts in this strong sense feels like cheating. Any satisfying epistemology of intuitions will have to explain how such a fortunate thing as concept possession in Bealer's sense could have come about, when we could so easily have possessed things which function rather like concepts but are not such that, by definition, their possession stands in the appropriate modal relationship with the truth of the intuitions they give rise to.

Notice that like Peacocke's account, Bealer's does not include any input step. An input step would be the right kind of thing to explain why we possess Bealer-concepts, rather than something less useful. Without an input step, the epistemology looks incomplete in a crucial regard. Unless Bealer

relevant kind of empirical input does not count as 'phenomenal experience and/or observation', in which case I am not an empiricist by Bealer's lights, or it does, in which case I am both an empiricist *and* a moderate rationalist by Bealer's lights. Neither result seems particularly happy.

can reassure us that a non-empirical input step is available, his moderate rationalism is missing something very important.

2.6 Alternatives to empiricism: Field

Field (2000, 2006) tries to motivate another alternative to empiricism, which is quite different from both traditional rationalism and the moderate rationalisms of Peacocke and Bealer. Though he too thinks that some propositions can be reasonably believed without empirical support, he does not think this is because they have positive justification through rational intuition or through our grasp of meanings or concepts.

He suggests, rather, that certain kinds of propositions are 'default reasonable', and as such neither need nor admit of justification from any source. They can be known without justification. Field proposes an 'evaluativist' approach to a priori knowledge, whereby our assessments of methodologies (and, presumably, propositions encapsulating them[16]) as 'reasonable' are taken to be merely evaluations of those methodologies. He goes on to suggest that some methodologies are 'default reasonable'—positively evaluated in the absence of justification. Default reasonableness is by my lights a priori reasonableness, since default reasonable propositions do not rely for their reasonableness on support from empirical evidence, hence aprioricity is accounted for without the need to postulate either rational intuition or knowledge underwritten by our grasp of meaning or concepts.

Evaluativism and default reasonableness are separable components of Field's view; others have defended something like default reasonableness without evaluativism (see e.g. Wright 2004, and Jenkins 2007b for a critical discussion of Wright's view) and something like evaluativism without default reasonableness (see Gibbard 1990). However, the evaluativism is supposed to play a key role in making the claim of default reasonableness palatable. At first blush we wonder what reasonableness could consist in, and where it could come from, in the absence of justification. As the evaluativist sees things, however, 'reasonableness doesn't *consist in* anything' (Field 2000: 127) and does not come from anywhere; 'entitlement is not a

---

[16] It is not entirely clear what sort of relationship Field envisages between the default reasonable rules and the default reasonable propositions. He postulates both, but most of his discussion and argument focusses on rules.

fluid whose creation needs explanation' (Field 2006: 74). Reasonableness in the absence of justification is perhaps less mysterious if in calling something 'reasonable' we are just positively evaluating it.

There is prima facie something deeply unappealing about evaluativism: our intuitions rebel at the suggestion that reasonableness is 'not a factual property' (2000: 127) and that '[i]n calling a rule reasonable we are evaluating it, and all that makes sense to ask about is what we value' (p. 138). What can Field say to convince us that it is nonetheless correct? Well, if he can convince us that there are default-reasonable methodologies, maybe evaluativism will seem the best option for making sense of the existence of default reasonableness. To make this watertight, Field would need to tell us what is wrong with all the alternative proposals for making sense of this phenomenon. But let's grant him that, and see whether we ought to follow him in his arguments for default reasonableness.

The principal argument for the existence of default-reasonable methodologies is found in Field (2000: 120–1). This is a 'familiar argument', which starts from the premise that 'certain methodologies, including deductive reasoning, inductive reasoning, forming beliefs as a result of observation or testimony or memory-impression, and so forth' must be default reasonable because 'no justification for anything could be given without using some of these forms of reasoning'. So, Field reckons, assuming we reject circular justifications, these methodologies must themselves lack justification. Hence, they must either be unreasonable, or reasonable despite having no justification; that is, default reasonable. He is unwilling to follow the sceptic in regarding them as unreasonable, so he concludes that they are default reasonable.

This argument has two main problems (at least, it has two which concern us here). The first problem, which is really a pair of related problems, is that the argument does not establish that all—or perhaps even any—of the basic methodologies he mentions are default reasonable. The premise of the argument is that, for every justification J we can give, not all of the basic methodologies Field lists can be eliminated from J. This is obviously very different from saying that all of the basic methodologies are ineliminable from J. Field's premise, as it stands, could be true just because for any justification J, inductive reasoning (say) is ineliminable from J. This makes it seem very much as if the most Field's argument can hope to establish as it stands is that *at least one* of the basic methodologies on his list is default reasonable.

Relatedly, we have not been shown that there is anything particularly special about the methodologies on Field's list. We could add all sorts of things to the list (including crazy methodologies like guessing and believing at least three contradictions regardless) without altering the fact that, for any justification J, not all the things on the list can be eliminated from J. But presumably Field would not want to draw the conclusion that all these things we might add are default reasonable.

Field could hope to have shown something special about the particular methodologies on his list if he could show that for each such methodology M, every justification J which we can give is such that M is ineliminable from J. But that would be a huge philosophical task, and I doubt whether he in fact believes anything of the kind (else he would not have used the weaker premise he actually employs in his argument). It is far from obvious even that for each of Field's 'default reasonable' methodologies M, every justification J *of M* that we can give is such that M is ineliminable from J.[17] *Maybe* induction and/or deduction are like this, though even that is highly controversial. As a claim about memorial and testimonial methodologies it is incredible; inductive justifications can surely be given for trusting one's memory or others' testimony.

The second, and for our purposes crucial, problem with Field's argument (2000) is that it relies on our taking it as read that justifications are arguments. He says that the giving of justifications for basic methodologies involves the use of some of those methodologies (i.e. some of these argumentative moves), and takes it that if no such justification can be *given* without relying on them then there *is* no justification that does not rely on them. In other words, he is taking it that *justifications* are the arguments that would be used if one were asked to *give* a justification. (We shall see in a moment that although the discussion of Field (2006) is more careful about this, no positive argument is offered there and the (2000) argument is not repaired.)

As such, Field's argument should be viewed with extreme suspicion by most epistemological externalists, and probably by many internalists as well. It is clear that, although Field thinks that the distinction between internalism and externalism rests on a presupposition that is shown to be false once his view is adopted (p. 138), he does not intend his argument to be convincing only to those who *set out* accepting a particularly restrictive

---

[17] Thanks to Aidan McGlynn here.

view of what justification is that most externalists would reject (or at least, if he does intend his argument to have such narrow appeal, he is not up-front about it).

I should note that in (2000: 121 n.) Field offers a definition of externalism which is importantly different from mine. He writes:

The externalist holds that a necessary condition on the reasonable employment of inductive procedures or perceptual procedures is that those procedures in fact be 'reliable' or 'truth-conducive' or whatever (where the 'whatever' covers any other intuitively 'externalist' condition that might be imposed). This is compatible with certain procedures being default reasonable: it just implies (i) that what procedures are default reasonable depends on which ones satisfy the appropriate externalist conditions; and (ii) that evidence in favour of the satisfaction of those conditions isn't also necessary for the procedures to be reasonably employed.

A few comments about this. First, Field's 'externalist' imposes a certain kind of necessary condition, whereas mine merely rejects one of the internalist's necessary conditions. Second, (ii) is not an implication of externalism as defined by Field. His attitude to (ii) suggests that the notion of externalism that Field really has in mind involves rejection of a necessary condition imposed by internalists (perhaps *alongside* the acceptance of certain necessary conditions that may or may not be acceptable to internalists).

Most importantly for current purposes, nothing Field says here has any tendency to undermine the objection to his 'familiar argument' which I am interested in here. It may be true that default reasonableness is *compatible* with externalism and other positions which reject his presuppositions about what justification is, but that is not to the point. The point is that those who reject these presuppositions should not be swayed by Field's argument for default reasonableness.

A certain kind of internalist might suppose that in order to be justified in accepting M, S must be capable of becoming aware of what her justification for M is, and that this will involve her being capable of providing a good argument for M. But for externalists[18] there is simply no reason to think that arguments need to get in on the act at all. Even internalists could deny that being capable of becoming aware of what one's justification is consists

---

[18] I suppose a certain kind of externalist could hold that S's being justified in accepting M consists in there *being* a good argument for M, although S herself does not need to be capable of becoming aware of it. But most externalists tend to think of justification quite differently.

in being capable of providing a good argument. So one can concede to Field that no non-circular *arguments* for basic methodologies can be given, without feeling pressure to accept that there are no non-circular *justifications* for them.

Field's talk of what sorts of arguments can be given, as opposed to what sorts of justifications there can be, is not merely a small slip of the tongue in the presentation of an argument which can easily be made kosher. To repair the argument, Field would need to show that any kind of justification for methodologies M that S can have—*whether or not* that amounts to an argument for M—will somehow rely on S's already accepting M. But there is no obvious reason to think this is so, and Field offers none. Most of the more interesting accounts of a priori knowledge are compatible with—or explicitly postulate—kinds of a priori justification which will falsify the required generalization: traditional rationalism, moderate rationalism in the style of Peacocke or Bealer, Quinean radical empiricism, and my Part II view, to name a few. Prior rejection of all these options would be needed in order to grant Field the premise he requires. And, while I am happy to reject most of them for one reason or another, I think the view to be discussed in Part II is still a runner.

Field is noticeably more careful about the difference between justifications and arguments in his (2006). Here, however, no positive argument for evaluativism is offered; evaluativism is presented merely as a 'suggestion'. There is no attempt to recast the (2000) argument to deal with the above problem. However, some of the things Field says might be a little misleading on this point, so let me clarify here. Field's suggestion in his (2006: 86) is that:

(A) Our entitlement to use a logic or inductive policy can't depend on our having an argument for it; we are entitled 'by default'.
(B) Nor need our entitlement depend on there being some kind of justification other than argument... [I]n saying that we're default-entitled to our logic and methodology, I'm merely expressing an attitude of approval...

A couple of things are noteworthy about this. One is that, despite appearances, the claim that follows the semicolon in (A) is far from being supported by that which precedes the semicolon, for the reasons just described. Another is that (B) doesn't say that there *can't* be non-argument justifications for our logic and methodology, but that there *need not* be any.

No attempt is made to show that there is no such justification, or even to inspire doubts on the point.

Field does attempt to argue in his (2000) that one form of reliabilism, which he calls 'naturalistic reductionism', is 'thoroughly implausible' (pp. 124–6). The name 'naturalistic reductionism' is a questionable name for the particular reliabilist view that Field has in mind, however, for reductions of reasonableness to other natural properties than reliability are available and these ought also to count as kinds of 'naturalistic reductionism'. It should also be borne in mind that some of those who should count as reliabilists might just offer necessary and sufficient conditions on knowledge (or justification or reasonableness or whatever) in terms of reliability, whereas 'reductionism' suggests more—something closer to conceptual analysis or a metaphysical-dependence view.

Field writes as if this kind of reliabilism were the only alternative available on which justifications are not arguments. Of the seven objections to reliabilism he describes, only two have any shot at being applicable to non-reliabilist views.[19] The first simply mentions a kind of internalist intuition, so I shall not discuss it further here. For those who feel the force of it, it might be well enough accounted for by admitting *an* internalist sense of 'reasonable' (cf. Section 2.2 above). The other states that the identification of reasonableness with a natural property 'seems to strip it of its normative force', and that when two people disagree fundamentally 'about which natural property is coextensive with reasonableness, it is difficult to take seriously the idea that one party ... is right and the others wrong'. Taking these two points in reverse order, I do not know why Field finds it hard to take this idea seriously. It seems to me that it should be taken *very* seriously, even if one disagrees in the end. The other worry, about stripping reasonableness of its normative force by identifying it with some natural property, is avoided by the sort of non-evaluativist who merely gives necessary and sufficient conditions on reasonableness in terms of some natural property. It is not clear in any case how convincing that worry is; for those who think normative properties are natural properties, to say that the natural property is inadequate because it has no normative oomph is just to beg the question against the view that that very natural property

---

[19] Not all the points Field makes against reliabilism seem convincing to me either, but as defending reliabilism is not my concern I shall not talk about them here.

is itself a normative property, and hence in possession of all the required oomph (see Jenkins 2007a for discussion of a kind of epistemic naturalism which has the resources to parry this type of objection).

So much, then, for Field's principal argument for his evaluativism. The only other positive point he makes in favour of his view is that it undermines sceptical arguments (2000: 143): arguments which, I am tempted to think, should not be so easy as that to undermine. Other than that, support for evaluativism in Field (2000) and (2006) derives solely from the apparent dearth of alternatives. I contend that the suggestion of Part II below is a live alternative, and that it offends fewer intuitions than evaluativism does.

2.7 Summary

In this Chapter, I briefly described the kind of epistemological externalism with which I shall be working. I then surveyed some objections to standard empiricist attempts to deal with the a priori. I acknowledged their force against their targets, but promised that I would propose a quite different strategy for the empiricist which would not be similarly affected. I also considered two non-empiricist approaches to the a priori, one a 'moderate rationalist' approach exemplified by Peacocke and Bealer, the other an 'evaluativist' approach due to Field. I argued that Peacocke's and Bealer's proposals are incomplete, and that Field's is counter-intuitive and not supported by argument. Now I turn to another epistemological preliminary to my discussion of arithmetical knowledge: a discussion of knowledge in general.

3

A Theory of Knowledge

3.1 Introduction

In this section, I propose that knowledge is true belief which can be well explained, to someone not acquainted with the details of the subject's situation (an 'outsider'), just by citing the proposition believed. I show how this differs from some existing theories of knowledge which also appeal to explanation. I then show that the proposal is immune to Gettier-type counter-examples, and that it helps make sense of the appeal and short-comings of various other philosophical theories and of certain intuitions. Finally, I consider and respond to potential objections.

The purpose of this section is to supply background for my discussion of arithmetical knowledge. Mathematical epistemology can be made to seem more difficult than it really is when some theory of (or condition on) knowledge is adopted which seems to render mathematical knowledge impossible. I aim to remove this sort of obstacle by establishing as plausible an account of knowledge which will present no special difficulties in the case of arithmetic. This section will also, I hope, throw some light on what exactly is required of a satisfying account of arithmetical knowledge.

3.2 A theory of knowledge

In Section 2.2, I suggested that there is a good sense of 'knowledge' and a good sense of 'justified' on which externalism is correct. In this section, I shall be discussing knowledge in that externalist sense. I allow that there may be another good sense on which knowledge is only possible in cases where one is able to cite one's grounds, or on which some other internalist constraint must be met. However, this internalist notion of knowledge (if there is one) will not be my concern, either here or in my later attempts to develop a theory of arithmetical knowledge.

Craig (1990) casts doubt upon the project of trying to give the traditional sort of necessary and sufficient conditions for *A knows that p*. He interprets the inadequacy of existing analyses of knowledge as evidence that our concept of knowledge is complex and diffuse, and concludes that we should aim to understand it by thinking about the role the concept plays in our lives, rather than by trying to find necessary and sufficient conditions for the truth of knowledge ascriptions.

There is surely something right about Craig's view: we are unlikely to succeed in any attempt to analyse away the intricacies in our concept of knowledge. We cannot realistically hope to uncover a set of necessary and sufficient conditions for *A knows that p* which are in all cases either clearly satisfied or clearly not satisfied. Nor, I suspect, is it possible to offer necessary and sufficient conditions for knowledge which are widely accepted as being more securely understood than knowledge itself.

But to conclude on this basis that we should therefore stop trying to find *any* interesting necessary and sufficient conditions for *A knows that p* may be going a step too far. Perhaps we can further our understanding of what knowledge is by uncovering necessary and sufficient conditions which *share* the complexities of the target proposition. We can aim, not to 'clean up' these problematic features, but to capture them in ways which may prove illuminating even if they do not amount to reductive analyses.

In this section, I attempt a project of this kind. I propose a necessary and sufficient condition for *A knows that p* which is, although recognizably similar to the traditional sets of conditions, arguably immune to the kind of counter-example which tends to deter philosophers from thinking that any illuminating conditions can be found.[1] I present this condition, however, not as an analysis of knowledge, but rather as a way of getting a handle on the concept and furthering the effort to understand what its role in our lives might be. Taken in this spirit, the current proposal is not at odds with the principles that motivate Craig's view. In denying my proposal the status of a reductive analysis, I am mindful of the fact that it will tell us little more than that knowledge is 'non-accidental' true belief. What it offers is an

---

[1] Besides Craig, this concern is notable in Williamson (2000: 2−5).

(I hope, elucidatory) way of spelling out what is meant by 'non-accidental' in this context.

In what follows, I shall write 'KAp' for 'A knows that p' and 'BAp' for 'A believes that p.' I shall propose that KAp just in case BAp and it can be said (under specific circumstances, to be described shortly) that A believes p *because* p is true. But this is not a causal account of knowledge. The 'because' signals not causation, but explanation.

Explanationist accounts of knowledge somewhat similar to mine have been proposed by Alan Goldman[2] (1988 and elsewhere) and Steven Rieber (1998). However, neither of these philosophers exploits what I take to be the most important strengths of an account of this type. Consequently Goldman's and Rieber's accounts face serious objections, which I think may be avoided by a sufficiently sophisticated explanationism. These objections will be discussed in Section 3.3 below.

Neta (2002) has offered an account of knowledge which he claims is a modification of Rieber's. In fact, however, it is significantly different: Neta proposes that KAp iff p is 'the reason that' BAp (p. 668). This sounds like an explanationist account, until we discover that 'reasons' are to be contrasted with 'non-rational causes', revealing that Neta's is essentially a kind of justified-true-belief account. His proposal is that KAp iff A reasonably believes that p on the strength of A's conclusive evidence that p (p. 668). Neta is an externalist about evidence, thus avoiding some of the familiar objections to this kind of view.[3] But, while explanationist accounts of the kind I am interested in do focus on 'reasons' for belief in some sense, it is not required on these accounts that they be epistemic reasons.

My own proposal is that KAp just in case the following condition is met:

---

[2] All further references to 'Goldman' in this chapter are to Alan Goldman unless otherwise specified.

[3] Nevertheless, there are still problems. One is that sophisticated Gettier-like counter-examples can be produced to which the account is vulnerable. Suppose A, an extremely reliable and totally honest informant, remembers that p and informs B that he does. (I am using 'informs' in a factive way here.) B, reasonably, trusts him. However, unknown to B, A is on this occasion improperly ignoring some evidence that he has recently had brain surgery resulting in a few false 'memories'. B's evidence is that A has informed her that he remembers that p. This is conclusive evidence in Neta's sense: A could not have it if p were not true. For A cannot inform B of something false, so he must in fact remember that p; and nor can A remember something false, so it must be that p. Nevertheless, since A is improperly ignoring evidence, it is plausible that he does not know p. It is therefore also plausible that B does not know p either, since B is relying on A's testimony.

K: p is a good explanation of BAp for someone not acquainted with the particular details of A's situation (an 'outsider').[4]

I shall say a bit more about outsiders in a moment. First, note that, with **K** in place, we do not need to include clauses stating that p and BAp are true, since (I take it as read that) only true propositions make good explanations, and only true propositions can be explained. Note also that **K** does not require that p be *the* good explanation of BAp, or even the good explanation for an outsider of BAp. Explanations may be more or less good depending on the interests and intentions of their recipients, which will vary from context to context. All **K** requires is that there be *some* context in which an outsider might ask 'Why BAp?' and be well answered by 'Because p'.[5]

An outsider, in the sense envisaged here, is a person O who meets three conditions:

(1) O is rational, and can understand the content of A's belief that p (i.e. is capable of entertaining the proposition p).

(2) O is aware of *commonplace* facts about people and their mental lives, i.e. facts about what it is like, in general terms, to be a rational thinking person.

(3) O is not aware of any *special* facts about A or A's situation. O is aware that A is a person and that A believes that p, but that is all.

In what follows, I shall motivate my condition **K** by showing how it avoids Gettier counter-examples (Sections 3.4–3.5) and how it accommodates the motivations for various other theories of, and intuitions about, knowledge (Section 3.6). I shall then respond to an objection, in Section 3.7. First, however, I must show how my account differs from Goldman's and Rieber's, and why some improvement on their accounts seems necessary. This will occupy Section 3.3.

---

[4] Note that I assume it is not necessary, for p to be a good explanation of BAp in a context C, that p *actually be cited* in C as an explanation of BAp. It is enough that if it were so cited it would be a good explanation.

[5] 'Well answered' skims over an important question: well answered in a subjective sense, whereby the recipient feels satisfied with the answer, or a more objective sense, whereby the recipient has been told what she needed to know? I have in mind the more objective notion here. While it may be somewhat harder to detect goodness of explanations in this more objective sense, I think we are generally able to do a pretty good job of detecting it. I talk more about explanation, including the difference between the subjective and objective kinds, in Jenkins (forthcoming *b*). Thanks to an anonymous OUP reader for some helpful comments here.

3.3 Other explanationist accounts

Goldman (1988: 22) proposes that KAp iff p 'enters prominently into the best explanation of BAp', and Rieber (1998: 194) suggests that KAp iff p 'explains' BAp.

Let us consider Goldman's account first. I do not object to this account on the grounds that it appeals to 'the best explanation' of BAp. In fact this is something of a red herring, as it is later undercut by disclaimers. For instance, on pages 25–6 we are told that 'the explanation for a belief relevant to its evaluation as a claim to knowledge may not be the explanation uniquely best for all explanatory purposes'.

Goldman's response to a certain kind of objection might be criticized, but this problem is not devastating either. The objection in question states that facts about the future cannot enter into the best explanations of current beliefs, so that on Goldman's account we cannot know such facts. In fact, I see no reason to doubt that facts about the future explain certain facts about the present, including facts about present beliefs, so the objection does not seem worrying to me.[6] Goldman, however, feels that some more substantial response is needed (perhaps because he has a probability-raising analysis of explanation, and envisages probability raising as being somehow causal or quasi-causal). He therefore weakens his account so as to allow cases where some common fact enters prominently into the best explanations of both p and BAp to count as cases of knowledge. He allows, for instance, that KAp whenever the existence of some evidence e explains both BAp and p.

This, of course, is isomorphic to the attempt made by Alvin Goldman (1967: 364 ff.) to rescue his causal theory of knowledge by allowing that there is knowledge wherever a single event causes both p and BAp. The strategy is problematic in both cases for the same reason: the resulting accounts seem too weak. Almost any pair of facts p and BAp have *some* part of their explanatory histories in common, if only the big bang. So almost any belief counts as knowledge.

Can this sort of worry be finessed by demanding that the common element be something 'prominent' in the 'best' explanations of both p and BAp? This is not clear; for one thing, the resulting account is still too weak by Goldman's own lights. For if we accepted it, we ought also to

---

[6] Daniel Nolan and I discuss backwards explanation in Jenkins and Nolan (forthcoming).

accept that, on buying a lottery ticket, I know it will not win. After all, the existence of a great many other tickets enters prominently into the best explanations both of the fact that my ticket will not win and of the fact that I believe it will not win. But Goldman thinks that I do not know my ticket will not win (1988: 52).

This is not a conclusive objection, however; some may be willing to accept that I know my ticket will not win. Maybe more worrying examples could be constructed, but I shall not linger on this point. As I have said, I do not think the objection which prompts Goldman to modify his account in this way is really worrying. So even if he has failed to address it properly, this does not show there is anything fundamentally wrong with his account.

What *does* seem to be wrong with the account is that, for reasons independent of the amendment to allow for future knowledge, it is too weak as it stands. For p might 'enter prominently' into the 'best' explanation of BAp in all sorts of cases where we would not want to ascribe knowledge. For instance, a bang on the head might, simply through having a certain kind of physical impact on my brain, and not via any rational process, cause me to believe I've just received a bang on the head. In such a case, Goldman's condition is surely met: a prominent part of the best explanation of my belief is the fact believed. Yet I do not *know* that I have just received a bang on the head.

To deal with such problems, Goldman complicates his account by imposing an additional constraint, which he calls 'Condition C'. In order to understand it we must note that, for Goldman, to explain something is to raise its probability. Condition C reads as follows:

The explanans for a belief, which explanans explains (type 1) or is explained by (type 2) the fact to which the belief refers, must be such that: if it is a type 1 explanans, its raising the probability of the belief is itself made more probable by its raising the probability of the fact to which the belief refers; if it is a type 2 explanans, its raising the probability of the belief is made more probable by its being made more probable by the fact to which the belief refers.

(1988: 36)

(Note that the 'type 2' explanation is supposed to be the normal case, while the 'type 1' explanation is the kind allowed by Goldman's amendment to deal with knowledge of future facts.)

Unfortunately, even when condition C is incorporated, Goldman's account is too weak. It is susceptible to counter-examples of the sort described by Gettier (1963). Suppose I see Professor Craig driving a BMW, and conclude that one of the Cambridge philosophy professors owns a BMW. Unbeknownst to me, the BMW Professor Craig is driving is owned by Professor Heal, who has lent him the car for the day. In this situation, we do not want to say that I *know* one of the Cambridge philosophy professors owns a BMW.

Let A be me, let p be *one of the Cambridge philosophy professors owns a BMW*, and let q be *Professor Craig is driving a BMW*. Now q surely features prominently in 'the best' explanation of BAp, and p plausibly features prominently in 'the best' explanation of q. Thus it may well be that p features prominently in 'the best' ultimate explanation of BAp, so that Goldman's original condition on knowledge is met. What's more, condition C is also met: q is a type 2 explanans of BAp, and [the fact that p makes q more probable] makes it more probable that [q makes BAp more probable]. This is because I am a rational person, and so the weight I attach to evidence like q in deciding whether to believe p is sensitive to the probabilistic relations between q and p in the way C demands. Indeed, Condition C is best thought of as a kind of rationality constraint, enforcing this kind of sensitivity. Viewing it as such makes plain why it is susceptible to Gettierization, since what Gettier cases show is that beliefs can be perfectly true, justified, and rational, and yet still fail to amount to knowledge.

Goldman's questionable analysis of explanation is another potentially weak point in his account. As I mentioned, it is a probability-raising analysis. More precisely, Goldman demands that an explanans must raise the probability of the explanandum, without there being some other background factor which wholly accounts for this difference (1988: 23). The trouble is that sometimes one proposition can explain another without raising its probability. Consider, for instance, 'fail-safe' cases such as the following. There is a probability of 0.5 that my cat will jump on to the bed at 7.29 a.m., knocking my alarm clock to the floor and breaking it, in which case there is a probability of 0.9 that I will wake up as a result of being jumped on (but no chance of the alarm clock going off). If she doesn't jump on me, then my alarm clock will go off at 7.30, in which case there is a probability of 0.9 that I will wake up as a result of hearing the alarm. Suppose she does jump on to the bed at 7.29. Then a perfectly good explanation of why I am awake at 7.31 is that she jumped on to the bed at 7.29. However, the probability of my being awake at 7.31 is not raised by her jumping on to the bed. Before she did so, the probability of my being awake at 7.31 was $(0.5 \times 0.9) + (0.5 \times 0.9) = 0.9$. And after she does so, the probability of my being awake at 7.31 is still 0.9.

There are ways of responding to this point by appealing not to the probability of the explanandum's being true if its explanans is not true, but to the probability of its being brought about *in the same way* if the explanans is not true (a manoeuvre that parallels the familiar Nozickian appeal to the 'methods' by which a belief is formed). Whether or not there is any mileage in this line of response depends on whether there is a stable notion of being brought about in the same way which is fine-grained enough to enable us to answer the objection without being so fine-grained that anything involved in the causal history of p will trivially count as explanatory of p (because if it had not happened p could not have happened in *exactly* the same way).

Unlike Goldman, I do not depend on any particular account of explanation. I shall rely on intuitions about explanation, such as the view that an explanation is an answer to a why question, and the view that why questions are implicitly contrastive (which claims are defended by e.g. van Fraassen 1980 and Garfinkel 1981). In defence of this strategy, I would say that these intuitions are so fundamental they ought to be respected by any account of explanation.

Rieber (1998) proposes an account of knowledge belonging to the same research programme as Goldman's and mine. He argues that KAp iff p 'explains' BAp. The main problem with this is that it is too unspecific to be helpful as it stands; one could interpret it as identical to the condition **K** which I propose, or as identical to the condition proposed by Goldman, or in various other ways. But in his note 7, Rieber states that Goldman's condition is sufficient for knowledge. This shows that, on his intended reading, p 'explains' BAp whenever p enters prominently into the best explanation of BAp. For this reason Rieber's account, like Goldman's, is too weak.

We can see this by considering one of Rieber's own examples:

An apple falls on Newton's head. By an amazing coincidence, Newton has a brain lesion such that, whatever rate the apple falls, the impact of the apple will (together with the lesion) cause Newton to believe that objects fall at precisely this rate. As it happens, the apple falls at 32 ft./sec.^{2}, and Newton walks away with the belief that objects fall at this rate.

(1988: 201−2)

Rieber rightly says that this is not a case of knowledge, and he also claims that his condition on knowledge is not met in this case, since explaining Newton's belief by citing the fact believed 'leaves out the most salient and important part of the explanation, namely that Newton has a very peculiar brain lesion'. But is he entitled to say that this means his condition is not met? It seems not. His condition does not explicitly demand that p be an explanation of BAp which cites the 'most salient and important facts'. Although doing so is required of a *good* explanation, and we might be moved charitably to interpret Rieber's condition as demanding that p be a *good* explanation of BAp, such an interpretation would be mistaken. Rieber explicitly does *not* appeal to explanatory goodness in his conditions for knowledge, because he thinks that goodness comes by degrees and knowledge does not (p. 195).[7]

Perhaps, however, he could say that, because it leaves out salient facts, the claim that objects fall at 32 ft/sec^2 simply does not 'explain' Newton's belief. But then Rieber owes us some account of when enough 'salient' facts have been included for one proposition to count as 'explaining' another. As we saw, his endorsement of Goldman's condition as sufficient reveals that he thinks it is enough for p to 'explain' BAp if p features prominently in the best explanation of BAp. It can do this without by itself supplying all the salient facts, or even the most salient facts.

Moreover, for people who *already know* about Newton's brain lesion, citing the fact that objects fall at 32 ft/sec^2 is enough to explain his belief to that effect. What counts as a 'salient and important' explanatory fact depends a lot on what background information one has (as well as what one is interested in). Rieber's account does not mention who the explanations of BAp should be explanations for, but this matters a good deal for determining which cases it will capture and which it will not.

Neta (2002: 667−8) has argued that the sort of response Rieber gives to the Newton problem does not resolve the underlying difficulties. I shall

---

[7] This seems to me a spurious reason for rejecting the phrase 'good explanation', and so I use it freely in my account. Even if explanatory goodness comes by degrees, so that (e.g.) some explanations are 'fairly good' and some are 'not very good', there might well be a (perhaps vague, but at least reasonably well-understood) boundary above which an explanation is 'good' *simpliciter* and below which it is not.

postpone discussion of Neta's argument, because it can also be construed as an objection to my own proposal, and will be considered as such below. But, as we shall see, Neta's argument is spurious. What Rieber says about the Newton case is the right sort of thing to say (though it is possible to be more explicit as to why this is so). It's just that Rieber owes us a few more details before he is entitled to say it.

3.4 Gettier immunity

I now return to my own proposal, whereby a belief that p counts as knowledge iff it can be well explained to an outsider just by citing p.

An important feature of this proposal is its ability to deal with Gettier-type cases: cases where a subject has a true belief which meets various supposed sufficient conditions for knowledge and yet does not amount to knowledge. It will be significant if a condition on knowledge can be shown to be immune to counter-examples of this kind, which have floored so many other proposals.

Whenever we are given a very simple explanation of something, we assume this is because all other relevant facts are as we would expect them to be. Suppose I explain my going out by telling you I want some chips. This is an adequate explanation if all other factors are normal (e.g. I believe the chip shop is open and I can get some chips there). But suppose I believe that all the shops are closed, and that going for a brisk walk will take my mind off my chip craving. Then explaining my going out just by saying I want some chips seems inadequate and misleading. Although my desire for chips will still form *part* of an explanation of my behaviour, it is no longer a good explanation *by itself.* That is, not unless you are already closely acquainted with my customary methods of dealing with unwanted cravings.

It may be helpful to introduce some terminology here: that of *collapsible* and *non-collapsible* explanations. Suppose I explain my going out to an outsider (someone not acquainted with any specific details about me) by saying I want some chips, I believe that the chip shop is open, and I believe that I can buy chips there. This explanation is *collapsible*: it would not mislead my audience if I left out the fact that I believe the chip shop is open and that I can buy chips there, and collapsed the explanation into a simpler one, citing only my desire for chips. By contrast, suppose I explain my going out to an outsider by saying I want chips, but I don't want to want chips, and believe that by going for a walk I can take my mind off my chip craving. This explanation is *not collapsible*: if I collapsed it into a simple explanation citing only my desire for chips, this would be misleading. The outsider would assume I was going out in order to *get* some chips. By contrast, if I were talking to someone I knew very well, the latter explanation *might* be collapsible: such a person would be likely to assume I was going out to try and forget about the desire for chips, knowing that this is what I usually do when I have that sort of desire.

The role of the outsider in my account of knowledge is to set a high standard for collapsibility. The less my audience knows about me and my circumstances, the less likely it is that explanations of my behaviour can be collapsed without being misleading. Hence, it is *difficult* for a belief to count as knowledge by the lights of condition **K**. This is what makes it preferable to Goldman's account, which (as we saw above) sets rather looser standards on knowledge, and is thus too weak.

My strategy in this section will be to argue that Gettier cases are cases where there is *some* explanatory connection between p and BAp, but where that connection is unusual in a way that must be mentioned when giving an explanation of BAp to an outsider. This means that to explain BAp to an outsider by citing p alone will be inadequate in such cases, because it will be misleading. Thus condition **K** is not met in Gettier cases.

To see how this is supposed to work, consider the following example. Suppose, as before, that I see Professor Craig driving a BMW, and as a result believe that one of the Cambridge philosophy professors has bought a BMW. As before, the BMW Professor Craig is driving has been lent to him by Professor Heal. Now, I believe that one of the Cambridge philosophy professors has bought a BMW, and what's more the fact that one of them *has* bought a BMW can figure in a good explanation of that belief to an outsider. Yet, we feel, I do not *know* that one of the Cambridge philosophy professors has bought a BMW.

This is because condition **K** is not met. In this unusual kind of case, we would need to say *more* to give a good explanation of my belief to an outsider than that one of the Cambridge philosophy professors has bought a BMW. If the outsider were given this simple explanation, he would assume that the professor who bought the BMW was the same as the one I think bought it (at least, if I have any belief as to which of them that is). But this is not the case; I think Professor Craig bought the BMW, though in fact it was Professor Heal. So the simple explanation is inadequate because it is misleading on this point. There is an explanatory connection between p and BAp here, but not one which is collapsible when talking to an outsider.

It should be clear that this strategy generalizes, allowing us to deal with any other Gettier-type case we care to contrive. The 'deviancy' of the link between p and BAp, which makes Gettier cases so problematic for other accounts of knowledge, is just what supplies us with a reason to say condition **K** is not satisfied in these cases.

Gettier cases are cases of justified but accidental true belief. We should note that the account I am defending also deals with cases of *un*justified accidental true belief. Suppose I am hit on the head with a hammer, and this causes a brain injury, one effect of which is that I lose my memory completely but irrationally start believing I have just been hit on the head with a hammer. In this situation one cannot explain my belief to an outsider just by citing the fact that I have been hit on the head with a hammer, since this would lead the outsider to think that my belief was rational (e.g. that I remembered being hit). So **K** is not met in this sort of situation either, and the problem faced by Goldman is avoided by my account.

In general, the account makes sense of the fact that we intuitively take justification to be necessary for knowledge. If A's belief that p is formed in an irrational way (without justification), then a simple explanation of BAp which cites only p will always be misleading to an outsider. Irrational methods of belief formation are unusual, so the outsider will assume that nothing of that kind is going on unless she is told otherwise. Hence, in cases of irrational or unjustified belief, condition **K** is not met, and we do not ascribe knowledge.

It may be objected that I seem to be suggesting nothing more than that to know that p is to have a belief that p which is acquired because of p and 'in the usual kind of way'. For I seem to be claiming that p is an adequate explanation of BAp just in case there is an explanatory link between p and BAp which involves nothing unusual or deviant (i.e. nothing which would need to be mentioned to someone who expects things to be as they usually are).

In reply, I should stress that I *agree* that what I am proposing is merely a development of the thought that knowledge is true belief acquired in the usual kind of way; I do not presume to have analysed away the notions of normality and non-deviancy which inform our concept of knowledge. What I do claim for my proposal is that it offers us a useful way of *dramatizing* this notion, and thus helps us to understand it a little better. I am trying to reduce the problem to a familiar one; namely, that of saying when an explanation is adequate in a particular context. (Without offering a full account of explanation,[8] I cannot say much more about the intuition that, in Gettier cases, p is *not* an adequate explanation of BAp to an outsider. But I trust that intuition is strong enough not to need support from any particular theory of explanation.)

The proposal certainly doesn't seem to be rendered inert by dint of being simply a development of the idea that knowledge is normal true belief. It can, for instance, help us understand why not *all* kinds of explanatory abnormality are relevant to knowledge ascriptions, which mere hand-waving at 'normal true belief' cannot do. Suppose a wartime diary is preserved despite the extreme unlikelihood of this happening. We can colour the story with tales of burning libraries and courageous escapees bearing concealed manuscripts. The diary contains a genuine account of its author's attempt to overthrow the current military regime, which was unsuccessful, and was so well concealed that this diary is the only remaining evidence for it. The diary is then published and I read it. Do I know that the author tried to overthrow the regime (= p)? We surely want to say I do. But don't we have to mention the unlikely escape and the burning libraries in explaining my belief to an outsider? They are hardly normal circumstances. So, surely, explaining my belief that p to the outsider just by citing p is inadequate, implying as it does that all factors not mentioned in the explanation are as the outsider would expect.

In fact, however, we do not need to cite these unusual factors to explain my belief that p. The reason is that, notwithstanding the unusual *features* of the explanatory connection between the truth of p and my belief that p in this case, the connection *itself* is of an utterly mundane kind: I come to believe p through reading the honest testimony of someone with first-hand experience of the relevant facts. By contrast, in Gettier cases *the very connection* between p and BAp is of an unusual kind. Seeing Professor Craig

---

[8] Jenkins (forthcoming *b*) makes some moves in the direction of a positive account but still falls far short of offering necessary and sufficient conditions.

driving a BMW is not a normal connection to the fact that one of the Cambridge philosophy professors has bought a BMW, when the person who has done so is Professor Heal.

It is a general fact about explanations that unexpected *features* of explanatory links do not need to be mentioned to avoid misleading one's audience, although unexpected *links* do. Suppose I explain why the light came on (p) by saying that I flipped the switch (q). This will be inadequate if what actually happened was that Anna saw me flipping a switch which she knew did not work and therefore kindly decided to turn the light on herself using another (functional) switch. The explanatory link between p and q is not a normal one, so we must say more than p to explain q (unless our audience already knows a lot about the situation under consideration).

By comparison, this explanation (q) of this fact (p) *would* be adequate if all that was odd about the case was that the switch was connected to the light insecurely, by forty-year-old wiring. For in this case, although the explanatory connection between p and q would have unusual *features* (the insecurity of the connection and the age of the wiring), it would be typical of the *kind* of connection you normally get between switches being flicked and lights coming on.

When knowledge is understood as I propose, this general fact about explanations enables us to understand the impulse to say that in the case of the wartime diary I have knowledge, whereas in the case of Professor Heal's BMW I do not. We understand which sorts of abnormality are relevant to knowledge ascriptions by understanding which sorts of abnormality are relevant to explanation.

My definition of an outsider has been doing crucial work in this section. Before we move on, therefore, we might take a moment to consider whether that definition is really correct. What kinds of 'commonplace facts' is the outsider aware of? If we give her too much, so as to include (e.g.) familiarity with typical human epistemic failings, we may end up allowing something to count as a case of knowledge where in fact it is only the output of a such an epistemic failing. If the outsider is aware that we humans typically conclude that p in circumstances C whether or not it is justified, and that whenever p is true circumstances C obtain, then explaining BAp by p may be adequate for that outsider, even when it is only by lucky chance that A's belief is in fact true in this case. For citing p will be adequate to explain to her why C obtains, and this will explain to her why BAp. This is so even if (say) only five per cent of cases where C obtains are cases where p, and A indiscriminately believes p whenever C obtains.

To avoid this sort of problem, the outsider must know nothing except the bare bones of what it is to be a thinking person. But there seems to be a risk that if she knows so little, condition **K** will become too strong. Suppose aliens who do not share our sensory modalities can count as outsiders by our definition.[9] Then, it seems, we may end up ruling out many perfectly ordinary explanations of beliefs of the kind we want to include, simply because they wouldn't be good explanations for these aliens. For instance, an alien from a world whose inhabitants lacked anything resembling a sense of sight (or other means of responding to the frequency of light waves) presumably would not find 'Snow is white' a good explanation of my belief that snow is white. But we don't want to say for this reason that I do not know that snow is white (or so the worry goes). Do we need, then, to specify that aliens of this sort cannot count as outsiders? If so, how many other kinds of rational being should be excluded? Could someone from a very different terrestrial cultural background fail to be an outsider?

Actually, I don't think we need be worried by this line of thought. It may be true that an alien who had no familiarity with visual perception would not find 'Snow is white' a good explanation of my belief that snow is white, but we need to consider *why* this is so. If the problem is simply that they would not understand the explanation, these aliens are already ruled out as potential outsiders by dint of clause (1) of my definition of an outsider. On the other hand, if they *can* understand 'Snow is white', why should we doubt that they will find it a good explanation of my belief that snow is white? Even if they have no idea how exactly I managed to come by that belief, they will not be misled by the explanation: presented with it, they will assume, correctly, that I used some sensible method of investigating the world around me and responded appropriately to the deliverances of that method. The definition of an outsider offered in Section 3.2 is adequate for our purposes.

---

[9] Thanks to an anonymous journal referee for bringing the general point, and this particular case, to my attention.

3.5 Neta's objection

I shall now take up the postponed discussion of Neta's objection, which is directed against Rieber's attempt to give a certain response to the problem case of Newton's apple. What Rieber says about this case is similar to what I have said about cases of irrational true belief where there is some explanatory link between the belief and the fact believed. Recall that Rieber claims that in the Newton's-apple case the explanation of BAp by p omits salient and important facts. My response to the case where one is hit on the head with a hammer and hence irrationally believes one has just been hit on the head with a hammer was that, in this case, the fact believed would not supply the kind of explanation of one's belief required by condition **K**. This is a development of Rieber's response, intended to make clearer exactly when a fact is 'salient' and 'important' enough to be indispensable for the relevant explanatory purposes.

I have already said that I think Rieber's response is correct in essentials: it is indeed the 'inadequacy' (to an outsider) of the explanation of BAp by p alone that prevents the Newton case being a case of knowledge (although, as we saw, is not clear that Rieber is entitled to use this response). But Neta (2002: 667–8) claims that the response *does not work* in more complicated cases. His argument for this claim is intriguing, and requires a rather intricate discussion.

Neta imagines a more complex version of the case of Newton's apple:

An apple falls on Newton's head. By an amazing coincidence, Newton has a brain lesion such that, whatever rate the apple falls, the impact of the apple will (together with the lesion) cause Newton to believe that objects fall at precisely this rate *and that he has a brain lesion*. As it happens, the apple falls at 32 ft./sec.^{2}, and Newton walks away with the belief that objects fall at this rate and that he has a brain lesion.

(667–8)

He argues that in this case:

Newton's conjunctive belief… is explained by the fact that objects fall at 32 ft./sec.^{2} and that he has a brain lesion. And yet even here Newton doesn't know that objects fall at 32 ft./sec.^{2}, and this is something he must know if he knows the truth of the conjunction. Rieber cannot protest that we have still left out a 'salient and important' part of the explanation: we can pack any such part of the explanation into the content of the explained belief as well. We thereby construct a case in which Newton's belief is caused by the fact believed but doesn't count as knowledge.

(I assume that 'caused' in the final sentence should read 'explained'.) It may or may not be true that, in *Rieber's* sense, Newton's conjunctive belief is 'explained' by the fact believed in this case. But it is not *well explained to an outsider* just by that fact, as **K** requires. Let p be *objects fall at 32 ft/sec²*, and let *q be Newton has a brain lesion*. To see why **K** is not satisfied here, note that if we just cited p&q in explaining Newton's belief that p&q to an outsider, we would mislead our audience. We would mislead them as to the way Newton acquired the belief that p&q. By not mentioning that anything extraordinary is going on, we would lead our outsider to suppose that Newton acquired the belief that q in an ordinary way; perhaps by being told by his doctor that his brain was damaged, or by having noticed characteristic impairments in his own cognitive performance. A good explanation to an outsider of Newton's belief that p&q will not simply cite p&q, but must also make clear that the connection between p&q and Newton's belief that p&q is an extraordinary one.

But what of Neta's claim that such further explanatory information can simply be 'packed into' the content of the explained belief to generate new, genuine, problem cases? Well, let's see what happens when we attempt to 'pack in' the appropriate information. Let r be *Newton believes p&q in an irrational way after his apple-bump, because of his brain lesion*. By 'packing' r into the content of Newton's belief, we arrive at a case where Newton, once the apple has landed on his head, comes to believe (for no epistemically respectable reason) that p&q&r. For Neta's objection to hold water against my account, it will have to be the case that Newton's belief p&q&r is well explained to an outsider just by p&q&r.

There are two points to make about this. First, look closely at what Newton supposedly believes in this case: he believes p&q and *that his belief that p&q is irrational*. This combination is psychologically unstable, and it is questionable whether it is really possible to believe a conjunction of claims which create such an obvious tension. So it is at least not obvious that

Neta's method can be used to construct a realistic counter-example to my proposal.

This line of thought might be resisted, though; perhaps to some it will not sound so surprising to say that people hold beliefs which are in tension in the way described. After all, people will often say things of the form: 'I think p is true, but I don't suppose I have any good reason to think so'. However, even if we allow that it is in some sense possible for Newton to believe p&q&r, a second point prevents us from supposing that p&q&r would then be, by itself, a good explanation to an outsider of his having that belief.

This is that the explanation would again be misleading: it does not make it clear that the third conjunct (r) is believed irrationally after the apple-bump because of the brain lesion. This must be mentioned, or else we give the impression that Newton's belief in r is acquired normally (e.g. through the testimony of a rational and reliable informant), regardless of how the other beliefs are acquired. This point obviously iterates if we simply continue 'packing' new propositions like *r is believed irrationally* into the content of Newton's belief.

What if Newton believes p&q as before, but also believes r for normal reasons; for example, on the basis of the testimony of a reliable informant? Then, we can say, he believes p&q&r and there seems to be no reason to deny that p&q&r is a good explanation of this belief. But he surely does not know p or q in this situation, although it seems we are forced to say he knows p&q&r, which (on any reasonable view) implies that he knows p and knows q. The earlier thought, that the explanation leaves out the irregularity of Newton's reasons for believing r, no longer applies, for those reasons are no longer irregular.

The explanation is nonetheless still misleading as to the relationship between explanandum and explanans. When presented with it, the outsider will not get a clear idea as to why Newton believes r. All of p, q, and r are needed just to explain why Newton believes p and q. The explainer then intends r to be used *again*, quite separately, to explain (together with some background assumptions about likely ways for Newton to have learned that r) why Newton believes r. But the outsider would not have reason to see things that way, when presented with the simple explanation p&q&r of Newton's belief. This simple explanation does not make it clear that r is being 'used twice' in this way. So the explanation is inadequate in this context.

To avoid this inadequacy, the explanation of Newton's belief will have to separate out the explanations for his believing these two parts of the proposition, and state that he believes p&q because p&q&r, and that he believes r because r. Since the simple explanation p&q&r does not do this, it will not be a good explanation to an outsider, hence condition **K** is not met in this case, and hence it is not a counter-example to my proposal.

The structure of an explanation matters, then. An explanation is not just a list of propositions, inadequacies in which can always be resolved by 'packing' more propositions on to the list. Neta's objection cannot be pressed against me without assuming a rather simplistic conception of what an explanation is.

There is one more possibility to be considered in our attempts to construct a counter-example along Neta's lines. What if we try using self-referential propositions to correct for the problems with the previous attempt at a counter-example? Let r′ be *Newton believes p&q&r′ in an irrational way after his apple-bump, because of his brain lesion.* Could a Neta-style case be contrived where Newton believes p&q&r′, and this belief is well explained to an outsider simply by citing p&q&r′? The problem described above will not arise: the idea here is that p and q and *part* of r′ (the part that refers to p and q) are used to explain why Newton believes p and q, then the rest of r′ (the part that refers to r′ itself) is used to explain why he believes r′.

However, even if we assume for the sake of argument that sense can be made of the kind of self-referential belief required here, the explanation will still be inadequate. The outsider receiving p&q&r′ as an explanation of Newton's belief that p&q&r′ is not given any clues as to the structure of the intended explanation, and so she could reasonably suppose (amongst other possibilities) that Newton's belief in each conjunct is supposed to be explained by the corresponding conjunct of the explanans, which is not the case.

Given that several attempts to press Neta's objection have now failed, despite the construction of various recherché cases, I shall assume that this is not a promising line to pursue further.

3.6 Other theories and intuitions

3.6.1 Causal theories

If some explanationist account of knowledge is correct, that reveals why a causal account is initially attractive for some kinds of knowledge (see e.g. Alvin Goldman 1967). For many, though not all, explanations are causal; and many, though not all, causal links are explanatory. The fact that a causal theory generates conditions on knowledge which are prima facie plausible but on reflection neither necessary nor sufficient suggests that some other concept, with which causation is loosely connected,[10] could be used to generate a more promising account of knowledge. Explanation is an obvious candidate.

Roughly speaking, a causal theorist of knowledge maintains that A knows that p just in case the fact that p causes A to believe p. By concentrating on explanation, we can see exactly why this sort of account goes wrong. Because some causal links are non-explanatory, a causal account of knowledge generates conditions which are insufficient. Such an account, as is well known, fails to make a principled distinction between the 'normal' and 'deviant' causal chains that can hold between our beliefs and the world. (This is why causal accounts are susceptible to Gettier-type counter-examples.) The explanationist can draw the needed distinction by saying that 'deviant' causal chains are those where citing the cause would not provide a good explanation of the effect to an outsider.

And because some explanations are non-causal, the conditions generated by a causal account will also be non-necessary. The account will have no natural way of dealing with (e.g.) knowledge of general truths such as *All emeralds are green*. For it is hard to see how such facts should be said to relate causally to our corresponding general beliefs. Note, however, that there is no reason to doubt that they can explain them (I shall discuss this point further in Section 3.7). Knowledge of future events is also prima facie problematic for causal accounts, as future events cannot cause present beliefs. But, again, there is no obvious objection to the claim that facts about the future explain present beliefs. They can certainly explain present actions: I am tidying my flat today because my brother is coming to visit

---

[10] In Jenkins (forthcoming *b*), I explain that I think the connection is that of realizer to role.

tomorrow. I also find it quite natural to say that I believe he is coming to visit tomorrow because he is coming to visit tomorrow.

It might be objected that what 'really' explains my tidying my flat is the fact that I *believe* that my brother will visit tomorrow (a fact about the present). After all, I would still be tidying even if he weren't coming, provided I believed that he was. Or that what 'really' explains my belief that he will visit tomorrow is that he has told me he will (a fact about the past). But what force would such an objection have? Bear in mind that all I need, for the current point to go through, is the claim that in certain contexts the fact that my brother will visit tomorrow can constitute *a* good explanation of my tidying, and that similarly the fact that he will visit tomorrow can constitute *a* good explanation of my belief to that effect. I do not claim that these are *the* good (or 'real') explanations, so we need not worry if the objector is just pointing out that the fact that I believe my brother will visit tomorrow *also* constitutes an adequate explanation of my tidying behaviour (or even that in most contexts it may be a fuller or better explanation). On the other hand, if there is meant to be more to the objection than this, I am not sure what it might be. If it is being claimed that the fact that my brother will visit tomorrow, although true, is never *a* good explanation of my tidying my flat, and that the fact that he will visit tomorrow is never *a* good explanation of my belief that he will, then I don't find the claim plausible.[11]

3.6.2 Nozick

It is quite plausible in many cases that if q is a good explanation of r then $\neg q \mathbin{\square\!\!\rightarrow} \neg r$ (where '$\square\!\!\rightarrow$' represents the subjunctive conditional). So, often, if p is a good explanation (to an outsider or anyone else) of BAp, then $\neg p \mathbin{\square\!\!\rightarrow} \neg BAp$. This counterfactual is one of Nozick's conditions on knowledge. Nozick's proposal (in outline) is that KAp just in case:

(1) p is true
(2) BAp
(3) $\neg p \mathbin{\square\!\!\rightarrow} \neg BAp$
and
(4) $p \mathbin{\square\!\!\rightarrow} BAp$

---

[11] See Jenkins and Nolan (forthcoming) for more on this topic.

Statement (4) is not supposed to be implied by (1) and (2) (as it is on the now standard Lewis–Stalnaker semantics for the counterfactual; see e.g. Lewis 1973: sect. 1.7). Rather, Nozick suggests interpreting (4) as the claim that at the close counterfactual worlds where p, BAp (p. 176).

Nozick's decision to include p $\Box\!\!\rightarrow$ BAp as a fourth condition stems from his noticing that his conditions (1)–(3) are in some cases inadequate to guarantee knowledge. I shall suggest in this subsection that the source of Nozick's concern is the feeling that in this kind of case, although there is some connection between p and BAp (which is why (3) obtains), there is something not quite right about that connection. This feeling, I shall say, is correct: in such cases, although there is some explanatory link between p and BAp, p fails to be a good explanation of BAp to an outsider, because there is something unusual about this link. Such cases must be ruled out by a successful account of knowledge. Nozick tries to rule out such cases by demanding p $\Box\!\!\rightarrow$ BAp, but I shall argue that this rules out too many kinds of unusualness in the connection between p and BAp, and thus generates familiar difficulties for Nozick. (Another problem is that there are a few cases where (1)–(4) hold but we do not have knowledge, so that the account is too weak in some respects as well as too strong in others.) Nonetheless, Nozick's conditions are comprehensible from our perspective: (1)–(3) are almost points of overlap with my proposal,[12] and (4) is a natural, if ultimately misguided, attempt to capture a further condition on explanatoriness.

To see that condition (4) is not necessary for knowledge, consider the case of the bystander who sees someone robbing a bank, and is able to identify him as Jesse James when his mask slips and she catches a glimpse of his face (Nozick 1981: 193). Clearly, condition (4) is not met here. In most close worlds where James robbed the bank, his mask did not slip and so the bystander formed no belief about who the culprit was. Yet we still want to say the bystander knows that James robbed the bank. (Nozick tries to resolve this problem by appealing to the idea of a method of belief formation, and specifying that the relevant nearby worlds are ones where the same method is employed.)

---

[12] Condition (3), however, creates some difficulties which my account can avoid. For instance, the case of the concerned Granny (Nozick 1981: 179) forces Nozick to amend condition (3) so as to take account of the 'method' by which a belief is acquired. We can accommodate the concerned Granny by noting that (3), although a symptom of the satisfaction of condition **K**, is not a necessary condition for **K** in all cases.

I suggest that the case is best understood as akin to that of the wartime diary: the fact that James's mask slips is an unusual *feature* of the connection between the fact that James robbed the bank and the bystander's belief that he did, but it will not need to be mentioned in explaining her belief to an outsider, since *the connection itself* (visual perception in favourable conditions) is entirely normal. Hence, we are inclined to say that the fact that James robbed the bank supplies a good explanation to an outsider of the bystander's belief that James robbed the bank. And therefore we feel that the bystander knows this. (If it had been the connection itself that was unusual—if, for instance, James's presence had triggered the projection of a holographic image of James, which the bystander then saw—we would not want to say that she knew James was there.)

To motivate (4) Nozick considers various cases where (1)–(3) are satisfied but we do not want to ascribe knowledge, because there is a 'deviant' link between the subject's belief and the fact believed. Amongst them is a case where a brain in a vat is given the belief that it is such by the vat operator (p. 175). All of (1)–(3) are satisfied here, yet the subject does not know it is a brain in a vat. Statement (4) is supposed to help rule out such cases (although one might question whether it actually does so in all the relevant cases, as we shall see in a moment).

Unfortunately for Nozick, the condition p $\Box\!\!\rightarrow$ BAp rules out *too many kinds* of unusualness in the explanatory link between p and BAp, and this is what creates the problem in the Jesse James case. Condition (4) rules out cases where there is a normal link with unusual features, as well as cases where the link itself is unusual. The unusualness of the mask's slipping is only an unusual feature of the link between p and BAp; the link itself is normal. Thus the unusualness of the mask's slipping does not interfere with the ascription of knowledge, because it does not interfere with our explaining BAp to an outsider by p alone. So condition (4), which rules out this kind of unusualness, is too strong. It forces Nozick to throw out the baby of glimpse-based knowledge with the bathwater of well-informed vat brains.

What Nozick needs to add to (1)–(3) is a condition which will rule out those cases where ¬p $\Box\!\!\rightarrow$ ¬BAp holds simply because p is *part* of a good explanation to an outsider of BAp, although it is not such an explanation by itself (such as cases where there is a deviant causal link between p and

BAp). To my knowledge, there is no better condition for this purpose than **K**.

It is also familiar that (1)–(4) are not only too strong, in ruling out glimpse-based knowledge, but also too weak, in failing to rule out some things we *do* want to rule out. These are cases where there is an unusual explanatory connection between p and BAp such that the unusualness would have to be mentioned in explaining BAp to an outsider, but where the truth-values of p and BAp nonetheless co-vary across close possible worlds, so that Nozick's conditions (3) and (4) are met. This might occur if I were a brain in a vat who formed a true belief that p on the basis of evidence fed into my brain by my benevolent vat operator, who likes to give me true beliefs (and who has arranged for others to continue doing so should she be unable to). For then it seems that in all close ¬p worlds she, being benevolent, will make sure I do not have a belief that p, whereas in all close p worlds she will make sure I have a belief that p. Here, again, the explanatory constraint supplied by condition **K** seems to succeed where Nozick's conditions fail: this is not a case of knowledge, because one would have to mention the strange link between p and BAp in explaining BAp to an outsider.

3.6.3 Other views

The reliabilist notion of 'belief acquired by a reliable method' is, in extension at least, fairly close to the notion of belief acquired in the sort of way an outsider would expect. Unless one is given a reason to suspect that something unusual is going on, one expects people to use reliable methods to form their beliefs. But the two sometimes differ in extension, because some reliable methods are unexpected (such as those employed by a brain in a vat which is reliably given true beliefs about its surroundings by a benevolent vat operator). Where this happens, it is reliabilism that seems to deliver the wrong result. (The vat brain does not *know* what its surroundings are like, although it is acquiring true beliefs on that subject by a reliable method.)

Armstrong (1973) has suggested that A's knowing that p is a matter of the existence of a law-like connection between A's belief that p and the state of affairs which makes p true. If **K** is a genuinely necessary and sufficient condition for knowledge, then, given the influence of the covering-law model of explanation,[13] the emergence of an account like Armstrong's should not surprise us.

Let me briefly mention three other points of interest here. (These points could stand further development, but I shall not pursue them here.) First, note that first-person beliefs about the sense-data one is currently and consciously experiencing are plausible candidates for beliefs which can be well explained under any circumstances by citing the fact believed. Surely it will never be misleading, even when talking with an outsider, to explain my belief that there seems to me to be an orange patch in front of me just by saying that there seems to me to be an orange patch in front of me. The explanatory connection between fact and belief is very tight, and very obvious, in this case: there is no room for interference from the factors which usually cause trouble for explanatory links between facts and beliefs (such as misleading evidence). It is no coincidence, I think, that knowledge of one's present sense-experiences has sometimes been taken to be a most certain kind of knowledge.

Second, many philosophers think there is something troubling about knowledge of abstract objects such as numbers and sets. This is understandable when we consider that such objects could not interact causally with our beliefs, and that the concepts of causation and explanation have often been associated and even conflated. Such association might make it appear that facts about abstract objects could not possibly explain our beliefs about them. Hence, to anyone implicitly construing knowledge as requiring the satisfaction of condition **K**, knowledge of abstract objects would naturally appear problematic.

Third, it is suggestive that the English word 'reason' is used both for explanations and for epistemic justifications.

3.6.4 Divided intuitions

The proposed account of knowledge enables us to make sense of a way in which our intuitions are sometimes divided as to whether A knows that p. Rieber has suggested that we can best understand a certain pattern of attitudes to scepticism by understanding particular aspects of the impact context of utterance can have upon both claims of explanatoriness and

---

[13] See Jenkins (forthcoming *b*) for my preferred take on the connection between explanation and subsumption under laws.

ascriptions of knowledge (1998: 195−7).[14] I agree, though I think we can do more to make the point perspicuous with condition **K** in place.

The point rests upon the view that explanation is contrastive; the view, that is, that when we explain why p, we are actually explaining why p rather than q for some 'foil' q. Where a foil is not explicitly mentioned, an implicit foil is determined by contextual factors. This sort of view is clearly expounded, for causal explanations at least, in Lipton (1990).

We can develop Rieber's own example (originally from Dretske 1970) to show how this view about explanation impacts upon sceptical debate in the light of condition **K**. Suppose Jane is looking at a zebra in a cage at the zoo. First, we can note, with Rieber, that *This animal is a zebra* is a good answer to an outsider who asks 'Why does Jane believe that this animal is a zebra rather than a tiger or lion or ... ?' but not to one who asks 'Why does Jane believe that this animal is a zebra rather than a cleverly disguised mule?'. To see the relevance of this, note that in most contexts we are only interested in how Jane forms beliefs when confronted with animals that look the way they're supposed to look. So we are asking questions like the first. This sort of question is well answered, even if an outsider asks it, by *This animal is a zebra*. We are therefore happy, in those contexts, to say 'Jane knows the animal is a zebra'.

In some sceptical contexts, however, we interest ourselves in how Jane would respond to animals which have been cleverly disguised. We do not feel that *This animal is a zebra* is a good answer to an outsider who asks why she believes it is a zebra rather than a cleverly disguised mule. This answer is misleading to the outsider because it suggests that Jane can tell zebras from cleverly disguised mules, which she cannot. And so we no longer want to say 'Jane knows the animal is a zebra'.

It does not seem as if one of these viewpoints is right and the other is wrong. Rather, we may be tempted to say that 'in an everyday sense' Jane knows the animal is a zebra, but she does not know this 'in the sceptic's sense'. And we can help spell out what is meant by this in terms of the two different types of why question which can be considered when we ask whether condition **K** is met. (Whether or not we ought, on reflection, to endorse the pretheoretic claim that the word 'know' has different senses in

---

[14] Neta also provides a helpful discussion of how contextualism about explanation can help us understand various puzzles about knowledge, which he lists in his (2002: 664).

the two contexts is a question that lies beyond the scope of this chapter. It may be preferable to say that 'know' has a fixed sense, albeit one which builds in a contextual parameter; a good recent discussion of this kind of issue can be found in Hawthorne 2004: esp. chs. 2 and 4).

What is important for our purposes is that it seems right to say 'Jane knows' when, and only when, it seems right to say 'Citing the fact that the animal is a zebra would be a good explanation to an outsider of Jane's belief that it is a zebra'. Context of utterance helps determine exactly what it would take for something to count as 'a good explanation', by determining which why question it has to answer in order to count as such. Context of utterance seems to affect the truth-value of knowledge ascriptions in a parallel way.

Like all accounts in this vein, my account of knowledge does not resolve our divided intuitions in one direction or the other, nor generate any argument that the sceptical intuition is mistaken. What this type of account tries to do is help explain those divided intuitions, and help us understand what is right about sceptical intuitions and how much is left unharmed by them.

Note that the proposal allows that simplistic epistemic-closure claims (of the kind rejected by e.g. Dretske 1970, Nozick 1981, and Rieber 1998) may fail. It might be, for instance, that we ordinarily know that we have hands ($= p$) although we cannot know that we are not brains in vats ($= q$), and this despite the fact that we know that p entails q and correctly infer to q on that basis. For it is not the case that whenever r is a good explanation of BAr, and s is an obvious known logical consequence of r believed on the basis of a correct inference from r, s is a good explanation of BAs. In the case of the two beliefs p and q just mentioned, the very nature of the shift in explanandum might be taken as forcing us to consider everyday standards of explanation such as are usually correct when talking about p inappropriate when we begin talking about q.

3.7 Inductive knowledge and deductive knowledge

This last point suggests the following objection to the claim that **K** is necessary and sufficient for knowledge. Suppose A believes that p because she knows that q and either infers to p as the best explanation of q, or else deduces from q that p. In this sort of situation, even supposing that q is a good explanation to an outsider of BAq, we cannot assume that p is a good explanation to an outsider of BAp. Obvious candidate explanations for BAp include BAq, q, and either BA(*p is a good explanation of q*) or BA(*p is a consequence of q*), but not p. But even if we don't allow that knowledge transmits across *all* good inductive or deductive inferences, it surely does in *some* cases. How can my proposal accommodate this?

Let us take the two cases of abduction and deduction separately. As regards the former, the solution to the problem is relatively straightforward. We simply note that in genuinely knowledge-producing cases of inference to the best explanation—where p explains q, q explains BAq, and BAq explains BAp, and all these explanatory links are standard—then one can collapse the explanatory chain and simply say that p explains BAp, even when talking to an outsider.

For example, if I believe that all emeralds are green on the grounds of an inference from known instances of green emeralds, it seems reasonable to say that the fact that all emeralds are green is what explains my belief that they are. For it is what explains the fact that all the emeralds I have seen so far have been green, and this is what explains my general belief. The central steps in the explanatory link between fact and belief are exactly what anyone with no special knowledge of my situation would expect them to be, so they can be safely omitted without rendering the explanation inadequate to such a person.

We do not need to worry about cases where p is *not* really a good explanation of the known fact(s) q from which A infers, because in these cases inferring p as the best explanation of q surely does not generate knowledge that p. But what of cases where p is a good explanation of q to the subject A, but not to an outsider? This can happen when A has information which is relevant to her understanding of the relationship between p and q, but which is not common knowledge. These cases need not trouble us either, however. Given that A reasons to p as the best explanation of q, which the outsider would not do, there are two possibilities: either A is *better* informed than the outsider, or A is *mis*informed. In situations where he is better informed, it is acceptable to explain BAp to an outsider by p alone. For the outsider will assume some rational process has lead to A's believing p, inference to the best explanation being one possibility. And the outsider will assume that if A has inferred to p as the best explanation of q, that is because p *really is* a good explanation of q (and A is aware of this). For, unless one has specific information about a person, one assumes that that person will make good abductive inferences. So the explanatory chain mentioned above (p $\rightarrow$ q $\rightarrow$ BAq $\rightarrow$ BAp) is once again collapsible for the outsider, since in particular the collapsed explanation will not mislead the outsider by suggesting that if A has arrived at the belief that p by abductive means, then the abductive inference she used was a good one. Cases where A takes p to be a good explanation of q because he is *mis*informed need not detain us, since they will not be cases of knowledge. (At best, they will be cases of accidentally justified true belief).

Deductive cases cannot be addressed in quite this way. We cannot assume that just because p is a consequence of q, p would be a good explanation of q to an outsider (or indeed, to anyone). So the first step in the chain by which p explains BAp in abductive cases cannot be assumed to hold in deductive cases. Nor can we simply stipulate that all propositions deduced from known propositions are known. For it seems that knowledge may sometimes fail to be transmitted in this way. For instance, as noted at the end of Section 3.6, it has seemed plausible to some philosophers that we know we have hands but do not know we are not brains in vats, although the latter is a known consequence of the former.

Nonetheless, it does seem that those cases where we want to say knowledge *is* transmitted across a deductive inference are precisely those where we are prepared to say that the resulting belief BAp would be well explained to an outsider by p. We can best see this by considering a concrete case.

Suppose Brian, a competent logical reasoner, knows that if Neil comes to his party he will get drunk, and knows that Neil is coming to his party. He deduces that Neil will get drunk. Is the fact that Neil will get drunk a good explanation to an outsider of Brian's belief to that effect? Well, first, note it is only because Neil *will* get drunk that the two premises from which Brian reasons are true together; that is to say, it is only because Neil will get drunk that Brian's argument is sound. What kind of 'because' are we dealing with here? One, I would suggest, which signals a familiar kind of explanation. For many explanations state the fulfilment of an obvious necessary (or almost-necessary) condition on the truth of the explanandum. For instance, I can explain why I arrived on time today by saying that, for once, nothing held me up. (But note that not all such conditions can be used in this way: more on this in a moment.)

Thus we can explain the soundness of Brian's argument by citing the fact that Neil will get drunk. In a similar vein, after noting that competent reasoners like Brian will (generally) only use sound arguments, we can explain the fact that Brian reasons as he does by citing the soundness of Brian's argument. Again, we are explaining the truth of the target proposition by stating that an obvious (almost-)necessary condition for it is met.

Finally, we note that, uncontroversially, Brian's reasoning as he did is what explains his belief that Neil will get drunk. So we now know that the fact that Neil will get drunk explains why Brian's argument is sound, which explains Brian's reasoning as he did, which in turn explains why Brian believes that Neil will get drunk. And the central stages in this explanatory link are entirely standard: people very often reason according to *modus ponens* in this sort of way. So these central stages can be omitted without making the explanation misleading, even when talking to an outsider. In other words, the fact that Neil will get drunk is, by itself, a good explanation to an outsider of Brian's belief that he will. And this is why we want to say Brian knows that Neil will get drunk. Of course, if Brian were an incompetent logician who drew conclusions randomly from his premises, or if he were using an unsound argument, I could not argue as I have done. But then we would not want to say that Brian knew Neil would get drunk.

A qualification is needed here, however. Note that explaining a fact by citing an obvious necessary condition only seems to work where it is, or at least could be, less obvious that the explanans obtains than that the explanandum does. In our example it is less obvious (to Brian at least) that Neil will get drunk than that the relevant instance of *modus ponens* is sound. (That is why Brian uses this instance of *modus ponens* to deduce that Neil will get drunk.) Similarly, my not having been held up today must be less obvious than the fact that I got here on time, if we are to explain the latter by the former.

Compare this with a typical case where, it is argued, warrant does not transmit across deductive inference. Michelle believes she has two hands and that brains in vats do not have hands, and she deduces that she is not a brain in a vat. What goes wrong here is that it can be no more obvious (to Michelle or anyone else) that she has two hands than that she is not a brain in a vat. And since knowing she has two hands is necessary for knowing that her argument is sound, it can be no more obvious that her argument is sound than that she is not a brain in a vat. This means we cannot satisfactorily explain to an outsider why she reasons as she does by citing the truth of her conclusion, as we could in Brian's case.

This analysis of the situation is, I think, confirmed by the fact that philosophers who argue that warrant does transmit across this kind of entailment (e.g. Moore 1939) assume that facts concerning our having hands *are* more obvious than facts concerning our not being brains in vats. Their opponents resist the transmission claim by arguing that this is not so (see e.g. Davies 2000: 400–1).

3.8 Summary

In this chapter, I have outlined an account of knowledge according to which a belief counts as knowledge iff the subject's having that belief can be explained, to someone with no specific knowledge of the subject's situation, just by citing the fact believed. I have not presented this theory as an analysis of the concept of knowledge, but as a way of dramatizing the notion of normality which is intimately related to that concept, and which it seems an account of knowledge must somehow elucidate.

What is most interesting about this account in the current context is that it holds out the prospect of a unified account of all kinds of knowledge: kinds which philosophers usually consider relatively unproblematic, such as knowledge of the physical world, and kinds which raise special philosophical problems, such as knowledge of logic and mathematics. For it is plausible that logical and mathematical propositions may be able to explain things—in particular, they may be able to explain our beliefs in the way required for the satisfaction of **K**. In this respect, explanationist accounts have an important advantage over causal accounts, which make mathematical and logical knowledge seem impossible, and Nozick's tracking account, clause (3) of which is trivially satisfied[15] whenever one believes a necessary truth.

---

[15] Assuming a Lewisian semantics for the counterfactual (Lewis 1973: sect. 1.6). Nozick's own view is that clause (3) 'does not come into play' for necessary truths, since no remotely satisfactory account of the relevant counterfactuals has yet been constructed (1981: 186).

There is reasonably widespread agreement that mathematical truths can serve as explanations (see Section 4.2). Of course, much work remains to be done to make the epistemology of mathematics comprehensible; we need to see how a mathematical truth could explain our having a corresponding belief. One might, reasonably, have doubts about whether one can explain the contingent, down–to–earth fact that I believe that $7 + 5 = 12$ by citing a necessary proposition which apparently deals in abstract objects. I shall try to address these doubts in Part II.

I said at the beginning of the section that the aim of the condition on knowledge to be offered here was to help us better understand the role that the concept of knowledge plays in our lives (the project begun in Craig 1990). Let me therefore add a few remarks on this. Traditionally, epistemologists sought a simple and reductive answer to the question of what knowledge is. But there is no reason to suppose there will be a simple reductive answer to this question; knowledge might just be 'normal' true belief, and what counts as 'normal' might be a function of the (complex and diffuse) requirements that we generally want our beliefs to satisfy.

However, this doesn't mean we can't say anything helpful about the notion of normality in play. One thing we can do is ask how the normality concept in play here relates to other concepts in regular use. What I have attempted to do is to relate the normality concept to the familiar (if philosophically intriguing) concept of explanation. If it is true that 'normal' true beliefs are just those of which **K** holds, then we may be able to learn more about what we tend to count as a 'normal' belief by considering under what circumstances instances of **K** are true.

PART II

An Epistemology for Arithmetic

4

A Theory of Arithmetical Knowledge

4.1 Introduction

The first task of this chapter is to show that there is nothing inherently problematic about arithmetical knowledge once we accept the explanation-ist condition on knowledge presented in Chapter 3, since arithmetical facts can explain our corresponding arithmetical beliefs. Even if this is granted, however, the arithmetical realist must be able say what *sort* of explanatory link there might be between the independent facts of arithmetic and our arithmetical beliefs. My aim in this chapter is to show how one might develop an account of this explanatory link—an account which respects both empiricism and the aprioricity of arithmetic.

4.2 Arithmetical explanations of belief

I believe that arithmetical propositions can sometimes be good explanations of why we have the arithmetical beliefs we do. I shall first say a little bit about the (relatively) widely accepted fact that mathematical explanation of *mathematical* facts is possible. I shall then argue that there is reason to countenance mathematical (and, particularly, arithmetical) explanations of *non*-mathematical facts, such as facts about what we believe.

Mathematical explanation is a somewhat neglected topic, but it has frequently been noted that there is such a phenomenon as mathematical explanation of mathematical facts, and various attempts have been made to make sense of this phenomenon. Steiner (1978), for example, has offered an account of the difference between explanatory and non-explanatory mathematical proofs. Resnik and Kushner (1987) take issue with this account, but do not deny that we need *some* account of when a proof is explanatory and when it is not. Sandborg (1998) offers arguments purporting to show that the (acknowledged) difference between explanatory and non-explanatory proofs should not be analysed in terms of why questions. Mancosu (1999, 2000) traces the history of philosophical reflection on mathematical explanation back to Aristotle. Intriguing remarks on the role of mathematical explanation in the work of Mill, Russell, Gödel, and Lakatos may be found in Mancosu (2001).

Although there exists as yet no agreed account of the *nature* of mathematical explanation, its existence is not disputed. Even paradigm causal theorists of explanation, such as Lewis (1986) and Lipton (1990), are generally careful to specify that their accounts are not meant to cover the kinds of explanation that might crop up in mathematics. Lewis, for instance, explicitly limits his account to explanation of particular events.

The following is a (non-exhaustive) list of candidate accounts of what makes for a good mathematical explanation of a mathematical fact.

(a) The explanans shows how the explanandum fits into a wider system of results. Or, more specifically:

(a*) The explanans is (shorthand for) a member of the explanatory store E. Members of this store are those deductions of elements of our total knowledge K which best systematize this knowledge (see Kitcher 1989).

(b) The explanans shows how the explanandum follows from *more general* theorems or from axioms. (This would be another way of following through the intuition that explanation is closely related to unification.)

(c) The explanans shows how the explanandum follows from *other previously accepted* theorems or axioms. (This would develop the intuition that explanation relates or reduces the explanans to something already familiar.)

(d) The explanans provides the recipient with 'new conceptual resources' for analysing the explanandum (see Sandborg 1998).

(e) Where the explanans is a proof of the explanandum, it must be presented so as to make it clear that the proof 'depends' (in a specific sense) on some 'characterizing property' of some relevant mathematical entity or structure (see Steiner 1978).

(f) The explanans is a good answer to some why question about the explanandum.

A detailed exploration of the merits of each of these proposals would be out of place here. But approaches like (f) have a strong intuitive appeal, and why-question approaches to explanation constitute a promising and popular trend in the philosophy of science (see e.g. van Fraassen 1980; Lipton 1990). Moreover, since (f) can be filled out with various accounts of what counts as a good answer to a why question, it allows us the leeway to include such insights as we wish to retain from other accounts of mathematical explanation.[1] So I assume here that (f) is on the right track (but not that it constitutes a thorough going account of mathematical explanation).

As mentioned above, Sandborg (1998) objects to a why-question account of explanation in mathematics, but I am not concerned by this. His principal objection rests upon the assumption that the why questions which a good explanation answers must all be questions that the enquirer could specify before receiving the explanation. I do not see why this should be assumed. One explanatory virtue might be answering an antecedently specifiable why question in a way which gives one new conceptual resources which allow one to consider and answer other subordinate why questions which were *not* antecedently specifiable but become specifiable (and obviously relevant) once the explanation gets under way. (Sandborg offers some other objections, but they are specific to van Fraassen's particular way of developing the why-question approach.)

What I want to stress here is that, once we grant that mathematical propositions can answer why questions, there is no obvious reason to suppose they can only answer why questions about mathematics. Unfortunately, there is not that much direct philosophical consideration of the phenomenon of mathematical explanation of non-mathematical facts in the extant literature. One of the best sources is discussion of the indispensability argument for the existence of mathematical objects, which sometimes attempts to make plausible the idea that mathematical existence claims could be explanatory of physical facts in some important way (see e.g. Colyvan 2001). I shall discuss these cases in a moment.

Occasionally other mentions of the phenomenon can be found in philosophical discussions of explanation more generally, and in everyday

---

[1] See Jenkins (forthcoming *b*) for more details of how this might work.

contexts; to these I now turn. It is relatively commonplace to regard claims about physically instantiated shapes, patterns, or numerosities as providing explanations of non-mathematical facts. We often say things like: 'The building was unstable, and eventually collapsed, because its top half was wider than its bottom half'; or 'Jim was unhappy because Daisy was given ten sweets and he only got five'. But these are examples of *applied* geometrical and arithmetical explanations of non-mathematical facts. Could explanations of such facts be given in *purely* mathematical terms?

Nerlich (1979) discusses examples which are closer to being explanations of non-mathematical facts in terms of purely mathematical (or more specifically, geometrical) facts. He shows that facts about (e.g.) the shape of a cloud of particles and the stress upon a membrane can be explained in terms of the (possibly variable) curvature of the space through which they are inertially moving.[2] Nerlich's explanations are more abstract than explanations in terms of the shape of a physical object: they appeal to the structure of space itself. (Another similar example can be found in Colyvan 2001: 47–9.)

Presumably, however, purely geometrical explanations should not assume anything about the shape of actual space. So these are still not quite the kind of thing we are interested in. Lipton describes an explanation of the alignment of a group of falling objects in terms of the number of horizontal and vertical dimensions there are (1990: 208). This seems even closer to an explanation in terms of pure geometry. But presumably a genuinely pure geometrical explanation should not even make assumptions about the number and kind of spatial dimensions there are.

Some geometrical explanations do not make any such assumptions, however, and therefore can properly be called explanations in terms of pure geometry. For instance, we can explain why an object X *would* behave in a particular way in some imaginary space by citing some conditionalized geometrical truth, stating that *if* space were as this imaginary space is, *then* it would have certain features which would constrain X to behave that way. Nerlich offers such an explanation (pp. 75–8). He imagines a volume of soft rubber passing through a space of variable curvature from a Euclidean

---

[2] These explanations are cited in the context of a contribution to the debate over the reality of space. Responding to the claim that space would have to be causally efficacious in order for us to know what it was like, Nerlich states that properties of space can *explain* observable behaviour and changes in physical objects without *causing* such behaviour or changes.

(non-curved) to a non-Euclidean (curved) region. His explanation of the change in the object's shape that would result is, roughly: If space were variably curved in the way envisaged, an object passing from a Euclidean to a non-Euclidean region 'must be stressed out of its Euclidean shape even to enter or occupy part of the latter [region] at all'. Nerlich's explanans here is in terms of pure geometry: no assumptions are made as to what space is actually like. And yet the explanans is pretty clearly non-mathematical: it is a counterfactual concerned with the movement and shape of a particular physical object in particular regions of space.

The mathematical explanations of non-mathematical facts which I have discussed so far have been *geometrical* and not arithmetical. There is somewhat less discussion of the possibility of giving an arithmetical explanation of a non-mathematical fact. It is not that philosophers deny that this is possible, but rather that, in general, they do not discuss it. Putnam (1979: 92–3) takes some arithmetical facts to constitute partial explanation of non-mathematical facts about how our counting episodes turn out, and what we find (or fail to find) counter-examples to. But we are interested in seeing whether such a thing could be an adequate explanation by itself, not just a partial explanation.

The literature on indispensability contains some notable exceptions to the rule. However, the holistic nature of the classic indispensability arguments means that there are few examples of the kind that interest us here; namely, examples of explanation of particular non-mathematical facts by appeal to facts of a purely arithmetical nature. (Colyvan 2001: sect. 4.4.1 might be appealed to as showing how real numbers can help explain certain commonalities in physical systems, though he himself is explicitly focussing on unification here rather than explanation.) Indeed, some worries about whether explanation of the non-mathematical by the mathematical is possible are raised in the context of discussions of the indispensability argument, though they tend to emanate from a conviction that explanation must be causal in some fairly restrictive sense (more restrictive than that of, say, Lewis 1986; see e.g. Field 1989: 18–19). For some convincing counter-examples to the thesis that all explanation is causal in such a sense see Lipton (1990: 34) and Colyvan (2001: sect. 3. 3). Baker (2005) contains a good summary of the debate over whether mathematical explanation of non-mathematical facts is possible. Some of Baker's examples look like good arithmetical explanations of non-mathematical facts (see esp. pp. 233–6).

One relevant consideration, I think, is that once we have admitted that (pure and applied) geometrical truths can explain non-mathematical facts, there seems to be no reason not to admit that (pure and applied) arithmetical truths can too. There seems to be no relevant difference between arithmetic and geometry in this respect.

One point which may seem relevant is that there is often thought to be a difference between the necessity of arithmetic and that of geometry. One might argue that the reason geometrical propositions (e.g. *There are two horizontal dimensions and one vertical one*) can explain physical facts is that they could be false. This property surely is not shared by arithmetical propositions.

However, in the case of *purely* geometrical explanations like Nerlich's above, the explanation offered seems every bit as necessary as an arithmetical proposition. We can deny that it is necessary that space actually be curved in a certain way, but it is more difficult to deny the necessity of the conditional proposition that if it were so curved then objects within it would be constrained to behave in a particular manner.

In Nerlich's explanation the non-mathematical explanans is also a counterfactual (*If an object were moving in such-and-such a space, it would behave in such-and-such a way*), which might itself be regarded as a necessary truth (at least if the explanandum is so regarded). Is it possible to give a mathematical explanation of a *non*-necessary non-mathematical fact? If not, the claims of Chapter 3 will create trouble for arithmetical epistemology, since propositions of the form *A believes that $7 + 5 = 12$* are non-necessary.

But mathematical (and in particular, arithmetical) explanations of non-necessary non-mathematical facts do in fact seem perfectly possible. Everyday cases are easy to find. The question 'Why is 12 Katherine's favourite number?' may be perfectly well answered by saying 'Because 12 is divisible by 2, 3, 4, and 6'. These necessary features of the number 12 explain the contingent fact that Katherine has selected 12 as her favourite number.

Some may be tempted to respond that in such a case 'the real' explanation of the explanans is that Katherine likes numbers with many divisors *and* 12 is divisible by 2, 3, 4, and 6. I find this unconvincing. This conjunction may be *another* perfectly good explanation of the explanans; perhaps it is better in some respects (because it is more explicit about the link between divisibility and Katherine's preferences). But that does not mean that the original, non-conjunctive, explanation is not also a good explanation.

It may be that when a necessary truth explains a non-necessary truth there will always be another contingency involved in some important way in the connection between explanandum and explanans. (In this case, *Katherine likes numbers with many divisors*.) It may even be that the explanation would be better (or at least more complete) if it were mentioned. But this does not affect my claim that arithmetical propositions can explain our arithmetical beliefs in the way required for those beliefs to count as knowledge. All that's required is that an explanation of the relevant arithmetical belief which cited just the arithmetical fact believed would not be misleading to an outsider. It could be that the reason it would not be misleading to an outsider is that on hearing it the outsider would make certain (correct) assumptions about other things which are contingently the case.

Further cases where an arithmetical proposition serves as an explanation of a non-mathematical fact are easy to come up with. Why did Sam get a bad mark on his arithmetic test? Because 9^2 is not 18. Why doesn't Katherine like the number 17? Because 17 is not divisible by anything except itself and 1. Why does Marcus want a twelfth person to join his dance class? Because 12 is an even number.

These explanations are not recherché or contrived. They are easy to understand and would readily be accepted as satisfactory explanations in everyday contexts. They are certainly no more puzzling than explanations of physical facts which appeal to geometrical propositions. In just the same way, they explain certain non-mathematical phenomena by appealing to aspects of the mathematical structure of the world which are responsible (though not, of course, causally responsible; cf. n. 2 above) for those phenomena.

We should not be dissuaded, then, by the fact that geometrical examples are more frequently discussed in the literature. We have every reason to believe that arithmetical truths can also explain non-mathematical truths of various kinds. For we can give plenty of apparently good examples of such explanations, and there is no reason to doubt that the appearance is veridical (once we are free of the assumption that all explanations are causal).

Therefore there is no reason to doubt that arithmetical propositions can, in particular, explain facts about what we believe.[3] If they can explain facts

---

[3] It is worth mentioning in passing here a worry corresponding to one discussed on p. 114 above. One might be tempted to say that 'the real' explanation of why I believe some arithmetical proposition

about our likes and dislikes, as suggested above, they should be able to explain other facts about our mental lives.

Of course, the difficult task is to give details of the fact-belief link which make it plausible that we have arithmetical knowledge. I shall hypothesize that this kind of explanatory link holds in virtue of three sub-links, one between the arithmetical facts and our sensory input, one between our sensory input and our arithmetical concepts, and one between our arithmetical concepts and our arithmetical beliefs. I shall outline my proposal in the remainder of Chapter 4; then in Section 5.4, I shall show how it fits the three-step structure just described.

4.3 Preliminaries

It may be easiest to understand my approach to arithmetical knowledge by contrasting it with two existing strategies which an arithmetical realist might find attractive. These are indispensability theory and neo-Fregeanism. Indispensability theorists, following Quine, believe that arithmetical truths are known because they are indispensable parts of our best scientific theory of the world. That theory is epistemically supported in virtue of its being the most explanatory, predictive, simple, fertile, and so on. They maintain that our arithmetical knowledge has no privileged epistemic status, beyond the fact that we are more reluctant to revise arithmetical beliefs than most others owing to the central role that arithmetic plays in our theory. Because it is so central, respect for the 'maxim of minimum mutilation' forces us to be very reluctant to revise arithmetic (see e.g. Quine 1951, 1960, 1981; Putnam 1973).

This proposal is attractive to realists in so far as the arithmetical knowledge so achieved is taken to be part of our knowledge of the independent world. But it fails to account satisfactorily for the special a priori status of arithmetic (see e.g. Parsons 1980: 151–2). It also seems worrying that any currently accepted theorems of arithmetic which turn out not to be indispensable for scientific purposes will also turn out not to be known.

---

is that (e.g.) I think I've seen a proof of it. As before, my reply is that as long as there are *some* contexts where the arithmetical proposition itself would constitute an adequate explanation of my belief, it makes no odds if there is *another* explanation which mentions my seeing a proof. The existence of such an explanation does not mean there is anything defective about the original one.

Neo-Fregeans defend a proposal considered, but rejected, by Frege in the *Grundlagen*. This is the thesis that our knowledge about cardinal numbers flows from our knowledge of a proposition known as Hume's Principle:

The number of Fs = the number of Gs iff the Fs and the Gs are equinumerous.

This biconditional is said to be epistemologically unproblematic. Sometimes this is said to be because its left-hand side is a recarving of the content of its right-hand side (see e.g. Hale 1997), and because instances of the right-hand side can be straightforwardly understood, since they involve no reference to abstract objects. In other places the recarving metaphor does not play this key role, but instead emphasis is placed on claiming that the status of Hume's Principle as an implicit definition of 'number' renders it epistemically tractable (see e.g. Hale and Wright 2000), given that the left-hand side is straightforwardly understood. It is well known that we can derive the standard axioms of arithmetic from Hume's Principle in second-order logic, which suggests that Hume's Principle could serve as a foundation for much of our arithmetical knowledge.[4] (Recent work on the neo-Fregean project is brought together in Hale and Wright 2001. Various important challenges for the project are helpfully listed in the appendix to that book.)

The neo-Fregean proposal might seem attractive to realists, since true instances of the right-hand side of Hume's Principle seem to be straightforwardly independent truths. But this does not by itself make neo-Fregeanism a realist view, since according to the neo-Fregean our knowledge of arithmetic does not flow from our knowledge of such instances, but from our knowledge of Hume's Principle itself. Is *this* knowledge of an independent truth?

We should note that adopting neo-Fregeanism could be associated with arithmetical anti-realism in my sense, if it were thought that Hume's Principle itself were *not* essentially independent: if, for instance, it were thought to be somehow the product of convention or stipulation. Indeed, the neo-Fregeans sometimes seem to be taking this route when they talk of Hume's Principle as an implicit definition of 'number'. (Recall from

---

[4] But not, for all that has been said so far, all of it—Gödel's incompleteness results show that there are some arithmetical truths which do not follow from the axioms (and that the same goes for all sufficiently rich axiom sets, not just the standard Peano axioms). Wright offers some reflections on this issue in his (1997: 4 n. 5). Thanks to Patricia Blanchette for helpful comments on this.

Section 2.3 that it is hard to see how an appeal to implicit definition can help us explain a priori knowledge if not underwritten by some sort of conventionalism.) They only occasionally call themselves 'realists', and then it is on the grounds that they believe mathematical objects exist (see e.g. Hale 1994 n. 7).

But if one took a different view of the status of Hume's Principle, realism in the sense of Chapter 1 might be made consistent with (most aspects of) the neo-Fregean view of how we know arithmetic.[5] In order for a realist to accept the neo-Fregean view that arithmetical knowledge flows from our knowledge of Hume's Principle, which has some special epistemic status, she need only hold that knowledge of Hume's Principle is knowledge of an independent truth. There is no obvious objection to her doing so. Of course, she will have work to do in explaining how independent truths of this kind are known in the special way envisaged. However, as we saw in Section 2.3, it is unclear that the conventionalist approach would make things any easier.

Two points arise from all this. First, something like a neo-Fregean epistemology might be attractive to realists, although it is not exclusively (or originally) their property. Second, and relatedly, a close examination of neo-Fregeanism reveals that *it does not, by itself, settle the philosophical question of how we know arithmetical propositions.* All it does is pass the buck on to how we know truths which are analytic (or implicitly definitional, or whatever), and what kind of truths these are (cf. BonJour's critique of 'moderate empiricism', discussed in Section 2.3 above). Realists and anti-realists will have to differ at this point.

Another problem for the neo-Fregeans is that it has not proved easy to establish that Hume's Principle is analytic or definitive in the required sense (see e.g. Boolos 1997 and Potter and Smiley 2001, 2002 for some objections on this score).

Both indispensability theory and neo-Fregeanism have met with various other objections, but the ones I have mentioned here are of particular relevance in the current context. To sum up what these are: Against the indispensability theorists, it is argued that they fail to account satisfactorily for the special epistemic status which arithmetical beliefs have and ordinary beliefs about the physical world lack, and that it is worrying that their

---

[5] Wright hints at something like this in his (1997: 278).

proposal may not account for all the arithmetical knowledge we like to think we have. Meanwhile the neo-Fregeans stand accused of being unable to defend the claim that Hume's Principle has the special (analytic or definitive) status they say it has; and I have furthermore argued that, even if they showed that it did have this status, that would not by any means suffice to explain how we know it.

The upshot, then, is that the indispensability theorists' epistemology is adequate to underwrite *some* sort of knowledge, at least of some part of arithmetic, but it does not accord arithmetic its distinctive status, and may not extend far enough. But while the neo-Fregeans fare well with respect to the special status of arithmetic, and may fare at least better with respect to the extent of our arithmetical knowledge, they do not offer an adequate account of how *any* of it is known. It is natural to wonder whether there might be a strategy available which is capable of combining the virtues of both theories and thus avoiding the pitfalls of each. I shall attempt to indicate that this may be so.

First, some terminological clarification is needed. I am aiming to preserve the (or at least a) standard meaning of each of the terms I define here.

(1) A way of knowing a proposition p is *empirical* iff it involves some epistemic use of the senses. A use of the senses is epistemic iff the role of the senses is not just that of awakening or preparing the mind so that it is ready to know things, but rather the senses play a key role in actually supplying us with the knowledge in question.

(2) A way of knowing a proposition p is *a priori* iff it is epistemically independent of empirical evidence; that is, there is no epistemic reliance upon any of the following:
   (a) immediate experiential knowledge of p;[6]
   (b) inductive empirical confirmation of p;
   (c) inference to, or deduction of, p from propositions which are known in one of the above ways.

(3) A proposition p is *conceptually true* iff p is a true proposition whose truth *follows epistemically* from certain concepts;[7] that is, iff a correctly

---

[6] That is, the kind of justification or knowledge which some philosophers think we have with regard to propositions reporting fundamental observations.

[7] I do not assume that the relevant concepts will always be exclusively concepts that are involved in p itself. It might be, for instance, that one needs to consider concepts besides those contained in p in

conducted examination[8] of the relevant concepts would suffice to ground a belief in p which, assuming there is nothing wrong with the concepts, will amount to knowledge. I shall also say that a proposition p which is not true *follows epistemically* from certain concepts iff someone who used those concepts could, on the basis of a correctly conducted examination of them, form a belief that p which would have counted as knowledge had there not been something wrong with the concepts (though these propositions, of course, cannot be called conceptual *truths*).

(4) *Concepts* are here taken to be sub-propositional mental representations, related to propositional mental representations in more or less the way that words and sub-sentential groups of words are related to sentences. I assume that concepts are typically available to armchair examination in the sense that we can access at least some facts about our concepts (in particular, facts about how they relate to other concepts) in the armchair, just by thinking. The type of epistemology I am planning to defend will be most attractive to those who individuate concepts more finely than by extension; on the kind of view I myself prefer, they are hyperintensionally individuated (so that even concepts which necessarily have the same extension may be non-identical).

(5) I take *possession of a concept* to amount to the use in cogitation of a concept. A concept is used in cogitation by a subject iff it figures in any of the subject's beliefs, desires, or other propositional attitudes (excepting attitudes in which it is merely mentioned). Use of a

---

order to grasp the proof which constitutes one's a priori method of knowing p. See Isaacson (1996) for an interesting discussion of such issues with respect to arithmetic.

[8] As I am an externalist (see Section 2.2 above), I do not wish to imply that such an 'examination' must be *consciously* conducted, nor that it must be something the subject is aware of or can reconstruct on demand. More on concept examination in Section 4.4 below.

I should also mention that *some* kinds of examination of one's concepts are not supposed to count. For instance, I can tell by examining my concepts that there are concepts, that I have some concepts, and that some of my concepts are colour concepts; but none of this is supposed to count. The relevant kind of conceptual examination is the kind which guides us to beliefs about the world as represented by our concepts, rather than just about the concepts themselves (except in the special case where concepts are themselves the things represented by our concepts).

An alternative line with which I am almost equally happy is that these kinds of examination do count but that the resultant conceptual truths are not the sort I'm interested in here. The reason I'm not so happy with this is simply that I think current usage of 'conceptual truth' is better tracked on the first than on the second strategy.

concept in cogitation is distinct from acceptance of any particular concept—or other—truths. Although such acceptance will often accompany concept possession and be intimately related to it, I do not claim that there are any concepts and corresponding conceptual truths such that it is impossible to possess those concepts without believing those truths. (Which is not to say I deny this either. I am neutral.)

Note that in defining conceptual truth I have not used the locution 'true *in virtue of* concepts'. A conceptual truth, by my lights, may be essentially independent of us (in the sense defined in Section 1.2). I take it that if, by contrast, all such propositions were true *in virtue of* their constituent concepts, their truth would seem to be somehow dependent upon us qua creators of those concepts. For it would then seem to be part (or all) of *what it is* for $7 + 5 = 12$ to be true that our concepts of 7, $+$, 5, $=$, and 12 are as they are.[9] In using the locution 'true in virtue of concepts' to define conceptual truth, one seems to beg the question against the view that essentially independent conceptual truths are possible. On my definition conceptual truth is an epistemic matter, rather than a metaphysical one: it concerns *our ways of seeing that a proposition is true*, not the nature of that proposition's truth or its truthmaker.[10]

I have avoided talk of 'analyticity'. The main reason for this is that this term has many different contemporary uses and connotations which could make for significant confusion, and because I can express everything I want to express without using it. One might, for instance, use the term 'analytic' as I am using 'conceptually true'. Or one might use it to mean 'true in virtue of meaning'. Or one might use it in a Kantian way, to describe propositions where the predicate concept is 'contained' in the subject concept. Or one might use it to describe sentences which 'define' some constituent word or words, or sentences which are such that their meaning what they do is sufficient for them to be true.

Readers will also have noticed that I do not define the a priori in terms of total epistemic independence from the senses. This is necessary if I am

---

[9] See Section 6.2 below, where this apparent consequence is discussed further.

[10] Boghossian (1997: 334) also appreciates the importance of isolating some epistemic notion akin to conceptual truth in my sense. That's why he distinguishes 'epistemological' from 'metaphysical' analyticity (see Section 2.4 above).

to claim that there is a way of knowing arithmetical propositions which is empirical although it is a priori. But is it fair? Why, given that the way of knowing that I'm interested in is empirical, do I not simply include it among the kinds of knowledge ruled out by the definition of 'a priori'?

The reason is that I think the (or at least, one) ordinary criterion for aprioricity *is and has always been* independence from (a)–(c) in the above definition of 'a priori'. This criterion is badly captured by the many definitions which talk of total independence of the senses. The existence of a certain empirical way of knowing has been ignored, and this has allowed philosophers to assume that to be independent of (a)–(c) is to be independent of the senses altogether. Once this new empirical way of knowing is recognized, we must ask without prejudice whether it is an a priori or a posteriori way of knowing. As we shall see below (pp. 148–50 and Section 9.5), it meets a range of (what are usually considered to be) sufficient conditions for aprioricity. So I shall argue that, contrary to popular belief, there is a widely accepted notion of aprioricity on which it is possible for some knowledge to be both a priori and empirical.

Let me quickly add a few more remarks about concepts here before moving on. First, I take it that concepts represent in a way which is in some respects language-like. They seem to exhibit systematicity and productivity best explained by compositionality (see Fodor and Pylyshyn 1988), features shared with linguistic representation. However, as will become clear later (p. 132), I think there are also some significant differences between concepts and representations in natural language. Second, I do not take it that concepts are mental images or clusters of abilities, though of course many may be closely *associated* with characteristic images and/or abilities. (In my Final Remarks I shall discuss to what extent versions of my proposal might be compatible with alternative views about what concepts are like.)

Third, although in the definitions above I helped myself to a notion of concepts 'figuring in' propositional attitudes, I do not mean by that to commit to the view that propositional attitudes are to be identified with token mental representations composed of concepts in my sense. That might well be what propositional attitudes are, but the notion of a concept's 'figuring in' a belief might alternatively be better understood in terms of that concept's appearing in a token representation which merely *accompanies* the relevant belief, or perhaps just in terms of that concept's appearing in a certain *type* of representation with *the same content* as that belief. No doubt there are other options too.

Finally, to avoid any potential confusion, I am not using 'concept' to mean anything like 'Fregean sense' or 'constituent of a proposition', nor in Frege's way to mean the referent of a predicate.

4.4 Grounding for concepts

On the view that I'm interested in arithmetical truths are conceptual truths; or, at least, enough arithmetical truths are conceptual truths to enable us to account for all of our a priori arithmetical knowledge once we add in knowledge secured by inference from other truths known in this way. That is to say, we can know about arithmetic by examining our concepts. This is a key aspect of my view; so before moving on it might be helpful to say a few words about how I think such conceptual examination might work. My particular take on this is not essential to the view under development; other accounts could be made to cohere with the central epistemological aspects of my proposal. However, it will probably be helpful to have something concrete on the table.

The way I think about it is that we (humans in general) are able to perform a process which we (philosophers) call 'attempting to conceive' of something's being the case. When we attempt to conceive of something's being the case, what we are doing is investigating how our conceptual representations fit together. For instance, when we attempt to conceive of a non-female vixen, we investigate whether our concept of *vixenhood* is a concept as of a property that includes the property of which our concept *female* is a concept. We find that it is, and hence report that we cannot conceive of a non-female vixen (or, sometimes, just that there aren't, and/or cannot be, any non-female vixens). When we attempt to conceive of $7 + 5$ not being equal to 12, we investigate whether our concepts of 7, 5, and 12 are concepts as of things that stand in the relation denoted by our concept $... + ... = ...$ We find that they are, and hence report that we cannot conceive of $7 + 5$ not being equal to 12 (or, sometimes, just that $7 + 5 = 12$, and/or that necessarily $7 + 5 = 12$). (Jenkins (forthcoming *a*) offers further discussion of conceivability and concepts.)

Notice that the locution 'as of' is quite important here. It is used to help capture the difference between information which is encoded in our conceptual representations and facts which are merely true of the things our concepts represent. A concept can be a concept *of* something F without being a concept *as of* something F. For instance, my concept of *grass* is a concept of, but not as of, green stuff. I cannot read off from my concepts that grass is green. This information is not encoded in my concepts. I have to learn it some other way; that is, through good, old-fashioned, empirical evidence-gathering. By contrast, my concept of *knowledge* is a concept as of a belief-involving state. So I can read off from my concepts that one only has knowledge when one has a belief.

It might sound wrong to say that we see $7 + 5 = 12$ to be true by conducting an examination of our concepts, because it might sound too psychologistic: when we think about whether $7 + 5 = 12$ is true in that distinctive way that leads to a priori knowledge, we don't seem to be thinking about *our concepts* but rather about *the numbers* 7, 5, and 12 and *the relations* expressed by 'plus' and 'equals'.[11]

I should like to respond to this thought by drawing a comparison which I hope will illustrate how broadly I want 'conceptual examination' to be construed. Suppose I look at a map of the British Isles and think to myself: *Aha! St Andrews is north of Cambridge, so I should drive north to get there.* When I do this I am thinking about St Andrews and Cambridge themselves, not about my map. Nevertheless, I am learning what I am about the relative positions of these two cities through an examination of my map. Because the map is a trustworthy and accurate representation, looking at the map is a way of learning about the cities themselves, not just about the map. And, importantly, because I trust the map, when I'm examining it and working out what it shows me, I am thinking about the cities themselves, not about the representations of them.

I suggest that much the same is happening in the arithmetical case. Our concepts are representations of the world; as such, they can serve as a kind of map of that world. Examining this conceptual map can—and probably often does—*amount to* thinking about the world and not about these representations of it. In doing conceptual examination we are allowing our concepts to guide us, but we need not be aware that they are what is

---

[11] I am grateful to Timothy Williamson for pressing me to clarify this point.

guiding us in order to count as performing an examination of them in my intended sense.

It might be argued, however, that in the case of map-reading we are always forming beliefs about the map *as well*. Is something similar also happening with conceptual examination? It doesn't really seem to be; often we seem to end up with no beliefs about our concepts, merely beliefs about the state of the world. But that things seem that way does not mean that we aren't relying on our concepts as guides to how the world is. Sometimes we are so at home with a kind of representation that we don't bother to form beliefs about the vehicle when we are relying on it in forming our beliefs about the world; or, at least, if we do, those beliefs about the vehicle go unnoticed and may well be unrecoverable to conscious reflection. For instance, when you hear people speaking your native language, you don't think much about the linguistic vehicles in which their utterances are couched—you skip straight to thinking about whatever they're talking about. Seconds later you may well be unable to recall which words they used or other similar details.[12]

Similarly, I think, we are often so at home with our conceptual map of the world, and so used to relying on it, that when we conduct conceptual examinations we don't notice the vehicle of representation but only what is represented (i.e. some fact about the world). If we do form beliefs about the vehicles, we don't really notice these beliefs or bother to remember them; our attention is wholly focussed on the worldly facts that we are learning via those vehicles. (Of course, none of this is to deny that sometimes conceptual examination *can* be done self-consciously: that is, with awareness that what one is doing is examining one's concepts, and with beliefs about those concepts formed as intermediaries on the way to beliefs about the world. Philosophers, at least, seem to do this fairly often.)

What is of crucial importance here is that most of the philosophers who accept that arithmetical truths are conceptual truths also consider that this claim does most or all of the heavy lifting in removing the epistemological mysteries of arithmetical knowledge. I don't agree. If $7 + 5 = 12$ is a conceptual truth, then I think we can *begin* explaining how we know it by

---

[12] One might, but need not, understand this as being because meanings are directly perceived (see McDowell 1981). Some of the remarks in Fricker (2003) are also conducive to my point of view here.

saying that, just by examining our concepts of 7, $+$, 5, $=$, and 12 we can see that $7 + 5 = 12$. But, if we are realists, this cannot be the end of the matter. For it is far from obvious that we can acquire knowledge about an *independent* arithmetical reality by examining *our concepts*—our own mental representations.

By way of filling in the rest of the story, I want to suggest that, if our concepts are somehow sensitive to the way the independent world is, so that they successfully and accurately represent that world, then an examination of them may not merely be an examination of ourselves, but may rather amount to an examination of an accurate, on-board *conceptual map* of the independent world. And I want to suggest that we might well be able to acquire knowledge about the independent world by examining such a map.

I suggest that, if it is to be possible for us to come to know essentially independently[13] true propositions by examining our concepts, then the concepts in question must be what I call 'grounded'. That is, they must accurately represent aspects of the independent world, and this accuracy must be due to a certain kind of sensitivity to that world.[14] Let me now explain in more detail what kind of sensitivity is intended.

First, some more definitions (and note that this time I am introducing new technical terms rather than trying to do justice to existing uses):

(6) I shall say that a concept *refers* iff it is a representation of some real feature of the world. I wish to allow here that property concepts can refer to properties, just as object concepts can refer to objects. I also wish to allow that to the extent that the world has other features besides objects and properties, concepts of the appropriate kind can refer to these other features (so, for instance, it might be that the world has logical features which our logical concepts—concepts of connectives, quantifiers, and so on—refer to). I am also allowing that a property may be a real aspect of the world even when nothing has that property, and even when *necessarily* nothing has it.[15]

---

[13] See Section 1.2 above for the definition of essential independence.

[14] The notion of grounding for concepts is novel, but it has something of a precursor. Locke (1689) took the units of justification and knowledge to be (at the level of) propositions, but acknowledged the existence of epistemically important links between experience and the (sub-propositional) mental entities which he called 'ideas'. See Section 6.7 below for more on Locke's view.

[15] This is probably not essential to the view, but certainly makes things much easier.

(7) Without wanting to get into too much detail as to what *concept composition* is, let me include a few words here to help avert later misunderstandings. The composition relation I have in mind is more like set-theoretic inclusion than mereological composition, in that I do not assume that a constituent of a constituent of a concept C is itself a constituent of C. It shares some features with the relationship between ordered n–tuples and their members, since I want to allow that the same constituents can be composed in different ways to make different concepts. However, I do not want to assume that each concept has a unique proper decomposition into constituents.

(8) *Correct* composition of concepts means composition that, non-accidentally, does not smuggle in extra content. Sometimes an attempt at composition could result in a concept which is not in fact a bona fide construct out of its constituents. For instance, suppose you try to compose a new concept from *red* and *square* and end up with *small red square*—a concept applicable only to small red squares. Clearly, extra content has been smuggled in; the correct compound would have been something applicable to large as well as small red squares.

(9) *Fitting* concepts are concepts which either refer themselves or else are correct compounds of referring concepts (or correct compounds of correct compounds of referring concepts, or ...). I appeal to composition here in order to avoid positing an ontology of features of the world as vast as our capacity to create new concepts from old. I want to leave open the option of believing in a relatively sparse ontology of aspects of the world. Another terminological device will help to make much of what is to follow more perspicuous. I shall sometimes say that something is true of a concept's *ultimate constituents*, meaning that this thing is true either of its constituents, or of the constituents of its constituents, or of *their* constituents, etc. (The locution 'ultimate' should not be taken to imply any kind of atomism.)

(10) I want to allow (at least for the sake of argument) that a concept may refer despite to some extent misrepresenting its referent.[16]

---

[16] I am indebted to Dave Chalmers, Daniel Nolan, Robbie Williams, and Crispin Wright for helpful discussions on this topic.

Hence, even fitting concepts may in some respects be (and/or be built of) partially inaccurate representations. We might be misled about how the world is by examining an inaccurate but referring concept. Given some purported a priori knowable proposition p, we can say that a concept C is *relevantly accurate* (or, sometimes, just *accurate*) iff C is fitting and neither C nor any concept from which C is composed misrepresents its referent in any respect relevant to our purported a priori way of knowing that p. (Note that which concepts count as 'relevantly accurate' depends on which item(s) of a priori knowledge we are interested in.) I shall say that a concept is *seriously inaccurate* if it is too inaccurate to count as fitting.

Although I allow this possibility for the sake of argument, however, I am not entirely clear on what it would be for a concept to misrepresent its referent. Concepts are not propositional representations; they cannot be false. However, it may be that falsity is not the only kind of misrepresentation. Perhaps, for instance, some definite descriptions succeed in referring to objects despite misrepresenting them (see Donnellan 1966). It is, perhaps, easier to see how a *group* of concepts might misrepresent their referents; for instance, by representing them in a way that makes it looks as if they stand in a certain relationship, when in fact they do not—in which case, accuracy may be ascribed to groups of concepts (and then, derivatively, to the concepts in the groups) even if not directly to individual concepts. I shall say more about representation by groups of concepts in a moment.

For those who do not think that a concept can misrepresent its referent, all fitting concepts will automatically count as fully accurate in my sense, and all conceptual inaccuracy will amount to unfittingness. That is fine by me.

(11) A concept is *grounded* just in case it is relevantly accurate and there is nothing lucky or accidental about its being so. (By analogy, a belief is *knowledgeable* just in case it is true and there is nothing lucky or accidental about its being so.) It is not required that the subject be aware of the relevant accuracy, though she should be appropriately *responsive* to it at some, perhaps entirely sub-personal, level.[17] Note

---

[17] Note that for one's possession of a concept to be responsive to some factor is not necessarily for one to have *acquired* it in response to that factor. It could be, rather, that because of that factor

that, by my lights, a non-accidentally correct compound of grounded concepts is itself a grounded concept. For it follows from the correctness of the composition that the new compound is accurate if the constituents are, and since this accuracy is non-accidental, the new concept is non-accidentally accurate; that is, grounded.

(12) It will also be useful to have a notion of a concept's being *justified*. Just as a proposition must be justified in order to be known, I take it that a concept must be justified in order to be grounded. However, more is required in each case, since justification can be present when a concept's accuracy or a belief's truth is accidental in a grounding- or knowledge-destroying way. I shall take it that a concept is justified iff it is rationally respectable[18] for us to rely on it as a relevantly accurate guide to the world. Justified concepts may not be relevantly accurate, or even fitting, since we may have misleading data which makes it rationally respectable to have inaccurate or unfitting concepts. A justified concept could alternatively be relevantly accurate but only accidentally so, since we could have data which makes it rationally respectable to have a concept which is in fact relevantly accurate although there is something 'deviant' about the way this is working. For instance, a brain in a vat might have a justified and relevantly accurate concept *table* which is not grounded because it is in the relevant sense accidental that this concept is accurate (e.g. because the vat operator has in fact given the brain sensory input that accurately reflects the world around the vat, though she could easily have done otherwise).

(13) I shall also occasionally say that a concept is *disjustified* iff it is rationally respectable for us to treat it as if it is *not* an accurate guide to the world. This is not the same a concept's being merely *unjustified*.

---

the concept has *not been discarded*. This is significant because it makes the debate over the innateness of fundamental concepts somewhat tangential to a discussion of their groundedness. More on this in Sections 4.5 and 8.3 below.

[18] I am employing an externalist notion of rational respectability here. It is not required for a concept to be justified that we are capable of recognizing that it is so, or that we are capable of recognizing what it is that makes it respectable. It might merely be, for instance, that our sensory input makes it highly (objectively) probable that the concept is relevantly accurate, and we are responsive to that fact at some—perhaps entirely sub-personal—level.

I shall say more about the kind of non-accidentalness required for concept grounding in a moment.[19] First, let me acknowledge at this point that some readers may be feeling uncomfortable with the whole idea of having epistemic grounding or justification for a concept. Perhaps they will be thinking that these things, by definition, accrue only to propositions. However, the concepts which I call 'grounded' and 'justified' could be described as '*proto*-grounded' and '*proto*-justified' if this were preferred. The only crucial points are that a concept can be non-accidentally relevantly accurate, and that it can be rationally respectable to rely on a concept as an accurate guide to the world. I do not think the feeling that epistemic grounding and justification can only accrue to propositions should interfere with *these* claims. And beyond this the issues are terminological.

To show what kind of non-accidentalness I think is required for grounding, I adapt the theory of knowledge presented in Chapter 3. As suggested in my definition of groundedness above, I think of groundedness for concepts as analogous to knowledge of propositions. I therefore suggest that a concept C is grounded iff its possession could be well explained to an outsider simply by citing the fact that C is relevantly accurate. But note that anyone not persuaded by my theory of knowledge could adapt a number of other standard externalist strategies to the purpose. A reliabilist, for instance, might say that our concepts are grounded as long as the mechanisms which determine which concepts we have are mechanisms which *reliably* lead us to have concepts which are accurate. Or a Nozickian tracking theorist might say that the grounded concepts are those we *would not have possessed* had they not been accurate, but do possess in close worlds where they are accurate.

I find my proposal more appealing then these alternatives because it seems best able to avoid difficulty with the analogues of Gettier cases, wherein a concept is justified and accurate but there is something accidental about the way it is justified. Reliabilism about concept grounding, for instance, could

[19] There is an interesting question in this neighbourhood as to whether a concept could be significantly similar to some feature of the world, or related to it in some other representation-like way, and yet fail to refer to it because the relationship was accidental. Even if non-accidentalness is needed to secure reference, however, note that it is not obvious that the kind of non-accidentalness needed to secure reference is the same as that needed for groundedness. It could be non-accidental that the concept C is so related to the property F-ness that it refers to F-ness, but accidental that C is a *relevantly accurate* representation of F-ness. Therefore it could be that we have concepts which genuinely refer to features of the world yet are not grounded.

not always handle such cases: a method for selecting concepts might be reliable for some accidental reason. (As suggested above, perhaps friendly vat operators reliably ensure that their vat inhabitants end up with accurate concepts.) In such cases I do not think we would want to say we could acquire *knowledge* through examining the concepts in question: we would arrive at true beliefs, but only accidentally. So we should not count these concepts as grounded.

Concept accuracy, justification, and grounding are important because, while we have no reason to suppose that examining just *any old* concepts will help us learn about the independent world, examining *accurate* concepts can help us acquire true beliefs about the world, examining *justified* concepts can help us acquire justified beliefs about the independent world, and examining *grounded* concepts can help us acquire knowledge of it.

It is not a new idea that concepts need to meet certain conditions in order for an examination of them not to lead us astray. Eklund (2002) has recently argued, tapping into a tradition encompassing Dummett, Quine, and famously Tarksi, that semantic competence or—equivalently in his view (see his n. 4)—conceptual competence can sometimes lead to our accepting falsehoods. (This is thought to be a promising diagnosis of what is going on with perennial paradoxes such as the liar.) I am in sympathy with much of what Eklund and others in this tradition are saying. Helpful steps are made with regard to the issue of determining semantic values for problematic expressions or concepts in Eklund's section 5 (although I think we should allow for the possibility that some words or concepts with sense meaning can fail to have what he calls a 'semantic value', rather than saying that 'the semantic values are whatever comes *closest* to satisfying the conditions laid down by the senses': p. 265).

A related way of allowing for the possibility that conceptual competence can lead to error is encompassed by what's known as the 'Canberra Plan'. Typically, Canberra Planners will associate a term or concept with a group of 'platitudes', and for some Planners the platitudes are meaning-determining propositions which competent users of the term or concept are disposed in virtue of their competence to accept (see Jackson 1998 for a good general discussion of this sort of methodology, and O'Leary-Hawthorne and Oppy 1997 for a discussion of one way of Canberra Planning 'true' which is interestingly related to the Eklund view mentioned above). If we take this approach, we may wish to claim that in some cases the platitudes are false or even inconsistent. Moreover, though they generally allow that the referent of a term may fail to satisfy *some* of the associated platitudes, Canberra Planners also generally allow that in some cases there may be nothing that satisfies the platitudes well enough to be the semantic value of the term under consideration.

These approaches seem to me to have got something importantly right about conceptual competence. However, many of the epistemologically important questions in the vicinity are as yet under-explored: in particular, questions about when we should trust the deliverances of conceptual examination. Clearly, if we are being led into contradiction by doing so, we should hold off. But that obviously does not mean that every piece of conceptual examination where we are *not* lead into contradiction is in the clear. Once we see that there is scope for error when we let conceptual examination guide our beliefs, we can start asking the kinds of questions which are central to this book. That is to say, we can start asking what kinds of errors these might be, and in what cases the possibility of such error might undermine our claims to have secured justified beliefs or knowledge through conceptual examination.

It might seem strange to propose that the notion of concept grounding can help explain any of our knowledge of propositions. Grounding for our concepts ensures that they or their ultimate constituents are non-accidentally accurate *referrers*, but how can it help us acquire knowledge of the *truth* of any proposition? What is the envisaged relationship between reference and truth?

One initial point to note concerns the way concepts represent. Although they do have some language-like features, concepts are also in one respect unlike linguistic representations. For an examination of concepts like *man* and *bachelor* can lead us to adopt beliefs (such as the belief that all bachelors are men), whereas an examination of the *words* 'man' and 'bachelor' is not so forthcoming. In this respect concepts (or perhaps conceptual schemes) are more like maps: the relationships between concepts serve as guides to the relationships between features of the world, just as the relationships between dots on a map serve as guides to the relationships between cities.

An important question worth considering here is whether on my view a *group* of concepts (e.g. *all, vixen, female*) might represent a proposition or propositions as being true (e.g. *All vixens are female*).[20] I do not intend to take a stand on this issue; my suspicion is that we should give the same answer here as we would give to the corresponding question in the case of maps and pictures, and I do not have a view on the latter issue at this time.

But suppose we *do* take it that groups of concepts represent propositions, and we assume that concepts acquire grounding in clusters or perhaps whole schemes. Then securing empirical grounding for groups of concepts might be taken to amount to securing empirical grounding for certain of our propositional commitments; that is, coming to know them in an empirical way. Similarly, it might be thought that securing empirical justification for groups of concepts would then amount to securing empirical justification for certain propositions. To the extent that my view is motivated in part by felt shortcomings in the traditional empiricism of Mill and Quine, this might be thought to be problematic. (In fact, I think it would be a little hasty to regard this as a serious problem, since my account's recognition of the significance of the role of concepts and conceptual examination in securing certain kinds of knowledge is itself an advantage over a simple Millian or Quinean view, even if it were simultaneously acknowledged that the way our concepts play this role is through representing propositions which get confirmed by experience in the familiar way.)

Be that as it may, the view is certainly less distinctive if, because groups of concepts represent propositions as being true, getting grounding for groups of concepts amounts to coming to know certain propositions. As far as I can tell, however, even if we do want to say groups of concepts represent certain propositions as being true, we should *not* conclude that getting grounding for these groups of concepts amounts to coming to know certain propositions, nor that getting justification for the concepts amounts to getting justification for the propositions.

One way to bring this out is to note that I construe concept grounding and justification as akin to having reason (in either a knowledge-conferring or merely justificatory sense) to trust a map. Even if we assume for the sake of argument that maps represent propositions as being true, I can have reason to trust my map of Scotland without having reason to trust any of the propositions it represents as being true, if only because I have no idea *which* propositions the map represents as being true. Similarly, I want

---

[20] Many thanks to Daniel Nolan here.

to say, I can have grounding or justification for groups of my concepts without having any (knowledge-conferring or merely justificatory) reason to believe the propositions (if any) that they represent as being true, if only because I have not done enough conceptual examination to work out which propositions those are.

I believe, for example, that someone may possess grounded concepts of *all*, *vixen*, and *female* without possessing justification or knowledge-conferring grounds for believing that all vixens are female, even if those concepts represent that all vixens are female. To transform the grounding or justification one has for one's concepts into justification or warrant for believing that proposition, one must do some conceptual examination. Analogously, to transform a reason to trust my map of Scotland into a reason to believe one of the propositions (if any) that the map represents as being true, I need to examine the map.

Perhaps there is some good sense in which groups of concepts represent propositions as being true: one can, after all, 'read off' certain propositions when one examines the concepts. However, this does not threaten to collapse the important epistemological differences between grounding (and justification) for concepts and grounding (and justification) for beliefs. Emphasis on this difference is the distinctive feature of the view under development here.

With all that in place, here's how I think concept grounding can help explain knowledge of (a certain special class of) propositions. A proposition p's truth is a matter of p's telling us how the world is. For the realist, the problem with conceptual truths is that justification for them seems to come too easily, *before* we have any reason to believe they tell us how the world is. We can justify them simply by examining our concepts; we don't need to examine the world outside ourselves. Yet the realist resists the apparent consequence, that their truth has nothing to do with how the world is, and has to do only with how we are.

But the link with the world can be restored, and the realist can be vindicated, if it turns out that our concepts are the way they are because they are appropriately responsive to the way the world is. If our concepts are sensitive to sensory input and hence the world, in such a way that they (or their ultimate constituents) are likely to represent real aspects of the world in an accurate way, then an examination of those concepts is no longer just an examination of ourselves, but becomes an examination of a reliable on-board conceptual map of the world. And if this is the case, we have reason to think that propositions believed solely on the basis of such an examination can supply us with knowledge of the independent world.

In short, grounding for concepts is an aid to knowledge because it transforms one's conceptual scheme from a work of art into a trustworthy map. Grounding ensures a non-accidental relationship between our concepts (or their ultimate constituents) and the world, which is what enables us to acquire knowledgeable beliefs about the world by examining those concepts. In just the same way, the fact that there is a non-accidental correlation between the dots on a map of Scotland and the Scottish cities enables one to acquire knowledgeable beliefs about Scotland by examining that map.

Grounding for our concepts does not enable us to secure knowledge of *non-conceptual* truths, of course. Conceptual truths are special. Most truths, once understood, can only be known if one gathers additional information; for example, through empirical testing. It is easy (or at least, easier) to see how truths known through empirical testing can be independent truths: empirical testing is obviously a source of information about the independent world. It is not so easy to see how truths knowable *without* reliance on empirical testing could be independent truths. What concept grounding does for us is ensure that *our concepts, like the results of our empirical tests, can be treated as a source of information about the independent world*. Our concepts are, for sure, a limited source of information: they cannot tell us everything there is to know. There are many things we will only be able to learn through gathering additional information. But concepts can give us access to some truths about the world, such as *All vixens are female* and, most importantly for our current purposes, the truths of arithmetic.

It is undoubtedly an interesting and important question *why* some and only some truths are knowable through conceptual examination: why, that is, some and only some information about the world is encoded in our concepts. Is there some metaphysical difference between the facts we build into our conceptual map and the facts we do not? Or is the difference purely epistemic—merely to do with our ways of accessing these different classes of facts? Important though these questions are, I cannot address them here (although I do discuss the relationship between conceptual truth and modality in Jenkins (forthcoming *a*)). I shall merely record my suspicion that the conceptual truth/non-conceptual truth distinction does indeed track some important metaphysical distinction, if not fully accurately, at least with some significant degree of accuracy. Postulating such a metaphysical difference seems to me a good explanation of the difference in our ways of recording the information. There are other, competing, explanations though, which I'm not in a position to rule out at this juncture. It could be merely useful for us to record certain pieces of information in a special way.

One way for a concept to be grounded is for it to be composed from grounded concepts. When things go well, we can compose grounded concepts like *man* and *unmarried* and thus secure a grounded compound concept like *bachelor*.[21] Even if we grant that we can learn truths about the world by examining non-accidentally accurate *referring* concepts, however, the reader might be wondering how the same can be said for concepts which are merely *composed* of non-accidentally accurate referring concepts (or composed of concepts which are composed of non-accidentally referring concepts, etc.). If nothing can be said to assuage doubts about this, we run the risk of discovering that much of our arithmetical knowledge is acquired through an examination of concepts which are mere compounds of non-accidentally referring concepts, and therefore not satisfactorily accounted for.

It may appear to be a mistake to assume that examining mere compounds of non-accidentally referring concepts will tell us anything about the world. They do not correspond to features of the world, so what could they be telling us about? Well, first, note that there is an important difference between a concept whose ultimate constituents non-accidentally refer and one whose do not. Remember that the aim is to explain how concepts can be treated as maps of the world rather than works of art. If the ultimate constituents of a concept non-accidentally refer, then that concept cannot be a work of art all the way down. It can, at most, be something we have created from previously existing map-like pieces. And if it is created

---

[21] I suspect it is more difficult to secure grounded concepts by *decomposing* grounded concepts. When we compose grounded concepts, there will always be enough bits of the world for propositions involving the new concepts to carry information about (more on this in a moment). But when we decompose grounded concepts, we risk imposing a structure which is more fine-grained than anything in reality.

from map-like pieces in the right way, then information about the world will be recoverable from it. For instance, when I examine my concept of *triangular circle*, I can learn something about those features of the world which correspond to its referring ultimate constituents (as it might be, the worldly properties of triangularity and circularity). So even if the compound concept does not itself refer to any genuine property, I can learn something about genuine properties by examining it.

Provided we stick to examining concepts whose ultimate constituents refer, there will never be a shortage of aspects of the world to learn about, and, provided the composition and examination are well conducted, we will only acquire true beliefs about those aspects of the world. The facts we thus learn will not necessarily be facts about features of the world corresponding to our complex concepts (since we do not assume such features will always exist), but may instead be facts about the features of the world corresponding to our more basic, referring concepts out of which our complex concepts are constructed.

In Section 4.5, I shall attempt to say a little more about concept grounding. While my externalism is an important permissive factor in the development of this account, my empiricism is an important limiting factor. I will not count as justifications and groundings some things which a rationalist would. I assume that *the only data which could be relevant to concept justification and concept grounding are data obtained through the senses.*

But, crucially for my purposes, such data need not always consist in conscious or conceptualized experience. (It *cannot* be such in all cases, on pain of making my proposal circular.)[22] The data may be mere 'sensory input', by which I mean that it may be merely a matter of the world's having a physical effect, via the normal functioning of our sensory apparatus, upon our brains, and hence upon our psychological mechanisms. Let me now

---

[22] Unless, perhaps, we are prepared to take a coherentist attitude to concept grounding. According to such a view, a set of concepts would be justified in virtue of being the most (*or a sufficiently*) coherent set. The aim would be to avoid the need for a foundation in (unconceptualized) sensory input (indeed, such a view might avoid the need for any connection with empirical input whatever, which would be worrying for an empiricist). I do not find a 'concept coherentism' of this kind appealing. For one thing, it is somewhat hard to imagine how competing sets of concepts could be compared for coherence (except, perhaps, in so far as one of them involves an *incoherence* which is obvious from the inside). In addition, there are objections familiar from the propositional case: for instance, just as we can worry about whether the coherence of a set of beliefs is any sort of guide to their probable truth, so we can worry about whether the coherence of a set of concepts (whatever that amounts to) is any sort of guide to their probable accuracy.

describe some ways in which sensory input, so conceived, might ground a concept. This is an attempt to describe the kind of 'input step' into a concept-examination epistemology which I claimed was missing from the moderate rationalisms of Peacocke and Bealer (see Section 2.5 above).

4.5 Cameras and filters

Even if many, or most, of our concepts are grounded simply through being correctly composed of other grounded concepts, at some point we will need to explain how it is possible for sensory input to ground a concept *directly* (i.e. *not* just through grounding its ultimate constituents). Here I shall offer two—purely hypothetical—stories about the mechanisms through which sensory input could ground concepts directly. I am no psychologist or neuroscientist, and I do not claim that either of these stories is true. All I claim is that it is plausible that something like one or both of them *could* be true. For convenience here, I shall sometimes refer to directly grounded concepts as 'basic' concepts. (This should not be taken to imply any kind of atomism about concepts.)

The first story goes as follows. From birth onwards, the normal func-tioning of a child's sensory mechanisms will lead to changes in her brain state. Whether or not she can be said to be 'conscious' or 'experiencing', she is receiving what we are neutrally calling sensory input.

Her brain, which is the product of natural selection, is well equipped with mechanisms which respond appropriately to the world around her. For instance, one mechanism (or group of mechanisms) causes her to feel pain when her body is injured. Another of these mechanisms will be responding to sensory input, in such a way as to generate further mechanisms which enable the child to respond appropriately to certain features of that input. Let us call these newly generated mechanisms her 'A-mechanisms' ('A' for 'acquired'). The important fact about A-mechanisms is that they, and the abilities which depend upon them, exist in *response* to sensory input. Note that, given that the child's brain is the product of natural selection, we can anticipate that only A-mechanisms which are *useful* to her are likely to be created in this way.

Continuing the story, let us suppose that the possession and exercise of certain A-mechanisms later leads to the possession of corresponding concepts. These concepts are mental representations of the features of the world to which the subject's various A-mechanisms are responsive. They provide a conscious overlay to the subject's pre-existing ability to respond to the relevant features of her sensory input. Let us also suppose that some of the concepts so acquired are basic[23] arithmetical concepts.

If this is how things go, then the A-mechanisms which underwrite the subject's basic arithmetical concepts are *useful* mechanisms. And we can further postulate that this usefulness is probably due to the fact that there exist *real features of the world* to which those A-mechanisms are enabling the subject to respond. Postulating such real features of the world *explains* why the A-mechanisms are useful: it is useful for the subject to be able to respond to real features of the world in which she must survive. Here, of course, I am relying on something very like a familiar kind of scientifically realist[24] assumption: I am assuming that the usefulness of responding to a feature of sensory input like this would be miraculous, or inexplicable, unless that feature of sensory input were correlated with a feature of the independent world.[25] It can then be hypothesized that the concepts which represent the features of the world to which A-mechanisms make us responsive are fitting, and moreover relevantly accurate.

If we accept this first story, then we have accepted that there is a link, mediated by sensory input, between the world and the subject's mental state, the existence of which makes it likely that the subject's basic arithmetical concepts (or their ultimate constituents) accurately represent real features of the world. For the A-mechanisms which underwrite the concepts probably would not exist if they were not responding to real features of the world, and therefore the subject's arithmetical concepts, which develop out of the exercise of the abilities for which those A-mechanisms are responsible, also probably would not exist unless they (or at least their ultimate constituents) likewise corresponded to real features of the world. Thus these concepts are

---

[23] Recall that by 'basic' arithmetical concepts I just mean those arithmetical concepts—like, perhaps, the concept of addition and concepts of small natural numbers—which are grounded directly rather than through composition of other grounded concepts.

[24] Scientific realists, in the sense I intend here, are those who believe that the reason science works so well is that, by and large, scientific theories accurately describe the way the world is. This is a standard notion of scientific realism and is not related to my definition of 'realism' in Section 1.2 above.

[25] For the vanilla 'no-miracles' argument for scientific realism, see e.g. Smart (1963: 39), Putnam (1975: 73), and Boyd (1981: 617–18, 1984: 59–60).

sensitive to the way the world is, and this sensitivity is due to the normal functioning of the subject's sensory apparatus.

We might call this the 'camera brain' hypothesis. For the central image is that of the infant brain, exposed to sensory input, generating A-mechanisms (and later concepts) which represent the structure of the world around her—much as a piece of photographic film, exposed to light, generates a picture which represents the structure of the world around it.

But what if, as some psychologists believe,[26] basic arithmetical concepts, or the mechanisms which underwrite them, are innate? Could there still be a sensory link between the world and these concepts which makes it likely that the concepts correspond to real features of the world?

Well, we can begin our second story by allowing, as before, that the sensory input the child receives from birth onwards leads to changes in her brain state, and that her brain, the product of natural selection, is, from birth, well equipped with mechanisms which respond appropriately to the world around her.

We can then suppose that some of these innate mechanisms are sensitive to sensory input, enabling the child to respond to important features of that sensory input (or else triggering other, latent, mechanisms which enable her to respond to such differences). As before, the exact nature of these mechanisms is immaterial; all that is relevant is the role they perform in the child's mental life. Let us call them (or the latent mechanisms which they trigger) 'I-mechanisms' ('I' for 'innate'). They are just like A-mechanisms except that they are innate, not generated.

The important fact about I-mechanisms is that, although they exist (actually or latently) from birth, they would not be maintained, or even used at all, if they were not *useful* to the child. As sensory input comes in, the I-mechanisms that are used to deal with that sensory input will be the ones which help the subject respond most appropriately to that input (which may, of course, be all of them).

Continuing this second story, let us suppose that the possession and exercise of certain I-mechanisms leads (directly or through further developments) to the possession of corresponding concepts. These concepts can be understood as mental representations of the features of the world to which the subject's various I-mechanisms are responsive. They provide a

---

[26] See e.g. Butterworth (1999).

conscious overlay to the subject's pre-existing ability to respond to the relevant features of her sensory input. Let us also suppose that some of the concepts so acquired are basic arithmetical concepts.

If this is how things go, then the I-mechanisms which underwrite the subject's basic arithmetical concepts are *useful* mechanisms. And we can now postulate, as before, that this usefulness is probably due to the fact that there are some *real features of the world* to which those I-mechanisms are enabling the subject to respond. Postulating such real features of the world explains why the I-mechanisms are useful: it is useful for the subject to be able to respond to real features of the world in which she must survive (relying, again, on the scientifically realist assumption that the usefulness of these mechanisms would otherwise be miraculous).

If we accept this second story, we have once again accepted that there is a link, mediated by sensory input, between the world and the subject's mental state, the existence of which makes it likely that the subject's basic arithmetical concepts accurately represent real features of the world. The I-mechanisms which underwrite those concepts probably would not be used or maintained in the light of the subject's incoming sensory input were they not responding to real features of the world. And therefore the subject's arithmetical concepts, which are developed through the exercise of the abilities for which those I-mechanisms are responsible, also probably would not exist if they (or at least their ultimate constituents) did not likewise correspond to (accurately represent) real features of the world. Thus, as in the first story, the concepts in question are sensitive to the way the world is, and this sensitivity is due to the normal functioning of the subject's sensory apparatus.

We might call this the 'filter brain' hypothesis: the idea is that utility in the light of sensory input acts as a filter, whereby only those I-mechanisms which enable the subject to respond to real features of the world are likely to be maintained to the point where concepts corresponding to them are developed.

It may be that our brains act in both ways, as 'camera' and as 'filter', with respect to different concepts. Or, of course, it may be that neither story is at all accurate. My purpose in presenting them has merely been to establish that there are ways in which our arithmetical concepts *might* be related to sensory input, in virtue of which those concepts could be said to be empirically grounded (whether or not the relevant input, and the nature of our responses to it, were accessible to our conscious minds). I do not wish to suggest that the two stories told here represent the *only* ways in which sensory input could ground a concept directly. The crucial point is that the supposition that some concepts are directly grounded in sensory input can be filled out in plausible ways.

I shall now consider a few responses to those who may, for various reasons, still be feeling uneasy about the claim that sensory input can justify and ground concepts.

First, I am suggesting that we should reject both halves of Sellars's view that justification is something which only propositionally contentful items can either possess or supply (Sellars 1956). For I am suggesting that concepts, *sub*-propositional mental representations, can be justified by *sensory input*, which is not necessarily conceptualized at all, never mind propositionally contentful. (More on this in Section 5.5) We have seen (p. 130) that the claim that only propositions can possess justification raises issues of terminology alone, but what of the thought that only proposition-sized items can *supply* justification? It is true, of course, that whenever we *cite* our justification for anything we will use propositions. But, as an externalist, I believe that someone can be justified in believing $7 + 5 = 12$ just by virtue of having arrived at it through an examination of justified concepts, even if she (and everyone else) is incapable of formulating any proposition which states that she did so. She is justified by what happened, not by a proposition stating what happened.

Sellars's view is crucially employed in his claims that 'the point of epistemological foundationalism is, presumably, to explicate the idea that empirical knowledge rests on a "foundation" of non-inferential *knowledge of matters of fact*' (1956: 15), and that 'givenness in its most straightforward form' is the givenness of the truth of 'observation *reports*' and of 'awareness *that* something is the case' (p. 73).[27] He is assuming that empirical foundations must take the form of empirically supported propositional beliefs. This is understandable, given that traditional forms of empirical foundationalism posit such foundations. But I think it is a mistake. 'Givenness in its most straightforward form', I suggest, may include—or may even be—the givenness of the sensory input which grounds our concepts. (In the

---

[27] All emphases in this paragraph are added, except for '*that*' in the final quote.

terminology of Chapter 7 below, Sellars is 'thinking too big'.) Sellars's arguments do not speak to this possibility.

Second, it seems plausible that the data which ground a concept C could also provide grounds for a certain *belief*; namely, the belief that C is accurate. (The data might need to be suitably conceptualized in order to provide grounds for a belief. Nevertheless, the sensory input that grounds the concept and that which grounds the belief might be ultimately the same.) This does not mean, however, that having grounding for C is equivalent to having knowledge of this proposition. According to the view I propose, one might possess C with grounding, although one has never even entertained the proposition stating that C is accurate, and indeed without even being able to understand that proposition, and hence without having a knowledgeable belief—or any belief—to that effect.[28]

Third, some might feel that mere sensory input cannot be a source of justification or grounding, not because it is non-propositional, but because it is unconceptualized. But they must allow that it affects brain state. And I assume that for a subject A to possess a concept C is a matter of, or at least a consequence of, A's brain being in a certain state. It follows that sensory input can at least *explain* A's possession of C. As an externalist, I further believe that all it takes for A's concept C to be grounded is that A's possession of C should be appropriately connected to A's sensory input. That is, there must be *the right kind* of explanation of A's possession of C in terms of A's sensory input.

I cannot here fully defend my view as to what *is* the right kind of explanation, or what exactly 'appropriateness' amounts to. But the situation is akin to those which arise when we try to explain what it means to say that A's belief that p must be 'appropriately' related to the fact that p in order for A to count as *knowing* that p, or that A's visual experience as of a banana must be 'appropriately' related to a banana in order to count as a veridical perception. I think the most promising approach is to say that A's possession of C is grounded iff one could explain A's possession of C to an outsider just by saying C is a fitting concept. But, as we saw on pp. 130–1, a number of other externalist strategies could also be adapted to help us spell out the kind of 'appropriateness' needed here.

---

[28] This issue is related to that mentioned on pp. 132–4, as to whether grounding for a cluster of concepts could amount to grounding for a proposition or propositions expressing (a) truth(s) involving those concepts.

I shall say more about unconceptualized sensory input in Section 5.5. For now, let me just register that I so far see no reason to suppose we are going to need to appeal to anything *other* than sensory input and our responses to it, in saying what it is that justifies and grounds our concepts. Given this, let us now see what can be done with the supposition that sensory input *does* ground some of our concepts.

4.6 Indispensable concepts

First of all, let us consider *which* of our concepts we should take to be grounded. When things go well, any concept which is justified will also be grounded. But we cannot tell from the inside whether things are 'going well' in this sense or not. Similarly, of course, we cannot tell whether our justified beliefs are knowledge or not: this is not a special problem about concepts. All we can do in the case of belief is say which of our beliefs we think are *justified*, and assume that most or all of these are knowledge. By the same token, all we can do in the case of concepts is say which of our *concepts* we think are justified, and assume that most or all of these are grounded.

But it is quite difficult even to say which of our concepts we should take to be justified. Which concepts do our sensory data make it rationally respectable to rely upon? This is a difficult question, because the ultimate source of concept justification is unconceptualized sensory input. I doubt whether any details can be given of the justifying relationship between particular concepts and the corresponding sensory input, at least without the benefit of a considerable amount of empirical research. Certainly I would not know where to begin in giving such details. I would not even presume to say what sorts of concepts are justified directly (rather than through being composed of other justified concepts).

Instead, I want to suggest that we have *evidence* that certain of our concepts are justified. I think that the structure of our sensory input is our best guide to the structure of the independent world. I furthermore suggest that concepts which are indispensably useful for categorizing, understanding, explaining, and predicting our sensory input are likely to be ones which map the structure of that input well. These two suppositions together mean that concepts which are indispensable for understanding our sensory input are probably ones which our best available data suggest correspond to the structure of the independent world; that is, ones it is rationally respectable to rely upon as accurate representations of—and guides to—the independent world.[29] These are concepts which count as justified by my definition. Note that concepts correctly composed of indispensable concepts are also such that we have evidence that we are justified, given my notion of concept justification.

In order to find out which concepts are indispensable for the relevant purposes, we would, I think, do well to seek out those concepts which are indispensably involved in our best scientific theories of the world. Quine (e.g. 1960) claims that we are justified in believing scientifically indispensable propositions. I think that we are similarly justified in possessing scientifically indispensable concepts. (This is not in tension with Quine's claim, of course; one can believe both.)

We should not draw the comparison with Quine too closely, however. I am not proposing that indispensability constitutes justification, but that it is *evidence* for it. The indispensability of a concept makes it *likely* that it is justified, but I don't postulate any constitutive connection between these two facts. I am not saying that our indispensable concepts are justified in a way which is *derived from*, or *dependent upon*, the indispensability of the scientific propositions in which they appear. Concepts are justified, on the view proposed here, in virtue of the fact that our sensory input makes it rationally respectable to rely on them as guides to the world. What I propose is that, as a way of finding out which concepts are like this, we should look to the concepts which are most useful to us in making sense of our sensory input. And, since in our most serious attempts to understand our sensory input what we use our concepts for is the formulation of scientific theories, it seems reasonable to try and track down the indispensable concepts by looking to the scientific theories which seem to be making best sense of what we experience.

---

[29] It is true, of course, that sometimes useful concepts are *not* taken as mapping real features of the world. Our colour concepts, for instance, are sometimes thought to be at least as much a product of our ways of responding to the world as of the world itself. However, colour concepts and concepts of other qualities thought of as 'secondary' are not indispensable for scientific purposes. It is the very fact that, for scientific purposes, we can explain colour perception without using colour terms (e.g. by talking instead about light wavelengths and the way our visual receptors respond to them) that makes us regard colour as a 'secondary' quality and not a real feature of the mind-independent world. The same point could be made about any purported secondary quality: if we have reason to regard it as secondary, that is because it is dispensable from a scientific point of view.

Not only is a concept's justification not constituted by the indispensability of any proposition containing it, it is—at least for all I have said—not even the indispensability of *the concept itself* that constitutes its justification. Although (according to the stories I told in Section 4.5) it is this sort of indispensability which results in a concept C being generated or maintained, it is *the fact that the sensory data makes it respectable to rely on C* which constitutes C's justification. The link which I postulate between justified concepts and indispensable ones is that, in general, when and only when our sensory data make it respectable to rely on C will C be indispensably useful to us in dealing with that sensory data. Hence, if a concept C is indispensable we have reason to believe that C is empirically justified.

Maybe, though, my appeal to indispensability appears to render my suggestion that there may be some other kind of justification for the relevant concepts otiose. Why *not* just say their indispensability justifies them? My main reason for not doing this is simply that I would prefer to leave my options open on this issue. I do not feel intuitive pressure in the direction of the claim, and nor do my theoretical commitments enforce it.

4.7 An epistemology for arithmetic

I think that grounding for one's concepts is necessary if one is to be able to acquire knowledge by examining those concepts. I do not say it is also sufficient. What else is required? An investigation of one's concepts, and a certain amount of correctly conducted cognitive processing. These are the processes which constitute step 2 of the kind of realist epistemology for arithmetic I am interested in. (Recall from Section 2.5 above that step 1 is input, step 2 is processing, step 3 is belief formation.)

Of course, there is room for error at this processing stage, just as there was room for error at the stage of concept grounding (where a concept could be justified by misleading data although it is not in fact accurate, or could be justified in a Gettier-like way even if it is accurate). One could mistake the nature of one's concepts, or forget exactly what they are like at some stage between conducting one's examination of the concepts and forming a belief about them, and so on. I will talk more about these different sorts of possible error in Section 9.2 below. For now, let me simply flag that, while there is no doubt plenty here for the epistemologist (and the empirical psychologist) to study, because these are issues concerning cognitive processing rather than the ultimate *source* of arithmetical knowledge, they are not at present the most pressing issues. What we really want to know, at this stage of the game, is whether there can be the right kind of worldly input into these processes to enable them to play a role in the epistemology of realistically construed subject matters.[30]

At this point it may be helpful to say a word about arithmetical concepts. What are they concepts of? A feature of my account is that many answers to this question are compatible with it. Arithmetical concepts may be thought of as concepts of objects and properties, concepts of properties only, higher-order concepts, structural concepts, logical concepts, concepts of how things stand with an abstract realm, ... All that matters is that they are mental representations of the right kind, and indispensable in the right sense. The nature we attribute to arithmetical concepts will have implications for the nature of the arithmetical knowledge one secures by examining them, of course. But this does not affect the shape of the epistemological story that I'm outlining here. (I say a bit about the account of arithmetical concepts I am tempted by in Section 5.2.)

I propose that whenever we have a belief in a conceptually true proposition p, which

(a) is held on the basis of a correctly conducted investigation of our concepts, and is such that
(b) all the concepts thus investigated are grounded,

then p counts as known. In other words, examining concepts which are non-accidentally accurate guides to the structure of the independent world enables one to acquire knowledge about that world. We might express this by saying that epistemic grounding for concepts can *flow through* to beliefs meeting conditions (a) and (b).

I take it that our concepts of 7, +, 5, =, and 12 are indispensable, and therefore I take it that they are justified. Assuming things are going well in this case, they are also grounded. This means we can come to know $7 + 5 = 12$ just by examining them. The new kind of epistemology for $7 + 5 = 12$ envisaged here can be thought of as having three stages, which

---

[30] I shall say a little more concerning the step from possessing concepts to believing conceptually true propositions in Section 9.4.

I shall present as (1)–(3) below. Please note, though, that (1)–(3) are not presented as stages in an *argument* for the conclusion that $7 + 5 = 12$ is known, and that I am not claiming that a grasp of such an argument is what transforms our belief that $7 + 5 = 12$ into knowledge. Rather, (1)–(3) provide an *overview of the process* owing to which our belief that $7 + 5 = 12$ counts as knowledge.

(1) A correctly conducted investigation of our concepts of 7, +, 5, =, and *12* leads us to believe that $7 + 5 = 12$.

(2) Our concepts of 7, +, 5, =, and *12* are empirically grounded.

(3) So $7 + 5 = 12$ is empirically known.

This way of knowing $7 + 5 = 12$ is a priori by my definition: there is no dependence on empirical evidence. The role of empirical input at step (2) is not an evidential role. Evidence is something that accrues to hypotheses or theories (i.e. propositions or groups of propositions), not to concepts. Evidence is evidence *that* something is the case.[31] We saw in Section 4.5 that, although the sensory input which grounds a concept may also be sufficient to ground (i.e. enable us to know) a proposition stating that the concept is fitting, the role of that input in grounding the concept is not simply that of grounding the corresponding proposition (see also pp. 132–4).

It might be argued that the kind of sensory data which I say grounds the concepts involved in $7 + 5 = 12$ would also suffice for a posteriori, inductive empirical confirmation of $7 + 5 = 12$ (or of some proposition which entails it). But, be that as it may, (1)–(3) above is not equivalent to any confirmation of this kind, nor does (1)–(3) depend upon the existence of such confirmation. Induction involves the formulation of a hypothesis, and the taking of certain (conceptualized) experiences as confirming or disconfirming it. No such undertakings are required at any stage of (1)–(3).

---

[31] Grammatically, evidence can also be evidence-*of* something, but I take it this reduces to some kind of evidence-that; for instance, evidence of X may be evidence that X exists, or has taken place, or has been nearby. The same goes for evidence-for, which may be evidence for a hypothesis (in which case it is evidence *that* the hypothesis is true) or evidence for something else, in which case it is evidence *of* that thing. The notion of evidence may also be linked with wh–questions; evidence may be evidence as to whether there is someone in the garden, evidence as to who committed the murder, and so on. In each case, I take it that in playing this role it constitutes evidence *that* there is someone in the garden, evidence *that* Professor Plum committed the murder, and so on. There are interesting questions here concerning whether evidence-that or evidence-wh or both are basic, paralleling a similar debate about knowledge (see e.g. Schaffer 2007). All that really matters for present purposes, however, is that evidence is not something that accrues to concepts.

Does the fact that (1)–(3) is an a priori way of knowing by my definition simply mean that my definition of 'a priori' is mistaken? Surely being a priori should not be compatible with being empirical? Well, my definition of 'a priori' is not thereby shown to be mistaken unless a lot of other definitions are too. Many of the usual claims about the special epistemic status of $7 + 5 = 12$ can still be made on my (empirical) account of how it is known:

(i) There is no need to conduct tests to confirm inductively the hypothesis that $7 + 5 = 12$.
(ii) $7 + 5 = 12$ is knowable just through examination of our concepts.
(iii) No experience we can conceive of would undermine $7 + 5 = 12$.
(iv) Our justification for $7 + 5 = 12$ would be undermined only if our current way of conceptualizing the world turned out to be inappropriate.[32]

In Section 9.5, I shall return in more detail to the question of whether we should allow some a priori knowledge to be empirical. For now, let us simply note that, if we accept (1)–(3) as an empirical way of knowing $7 + 5 = 12$, then we must either accept that some empirical ways of knowing are a priori, or else deny that things like (i)–(iv) are characterizing properties of a priori knowledge. I think the most productive option is the former. If we take this option we can use the term 'non-empirical' to describe knowledge which is altogether independent of the senses, while 'a priori' is used to mark another important distinction (between knowledge which has properties like (i)–(iv) and knowledge which does not). Otherwise we will need a new term to mark this distinction. Why use 'a priori'/'a posteriori' to mark exactly the same distinction as 'empirical'/'non-empirical', when we can more efficiently use these terms to mark two different distinctions?

In fact, though, the current proposal really would not lose any of its appeal if we chose to relinquish the term 'a priori'. What is essential is that we are preserving and explaining the unusual features of arithmetical knowledge which have led philosophers to *describe* it as 'a priori'. Whether or not we decide to continue using the phrase 'a priori' for arithmetical knowledge,

---

[32] By comparison, our justification for *Dogs bark* could be undermined either through our discovering the inappropriateness of the concepts involved or through our discovering that we had been straightforwardly misinformed about a world to which those concepts were yet appropriate.

my empiricism respects the special epistemic status of $7 + 5 = 12$: its independence of empirical evidence (in any conventional sense); the fact that we can know it as soon as we can understand it; the fact that no conceivable experience would undermine it; and so on. This sort of empiricism is designed to respect *the phenomenon described as* aprioricity, and is thus very different from that of Mill or Quine, however we decide to use the term 'a priori' in future.

I'd like to try and forestall a couple of misunderstandings before moving on. First, some might suppose that, in order for one's sensory input to ground a proposition or a concept, it must be that one's sensory input *could have been otherwise*, so that it would not have grounded that proposition or concept. This claim will have some plausibility for those inclined to think that, if our sensory input could not *but* ground some proposition or concept, we do not need to wait for the input in order for the proposition or concept to be grounded. But it would certainly be more difficult to defend my view if it implied that our sensory input could have been such that it grounded radically different arithmetical concepts.

For all I know, it may be the case that no reasonable amount of sensory input could fail to ground the concepts 7, $+$, 5, $=$, and 12. Even so, there is no reason to suppose that those concepts could be grounded *without* reliance on sensory input. This sort of conclusion simply does not follow: by analogy, the fact that any experience will serve to ground *I am having an experience* does not mean that this can be known without reliance on *any* experience. And the fact that any switch will turn the light on does not mean the light can come on without reliance on any switch being flipped.

A second point worth mentioning briefly is that there are, naturally, ways to be sceptical about arithmetical knowledge as I conceive of it. It is possible that our arithmetical concepts are *not* sensitive to sensory input in the way I have supposed, so that they are not best regarded as accurate on-board conceptual maps of the world. And it is possible that the sensory input we have is highly misleading, so that we have ended up with inaccurate concepts. And so on. This sort of scepticism, it seems to me, is ultimately irrefutable: we cannot stand outside our own skins and *check* that our concepts are accurate. But the problem seems no worse than the problems raised by traditional forms of scepticism about our knowledge of the physical world. We can no more stand outside our own skins in order to check that our beliefs about the physical world are true than we can do so to check that our arithmetical concepts are accurate. There is ultimately no refuting the suggestion that my arithmetical concepts are mistaken in some way, but then there is ultimately no refuting the suggestion that I am a brain in a vat. (For all that, I tend to think that everyday knowledge-ascriptions are true; see Section 3.6.4.)

What reasons are there for thinking that arithmetical concepts are indispensable (or compounds of indispensable concepts)? Here we can piggyback on the arguments of indispensability theorists (such as Putnam 1975; Quine 1981; Resnik 1997; and Colyvan 2001) to the effect that arithmetical propositions (including those which quantify over natural numbers) are indispensable parts of our best scientific theories. If that is so, then the arithmetical concepts involved in such propositions are indispensable by my lights too. There is a large literature on indispensability arguments, and various objections have been mounted against them (see e.g. Field 1980; Maddy 1992; Sober 1993). Many of these objections (most of Maddy's and Sober's, for instance) are largely irrelevant to the question of whether arithmetical concepts are indispensable, as they address the issue of whether we are really obliged to believe in the entities indispensably quantified over by our best theories.

Field (1980) attempts to nominalize a substantial portion of our best scientific theory, in order to demonstrate that is possible to remove quantification over numbers from our best theories without rendering them unworkable or unacceptably unattractive. Some ways of addressing this concern cover well-trodden ground. Even if Field's nominalized theory is only somewhat less virtuous than the original, nonetheless quantification over numbers is required in our *best* theories. The existence of other, less good, theories does not threaten this fact. It is a judgement call how much better a theory must be (in terms of simplicity, elegance, etc.) to justify the ontological cost of quantification over extra entities, but it is widely agreed that Field's nominalized theory is substantially less simple, elegant, and so on than the theory it is supposed to replace.

In addition, it is worth pointing out that, since my epistemological proposal is compatible with various different views as to what arithmetical concepts are like, I actually require considerably less arithmetical indispensability than most extant indispensability theorists try to establish. For instance, a version of my epistemological view can be made to cohere with the claim that adjectival number concepts are indispensable even though quantification over arithmetical objects is not. Thus, even if Field's project of removing quantification over numbers from our best theories were to succeed, this would not necessarily constitute a threat to the views under development here.

While we are discussing indispensability, it is worth noting that not only does my approach promise an epistemology for arithmetic, but similar accounts could also help us understand other kinds of a priori knowledge, including knowledge of other areas of mathematics. Knowledge of logic also seems particularly amenable to this treatment: our logical concepts (certain basic ones at least[33]) are surely indispensable, and logical truths are conceptual truths if any are.

To conclude this central section, let me stress that, despite respecting the special epistemic status of arithmetic relative to (e.g.) physics and chemistry, my proposal maintains the naturalistic appeal of more conventional forms of empiricism. The only source of knowledge posited is one that relies in an essential way on the use of our familiar sensory apparatus. We do, it is true, also require that there is some faculty which enables us to derive $7 + 5 = 12$ by considering the concepts involved. But the existence of this faculty seems far less philosophically troubling once we realize that it is merely a processing faculty, and not a source of knowledge by itself (as rationalists suppose).

My proposal, then, would appear to unite the advantages of neo-Fregeanism and indispensability theory: the goal I described early in this chapter. It accounts for the special epistemic status of arithmetic, yet it is attractively naturalistic. The first of the two objections to indispensability theory which I mentioned in Section 4.3, namely that it does not account for the special epistemic status of arithmetic, is thus (obviously) avoided. Less obviously, but equally importantly, my proposal has resources to deal with the second objection, that on a Quinean account any dispensable

---

[33] It might be imagined that no set of basic logical concepts is indispensable, but that it is merely indispensable to have *some* set sufficiently rich to enable us to define up (construct) every logical concept we need. Since there are various non-overlapping sets which would enable this, no set is itself indispensable. However, the indispensability of a concept C does not imply that one could not *get by* without using C, but only that our *best* theory requires the use of that concept. Whichever logical concepts appear in our best theory are then indispensable, even if they could be constructed from other logical concepts.

parts of arithmetic will turn out not to be known. On the sort of view I advocate, it is not necessary that an arithmetical *proposition* be indispensable in order for the account to apply: it is sufficient if the *concepts* it involves are indispensable. And it is not even necessary that the concepts should be indispensable: it suffices if their ultimate constituents are indispensable. While it is quite plausible that some accepted arithmetical propositions will turn out to be dispensable, I cannot imagine how one would argue that any accepted arithmetical proposition contains *concepts* which are neither indispensable nor even ultimately composed of indispensable constituents. This seems to me to mark a key advantage of my proposal over Quine's.

Still, one might reasonably wonder whether my concept-grounding story can account for *all* of our knowledge of arithmetic. By itself, it is not intended to; like (nearly) everyone else I think much of our arithmetical knowledge is secured by deduction or inference from previously known facts (arithmetical or otherwise), and much of it is secured through testimony. The proposal of this book is primarily a proposal about those parts of arithmetic which are *not* known in these derivative ways. I also suspect that, in a similar vein, many of our grounded arithmetical concepts are secured by construction from previously grounded arithmetical concepts. This could be true of even some quite straightforward concepts. Very few arithmetical concepts need be grounded directly in order for my proposal to do all that is required of it. Indeed, it might even be that *no* arithmetical concept need be so grounded, because all arithmetical concepts can be constructed from (compounds of) grounded non-arithmetical concepts (such as logical concepts[34]).

To account for *all* of our knowledge of arithmetic is a tough call, even when we allow that much can be achieved by deduction from previously known arithmetical facts. Gödel's incompleteness results are a measure of how tough a call this is. Gödel proved that, for any axiom set rich enough to count as an axiom set for arithmetic, there are some true arithmetical propositions which cannot be proved from those axioms. (Smith 2007 is a good introduction to these results for those unfamiliar with them.) Therefore it is not enough—although I think it is true—to say that the standard Peano axioms of arithmetic follow epistemically from examination of our arithmetical concepts. For there are some truths of arithmetic which

---

[34] Vindicating, perhaps, something of the intuition behind logicism.

do not follow from these axioms; yet these are truths which we can know (by following Gödel's proofs). But I am not proposing that all we need our concepts for is to secure knowledge of some set of arithmetical axioms, from which everything else we know about arithmetic can be derived. It is my view that arithmetical knowledge is often expanded not through logical deduction from known premises, but through the re-examination of old concepts or the construction and examination of new ones.

There may be a conceptual analogue of the Gödel result.[35] It may be, for all I know, that for any set S of concepts which is sufficiently rich for a set of axioms for arithmetic to follow epistemically from S, there is some arithmetical truth p which does not follow epistemically from S or follow logically from the axioms. But if this is the case, I submit that any proof of the truth of p must involve some concept(s) outside S.[36] For how else could p be proved? Examining the concepts involved in S, and making deductions from whatever so follows, does not suffice. Hence, there will be a way of knowing p which is consonant with my view: introduce and examine the required new concept(s). That is what we are doing when we run through the proof.

These considerations fall short of an argument that all our arithmetical knowledge can be accounted for once we take concept grounding on board. But I hope they go some way towards addressing the kinds of concerns which might lead to doubts on that score.

On my view, I shall now argue, we also avoid the objections to neo-Fregeanism described in Section 4.3. One of the objections I focussed on pointed out that to say that Hume's Principle is analytic or implicitly definitive is not to say how it is known. But I have not assumed that claiming that an arithmetical proposition is a conceptual truth is sufficient to explain how it is known. I have offered a substantial *account* of how we know these conceptual truths, appealing to the thought that, in order for us to learn about the world through examining our concepts, those concepts must be grounded.

Neo-Fregeans (at least sometimes—see e.g. Wright 1997: 278) suggest that number concepts can be introduced, in some epistemically significant sense, via Hume's Principle, because the content of the left-hand side of

---

[35] Thanks to Patricia Blanchette for helpful comments on this topic.   [36] Cf. Isaacson (1996).

this principle is a 'recarving' of that of its right-hand side. But it has proved difficult to argue that recarving the content of the left-hand side of Hume's Principle is adequate to generate sufficiently rich concepts of numbers: witness, for example, the Julius Caesar problem (Frege 1884: sect. 66). This is the worry that grasp of the right-hand side of Hume's Principle is an inadequate basis for a grasp of the left-hand side because Hume's Principle alone does not give us a rich enough concept of natural number to enable us to settle the question of whether or not the number zero is identical to Julius Caesar.

My claim that arithmetical truths are conceptual truths is different from the claim that Hume's Principle is analytic or definitive in the required sense. I am not committed, for instance, to the view that it is possible to use Hume's Principle to introduce the concept of a natural number. I propose that our concepts of natural number (or at least their ultimate constituents) are grounded in sensory input, so that we do not depend on our understanding of the right-hand side of Hume's Principle to provide all the substance of these concepts. Unlike the neo-Fregeans, therefore, I do not face the unenviable task of saying how a grasp of the right-hand side of Hume's Principle could suffice for a proper grasp of the left-hand side. All I need to claim is that a grasp of *the whole proposition* enables us to see that it is true (although in fact I also suspect that it may be our grasp of the left-hand side which enables us to grasp the concepts on the right-hand side). The Julius Caesar problem is avoided by claiming that sensory input grounds arithmetical concepts rich enough to enable us to conclude that no number is equal to that same familiar conqueror of Gaul.

4.8 Summary

I have explicitly shown how my approach to arithmetical knowledge is designed to respect both apriorism and empiricism. To complete the trio of intuitions which it is my aim to preserve, therefore, we need only note that the proposal also respects arithmetical realism as defined in Section. I hope it will already be obvious that this is so. If our arithmetical concepts are grounded, then they accurately represent real features of the world as it exists independently of ourselves. This, I have argued, means that we can learn truths about that independent world by examining our arithmetical concepts. Thus, according to the account proposed in this chapter, the arithmetical truths which we learn through examining our grounded arithmetical concepts are essentially independent truths.

This concludes my exposition of the main thesis of this work. I have, in this section, sketched a kind of epistemology for arithmetic which I believe, if successfully developed in detail, could help resolve some deep philosophical tensions between realism, empiricism, and apriorism. I have suggested that we can know arithmetical truths, through examining our arithmetical concepts, in a way which is a priori (or, at least, has many of the traditional characterizing features of a priori knowledge). But I have also suggested that those concepts are grounded in sensory input, so that the arithmetical knowledge so obtained is also empirical.

I want to stress at this point that my purpose here is modest. I have not tried to offer a fully worked-out account of arithmetical knowledge. Nor, importantly, have I claimed that all arithmetical knowledge is of the kind sketched herein or that all arithmetical truths (or even all knowable arithmetical truths) can be known in this way.

The intention is just to invite readers to rethink the epistemic relations between the senses, our concepts, and the arithmetical propositions we believe, along the lines I have described, and then see whether some account of the kind indicated might not supply attractive answers to the otherwise intractable-looking question of how apriorism, realism, and empiricism can all be true together. It matters less whether the reader finds merit in (e.g.) my sketches of how the details of empirical concept grounding might work, or my intuitions as to which concepts we should take to be grounded. My real goal is to get off the ground with the idea that conceptual examination might be a way of recovering information previously obtained through the senses.

5

Development

5.1 Introduction

This section is something of a mixed bag, consisting of further development of certain key ideas from the previous section. I begin by sketching an account of arithmetical concepts which I think sits well with (though it certainly is not implied by) the epistemological story so far. I then distinguish my notion of empirical concept grounding from a more simplistic notion with which it should not be confused. Next I show how my epistemology for arithmetic relates to the theory of knowledge developed in Chapter 3. After this, I focus on the unconceptualized sensory input which I have suggested is the epistemic basis for our arithmetical concepts; I attempt to distance the notion of unconceptualized sensory input from that of 'non-conceptual content' (as defended by e.g. Evans and Peacocke). Finally I elucidate the notion of concept grounding a little further, by saying a little bit about ungrounded and inaccurate concepts. Among other things, I ask what happens to truth and validity once inaccurate concepts are around.

5.2 Concepts of structure

I have talked a good deal about arithmetical concepts. But so far I have not said much about what I take them to be like, nor about what I take the 'features of the world' to which they correspond to be. I have not even made any assumptions about which, if any, arithmetical concepts are grounded directly and which, if any, are grounded merely through being composed of other grounded concepts. If I were forced to guess, I should say it was likely that there are some of each, and that concepts like *natural number* and *plus* are good candidates for being epistemically primitive concepts. But this is merely a guess.

I have mentioned that many different opinions concerning the meta-physics and the nature of arithmetical concepts are compatible with my epistemological proposal, which I take to be an important feature of that proposal. Here, however, I shall describe the views that I am tempted by. This discussion is strictly supplementary to the core epistemological account, and does not have to be accepted along with it.

I incline towards some form of structuralism on both points: arithmetical (and other mathematical) concepts seem to me to be best thought of as concepts of structure; the arithmetical features of the world to which they correspond seem to be best regarded as structural features. Structuralist accounts of mathematics are amply discussed and defended elsewhere (see e.g. Resnik 1997, Shapiro 1997, Parsons 2004) and I shall not rehash the arguments here; I shall discuss only such points as my approach to arithmetical knowledge makes relevant.

There are, to borrow terminology from Parsons (see e.g. his 2004), eliminative and non-eliminative forms of structuralism. The eliminative kind tries to do away with or at least severely downplay ontological commitment to mathematical objects. It is exemplified by Hellman (1989), who aims to show that mathematics is not really committed to distinctive kinds of object, but only to the possibility of there being objects satisfying certain structural requirements. The non-eliminative kind of structuralism maintains that mathematical objects exist and tries to say something about their nature by talking about structure. The sort of structuralism by which I am tempted is of this non-eliminative kind. (However, I think it would also be possible to hold a Hellman-style eliminativist structuralist view in conjunction with a concept-grounding epistemology. This would require an account of the relationship between conceptual examination and modal knowledge; I take some steps towards such an account in Jenkins (forthcoming a).)

Structuralists say that mathematics is the study of structures, and the nature of a mathematical object is exhausted by its being a place in one or more such structures. Non-eliminative structuralists are also at liberty to say—and I myself am tempted to say—that the existence of these structures is essentially independent (in the sense of Section 1.2 above) of their being instantiated by any (other) objects.

Extant structuralists espouse other views to which I am not committed. I do not, for instance, endorse Shapiro's ontological relativity (see his

1997: 80–2), nor Resnik's resistance to language-transcendent facts of the matter, nor his claim that there is no fact of the matter whether the number 2 is a set (see his 1997: ch. 12), nor Parsons's claim that talk of structures is metalinguistic (see his 2004: sect. II). The kind of structuralism I would find attractive would be robustly realist and non-relativist. According to this kind of structuralism, the existence and nature of mathematical structures are essentially independent of our minds and languages, and there are robust mind-independent facts of the matter about the identities holding between them; mathematical structures are instantiable abstract objects, rather like word types; and a mathematical object is a part of a mathematical structure which essentially depends on its relationships to other parts of the structure (so that, for instance, being the successor of 1 is part of *what it is* to be the number 2). That, at least, is the kind of structuralism that appeals to me.

As things stand, such a structuralism seems to me to suffer as much as any other extant philosophy of mathematics for want of a convincing epistemology. The view certainly has its attractions; we might well want to say, for instance, that any sets (or other objects) which model the natural numbers can serve as *representations* of them, just because they have the right structure, but that none has any special claim to *be* the natural numbers, since many other models share that same structure. And our intuitions on this point seem to be well captured by saying the natural numbers are places in a structure which various collections of sets and/or other objects can exemplify or instantiate, but none is identical to.

But what sort of epistemology can go with this kind of view? Resnik (1997) and Shapiro (1997) describe various means of learning about structures through experience, abstraction, and extension. But their ways of developing these thoughts are problematic. What Resnik offers is a specially tailored form of Quinean holism (see esp. his ch. 3 and pt. 2). I have discussed some of the pitfalls of this sort of view in Section 4.3. Shapiro, sensitive to its counter-intuitiveness, tries to defend (at least the appearance of) a special a priori status for mathematical knowledge, by relating mathematical epistemology to our use of language (see his ch. 4). According to him, we learn about very simple structures through experience of their instances, but there are two 'linguistic' processes by which we can extend our knowledge of structures beyond knowledge of these simple structures. One is 'a linguistic abstraction, of sorts' (sect. 5) and the other is 'implicit definition' (sect. 7). Shapiro's aim in appealing to these linguistic processes is, presumably, to secure some of the supposed explanatory power of linguistic conventionalist approaches to the a priori.

Whether such approaches *have* any explanatory power was left in doubt in Section 2.3. Additionally, other, non-linguistic, methods for advancing beyond knowledge of basic structures are described by Shapiro earlier in the chapter (sects. 3–4). These are methods *applicable* to learning about language patterns too, but not *based* in linguistic ability. Why, then, does Shapiro appeal to the two 'linguistic' methods as well? They seem like epistemic spare wheels, added in an attempt to salvage some appearance of aprioricity. Shapiro claims that implicit definition is necessary in order to acquire knowledge of structures beyond a certain size (p. 129). But that still leaves the other linguistic method looking otiose. And this other method, called the 'sublanguage procedure' (this is the 'linguistic abstraction, of sorts'), carries unattractive baggage. We need not go into details here; suffice to say that, by Shapiro's lights at least, it seems to enforce an ontological 'relativity', whereby whether numbers count as objects depends on whether we are talking the right language. In Shapiro's words, 'the idea of a single, fixed universe, divided into objects a priori, is rejected' (p. 127). Shapiro is happy with ontological relativity, but anyone suspicious of it might well be equally suspicious of taking the 'sublanguage procedure' to be a source of mathematical knowledge.[1]

In any case, a serious cause for concern about both Shapiro's 'linguistic' methods of knowing about mathematical structures is that, like any kind of linguistic conventionalism, they seem to enforce anti-realism. I shall argue this point in Section 6.2. If language is really an *ultimate source* of (some of) our knowledge of mathematics, then the parts of mathematics known about in this way must be regarded as dependent upon us. For how could merely

---

[1] I am not sure how much of what Shapiro wants could be preserved by invoking a kind of contextualism instead—insisting merely that the meaning of 'object' is sensitive to (theoretical) context. While this is all that seems to be motivated by his remarks on pp. 126–8, it would not underwrite the thesis of language dependence to which he seems committed. Contextualism does not entail any interesting kind of language dependence. According to contextualism, which propositions I express by certain sentences depends on my context, but that does not mean there is anything mind-dependent about the truth of those propositions or the obtaining of the facts they pick out. Ontological contextualism is a theory about how ontological language works, not a theory about the ontological facts.

studying a language created by us tell us anything about the independent world? Shapiro tries to resist the anti-realist conclusion at p. 137, but I am not sure how to reconcile his claim that '[t]he natural number structure has objective existence and facts about it are not of our making' with his claim, later in the same paragraph, that '[t]hrough successful language use, *we structure* the objective subject matter' (emphasis added). However 'objective' the 'subject matter' of the world, if it is indeed we who *structure* it, then facts about the structure *are* of our making. On the other hand, if its structure is *not* imposed by us through language use, Shapiro fails in his attempt to maintain a semblance of aprioricity by making mathematical structure somehow linguistic.

Shapiro says again on p. 261 that his claim that 'the way the universe is divided into structures and objects ... depends on our linguistic resources' is 'not meant to be an affront to objectivity'. He argues, to that end, that mind–independence counterfactuals are true on his view, because these counterfactuals 'must themselves be formulated in our language and form of life—for we know no other'. He thinks that adherence to the truth of these counterfactuals makes him an 'unrepentant philosophical realist'. However, as I argued in Chapter 1, counterfactual notions of mind-independence are not well suited to characterize mind-independence realism, precisely because they may be appropriated by anti-realists in the way Shapiro is suggesting.

What of Shapiro's worry that, without implicit definition, we cannot advance much beyond knowledge of 'structures with continuum-many places'? We can actually be fairly concessive to Shapiro here. Although these more complex mathematical structures are not the topic of the current work, it is worth noting that, if we adopt an epistemology along the lines of Chapter 4, then we will be able to buy into something *very like* what Shapiro calls implicit definition, while remaining realists in my sense (i.e. maintaining the essential independence of arithmetic). Implicit definition is, according to Shapiro, the characterization of a structure through listing its places and their relationships to one another (pp. 129–30). Such characterization can still be achieved once we acknowledge the empirical basis of the concepts used, but it can now be construed as a kind of conceptual composition. A new structural concept can be composed out of the concepts used to describe the places in the new structure and their relations to one another. And the resulting structural concept will be grounded, provided these constituent concepts are grounded and the composition correct.

Once we acknowledge concept grounding, then, we can say that something other than our own linguistic practice ultimately grounds our beliefs about the complex structures characterized through what Shapiro calls 'implicit definition'. Grounding can be traced, from belief in the conceptually true propositions characterizing the new structure, back to the concepts these propositions involve, and ultimately to the sensory input which grounded these concepts or their ultimate constituents.

The kind of epistemology I have sketched in Chapter 4 is, I think, well suited to filling out a realist, structuralist account of arithmetic of the kind I find appealing. If we think of sensory input as arithmetically structured, we can understand why arithmetical concepts, that is concepts enabling us to represent certain aspects of this structure which both our sensory input and the world instantiate, are indispensable to us in our attempt to make the best sense we can of this input and hence the world. The idea is that the world has structure S, and so our sensory input shares that structure S. As a result, we have grounded concepts enabling us to (accurately) represent structure S. Since these concepts accurately represent the structure of the mind–independent world, we can learn facts about that structure just by examining them—that is, through an a priori, armchair method.

My epistemological account is compatible with a variety of different forms of structuralism about arithmetic. I have mentioned two so far: a robustly realist conception of arithmetical objects as abstract places in structures, and an eliminativist modal structuralism. A third option is to say that the arithmetical structure of the world consists in the obtaining of certain structural *relations* between objects in the world, and that there are no mathematical objects, structural or otherwise. Structural relations are, as far as I can tell, well suited to serve as features of the world to which our concepts can correspond. So one might argue that our arithmetical concepts are concepts of mind- and language-independent structural relations (not necessarily instantiated relations), and that in examining them what we learn are facts about these relations.[2]

---

[2] But see the second section of my Final Remarks for further discussion concerning arithmetical objects.

5.3   A simplistic view of empirical concept grounding

One might think that a problem could be created for my proposal by noting that some fundamental features of the world, and the corresponding concepts, create divisions such that everything falls on one side of them. Indeed, some concepts create divisions such that *necessarily* everything falls on one side of them. Take the concept of *thing* for example: necessarily, everything is a thing. The envisaged problem is that, according to Chapter 4, a crucial part of our reason for regarding certain concepts as justified is that sensory input renders them indispensably useful to us (or that they are composed of concepts which sensory input renders indispensably useful). But how can a concept be useful for classifying one's sensory input if it corresponds to a division in the world which is such that, necessarily, everything falls on one side of it? It is easy to see how it could be useful to represent a division in the world if one day we bumped into something that fell on one side of it, and the next day we bumped into something that fell on the other side, and we subsequently felt the need to categorize the difference between the two things. But nothing like this can be what is happening in the case of concepts like *thing* (or for that matter *natural number*). It also seems difficult to argue that concepts so fundamental as *thing* are compounds of other indispensable concepts, so we cannot easily avoid the difficulty that way.

A further worry, concerning arithmetical concepts in particular, is that even if we admit that some number concepts are indispensably useful in cat-egorizing and understanding sensory input, it might seem that these will be, at best, *adjectival*, as opposed to substantival, number concepts. They will be concepts like *being four in number* as opposed to concepts like *the number four*. It seems relatively plausible that unconceptualized sensory input might be structured in such a way as to render it indispensably useful to be able to rep-resent to oneself the difference between four orange patches and two orange patches. But that is not at all the same thing as rendering it indispensably use-ful to be able to represent *the number four* and *the number two*. And some philo-sophers may consider an epistemology for arithmetic inadequate if it fails to account for our knowledge of propositions about arithmetical objects.

The first of these two lines of argument really should not trouble us at all. The thoughts that lie behind it are over-simplistic in two ways. First, it is not always difficult to see how a concept which is in some sense fundamental could be obtained by constructing it out of other concepts, provided we do not imagine that the only way of composing new concepts is through *conjunction* of old ones. In the case of *thing*, for instance, we seem to be able to make some progress by thinking about *disjunction* of concepts (*the table or the chair or the cat or me or ...*). Second, and more importantly, it is not the case that a concept can only be useful to us in our attempt to understand our sensory input by enabling us to represent some distinction both sides of which are occupied by objects that we have experienced. The concept of *thing*, for instance, does much useful work by enabling us to quantify (due to its role as component of the more complex concepts *something* and *everything*). We need all sorts of concepts to enable us to formulate the complex theories we need to best explain and predict our sensory input; we do not merely use concepts to label the objects of our experience in ways that differentiate them from others. Any concept which can be used in a theory may turn out to be an indispensably useful concept in the sense that is relevant for my purposes. If theory T is the best theory we have, every concept it contains is indispensable in the sense I'm interested in.

Appreciating this fact also enables us to address the second worry, that only adjectival number concepts could be indispensable. Those who think I am obliged to account for the groundedness of substantival number concepts should note that, although the usefulness of adjectival number concepts in making sense of our sensory input is, perhaps, more obvious and more easily comprehended, it could also be argued that substantival concepts are indispensably useful. Although they are not used for the most simplistic kind of labelling of experiences, if they appear indispensably in our best scientific theories—if, for example, quantification over numbers appears indispensably in these theories—then the best explanation of this fact is that there is something about our sensory input which we need these substantival concepts to make best sense of. And, as argued above, the best explanation of the fact that our sensory input is such that certain concepts are required to make sense of it is that there are features of the world which are accurately represented by those concepts.[3]

---

[3] Or at least their ultimate constituents. Whether the features of the world in question would need to be *objects* is another matter. Perhaps, if only the constituents of substantival numbers concepts refer, and the concepts themselves do not, we can account for the groundedness of substantival number concepts without positing an ontology of numbers. But it is an interesting question, requiring further

The moral of my comments here is that we must take a rather more sophisticated view of concept grounding than that which underlies these objections. One could be forgiven for overlooking this, however. For, leaving concept *grounding* aside for a moment, one prevailing attitude to empirical concept *acquisition* is of the simplistic kind. For instance, the well-known Humean problematization of the concept of *cause* (Hume 1748) is founded on the assumption that experience cannot generate that concept since

(a) we do not directly experience (i.e. see, hear, etc.) causation, and
(b) the concept of *cause* cannot be built out of concepts whose instances we can directly experience.

Hume assumes that concepts can only be empirically acquired if they are concepts of things we directly experience, or if they are built out of such concepts. No provision is made for a subtler relationship between experience and the acquisition of concepts which are indispensably useful for understanding it for other reasons. And Hume's views on this point have been preserved in later philosophers. Carruthers (1992: 56–8), for instance, unquestioningly adopts the Humean assumptions (although he argues, contra Hume, that, since experience cannot generate certain concepts, such as our concepts of *cause* and of an independent physical reality, these concepts must be innate). Further evidence of this may be found in Cowie (1999: 28–9), who defines the 'classical empiricist' as one who asserts that all 'simple concepts' are 'acquired directly from experiences *of their objects*' (emphasis added).

Although Hume and these later philosophers are concerned with the acquisition, not the grounding, of concepts, one can easily see how such an attitude could be uncritically carried across to the case of grounding. It might be thought that if experience could not be rich enough to lead one to *acquire* a concept of *cause*, because we cannot experience causes, it could not be rich enough to *ground* that concept either, for the same reason.

There is good reason to doubt whether an empiricist need take such a limited view as Hume's of empirical concept acquisition. It is clear

investigation, whether a concept as of an object could be correctly composed from referring concepts without itself being a referring concept.

If substantival number concepts do turn out to be grounded, however, this might mean that we should believe in numbers for a different reason: see the second section of my Final Remarks.

that other concepts, besides those which we can directly experience things as falling under (or those which are built out of such concepts), might be indispensable in helping us make best sense of our sensory input. Why couldn't our sensory input lead us to acquire a concept by rendering that concept thus indispensable? But, in any case, even if such indispensability were for some reason considered insufficient for empirical concept acquisition, it constitutes good evidence of empirical concept justification, by my lights.

One more instance of a simplistic view of the kind under discussion here is worth mentioning, in order to demonstrate that such views are taken to have consequences for the philosophy of arithmetic. Potter (2000) seems to be even stricter than Hume: he says that 'it is hard to see how the world could supply the infinite content we require [for arithmetic] unless there are in fact infinitely many things' (p. 282). And even if there were, he argues that it would be impossible for a finite human being to experience them as such, and therefore 'it is senseless to look for [the] content [of arithmetic] in the world' (p. 287). It seems Potter would not even want to allow, with Hume, that a concept can be 'supplied' by experience of the world when it is a compound of concepts which experience of the world has supplied. His assumption is that *experience of infinity* is required in order for our sensory input to supply a concept of infinity.

But, without further explication or defence, this seems as bad as saying that experience of the world cannot supply a concept of *black swan* unless we have actually seen a black swan. Experience *can* supply such a concept, even if we haven't seen a black swan, because we can combine and think about the concepts *swan* and *black*, each of which could presumably be 'supplied' by our experience of the world in whatever sense Potter has in mind without our having seen any black swans. We might, similarly, arrive at the concept of infinity by composing concepts of negation and finiteness. Potter gives us no reason to doubt that possession of these concepts can be supplied by sensory input. (Maybe there are such reasons, but he does not say what they are.) And, even more importantly, nothing Potter says gives us reasons for doubting that experience can *ground* our concept of infinity. In addition to the possibility of composition from grounded concepts, the concept may itself be one which is indispensable for formulating our best scientific theories (for all Potter tells us), and hence one that we should take to be empirically justified.

It is, of course, a further question what grounds the belief that anything *falls under* the concept of infinity. I am inclined to think that, among other things, an examination of the concepts *number of natural numbers* and *infinite* can ground that belief. Does this amount to claiming that it is possible to analyse infinitely many things into existence? Not at all. It is simply to say that we can *know*, through an examination of our concepts, that infinitely many things (namely natural numbers) exist.[4] It is not the process of examining the concepts that brings the numbers into being: our belief that infinitely many natural numbers exist is knowledgeable because our concepts of *number of natural numbers* and *infinite* are grounded, not just because we happen to have those concepts, or because we happen to have examined them and thereby arrived at that belief. Whatever problems there might be with the epistemological claim that we can *know* about numbers by examining concepts, these must be kept separate from the obvious difficulties with saying that our concepts or our analysis thereof is *responsible for the existence* of numbers.

5.4 Relating the arithmetical epistemology to the account of knowledge

If some epistemology of the kind described in Chapter 4 is correct, then when we have arithmetical knowledge of the distinctive, non-derived, a priori kind, there is a three-stage explanatory link between the arithmetical facts and our corresponding arithmetical beliefs. First, facts about the arithmetical structure of the world explain the nature of our (unconceptualized) sensory input. Second, the fact that our sensory input is the way it is explains our possession of arithmetical concepts; for that sensory input is what renders our arithmetical concepts (or their constituents) useful to us, and this explains our possession of them. Third, our possession of these arithmetical concepts explains why we come to believe arithmetical truths: for it is by examining these concepts that we come to believe things like $7 + 5 = 12$.

In Chapter 3, I discussed cases where it is permissible to 'collapse' complex explanatory links with several stages into simpler explanations.

---

[4] Cf. Wright (1997: 278), where Wright argues that neo-Fregeanism is similarly uncommitted to analysing numbers into existence. Note, however, that Wright's claims as to what 'abstraction' is capable of are considerably stronger than my claims as to what conceptual examination is capable of.

Collapsing is acceptable when we will not mislead our audience by leaving out the extra stages. Now, the three-stage explanation I have just sketched between the arithmetical facts and our arithmetical beliefs appeals to processes which, I would suggest, are utterly normal and indeed central to our mental lives. For that reason I think this sort of explanation is collapsible, even when talking to an outsider; I think it is acceptable to explain my belief that $7 + 5 = 12$, even to an outsider, just by citing the fact that $7 + 5 = 12$. That is why this belief counts as knowledge by my lights.

It is true that the detailed three-stage explanation I just outlined is not what springs to mind when, pretheoretically, we are asked to give a suitable expansion for the collapsed explanation. I do not think this renders the collapse unacceptable, however. What collapsing implies is that the omitted stages in the explanation are *normal*; and in this case I think they are, even though most people could not say what a normal link of this kind looks like.

If readers harbour doubts about whether the collapse is acceptable in this case, perhaps these doubts can be assuaged by considering an analogy. When I predict where a ball will land in order to catch it, I watch its trajectory and, at a sub-personal level, various calculations are performed which result in my putting my hands in the right place. Most people could not tell you what sort of thing is going on at the sub-personal level, and would have no idea how to perform the necessary calculations on paper. But, since the method by which I work out where to put my hands is perfectly normal (and certainly rational), it seems acceptable to explain my belief about where the ball will land, even to an outsider, just by saying that it *will* land there. And for this reason we want to say I *know* where the ball will land. If this is right, then some explanations are collapsible even though most people—including the recipients of the explanations—do not know exactly what the uncollapsed versions would look like.

5.5 Unconceptualized sensory input

I have appealed to unconceptualized sensory input in explaining concept grounding. But I have deliberately avoided using such phrases as 'non-conceptual content' or 'non-conceptual information' (prominent in e.g. Peacocke 2001 and Evans 1982) in this connection. I do not say that sensory input can be *contentful* without being conceptualized, or that *information* can lack conceptual shape. Whatever the merits or philosophical interest of such claims, I do not need or want to make them. I have only referred to unconceptualized *input*, which need not be understood as a kind of representation. It can be thought of as merely a certain kind of structured causal influence on the brain.

However, I do not wish to suggest that only the sorts of things which seem to some to be *obviously* non-representational, such as the 'raw feel' of pain, can count as unconceptualized sensory input. We might perhaps take unconceptualized sensory input to consist in or be closely related to what are sometimes called 'raw feels', but would need there to be 'raw feels' which can be accurately described (if not necessarily by the subject) as the raw feel of seeing a cat, or the raw feel of seeing four apples.

It may be helpful to note that my notion of unconceptualized input is not only different in nature from Peacocke's notion of non-conceptual content, but it is also intended for quite a different role in my epistemology. (These two differences are related.) While Peacocke claims that experience with non-conceptual content 'makes available' certain concepts and helps supply a 'causal explanation' of our possession of them (2001: 242), he shies away (almost deliberately, it seems) from saying anything about justification or grounding in this context. Although Peacocke thinks *whole judgements* can be made rational by our having certain experiences with non-conceptual content, acquisition of concepts is only said to be *causally* influenced by such experiences. By contrast, my notion of non-conceptual input is designed to allow for the possibility that concepts are epistemically grounded in sensory input (which in fact can, *in turn*, make certain judgements rational).

Sedivy's commentary on an earlier work of Peacocke's (Peacocke 1992; Sedivy 1996) is potentially misleading on this point. Peacocke does use the word 'grounding' in connection with concepts; he says that possession conditions for concepts must be 'grounded' in the sense of being capable of non-circular explication. Sedivy, misleadingly, claims that Peacocke regards this 'grounding' of concepts as an epistemic matter (Sedivy 1996: 414), like the grounding of 'empirical thought' in non-conceptual experience. But Peacocke says nothing to suggest that he thinks non-conceptualized experience can ground a concept in the epistemologically significant sense I described in Chapter 4.

Peacocke does say, in his (1992), that non-conceptualized *proposition-sized* experiential representations (experiences with 'proto-propositional' contents) have an epistemic role to play in accounting for our empirical knowledge of *propositions*.[5] But he seems to think that any rationalizing link between concepts and non-conceptual experience consists solely in the fact that the concepts appearing in a justified empirical belief will (somehow) map on to corresponding aspects of the proto-propositional non-conceptual content which underwrites that belief.

So the primary rationalizing role of unconceptualized experience, on Peacocke's view, consists in the link between experiences with proto-propositional content and the corresponding propositional beliefs. He thinks any link between unconceptualized experiences and concepts is derivative from this. He makes no attempt to argue, as I have done, that unconceptualized sensory input rationalizes trust in certain concepts, independently of whether it rationalizes belief in any proposition, simply because it makes it likely that these concepts are accurate guides to the independent world. In fact, there is no attempt to argue that unconceptualized sensory input can guide us towards accurate concepts at all.

I am inclined to agree with Sedivy (p. 431) that unconceptualized sensory input is best thought of as something which is received and dealt with at a sub-personal level. I am also prepared to grant her, for the sake of argument, that for this reason it should not (contra Peacocke) be thought of as a kind of representation. But Sedivy, being an internalist, believes that the sub-personal status of such unconceptualized input renders it epistemically inert. As an externalist, I reject this part of her view.

To sum up, my notion of unconceptualized input is different from Peacocke's notion of non-conceptual content in (at least) two important respects. First, the former is not conceived as a kind of representation, while the latter is; and, second, the former is supposed to supply an epistemic basis for concepts, which the latter is not.

---

[5] Although, in this work, he seems to regard such experiences as potentially rendering certain beliefs justified solely because it is possible for these experiences to represent things as they really are (see e.g. p. 80). He neglects to consider that an experience (of whatever kind) might be *accidentally* veridical, in such a way that to rely on the experience in formulating a belief would be quite *ir*rational and the resulting belief would be unjustified. This neglect is comparable to his failure to respect the requirement that our concepts be non-accidentally accurate if the beliefs we secure through examining them are to count as knowledgeable (see Section 2.4).

This might suggest that the debate over non-conceptual content, as conducted by people like Peacocke, Evans (1982), McDowell (1994), and Brewer (1999: sect. 5.3), is irrelevant to my project. That would be a mistake. For instance, one standard objection to theories of non-conceptual content is also an objection to the way I attempt to use the notion of unconceptualized input. Consider McDowell's claim (McDowell 1994: 52) that rationality requires the possibility of scrutiny of the links between experience and judgement. This, if true, seems to undermine both Peacocke's claim that experience with non-conceptual content can be rationally related to judgement, and my claim that non-conceptualized sensory input can be rationally related to concept possession and hence to belief in conceptual truths. For in both cases it may seem prima facie difficult to see how the non-conceptual, or its relationship to the conceptual, could be 'scrutinized'.

Peacocke's response to McDowell is to argue (2001: 255–6) that one can scrutinize, and even talk about, the non-conceptual (and understand its relationship to the conceptual) by using demonstratives to refer to the non-conceptual parts of experience. But I should not like to judge here whether or not it is possible to refer demonstratively to parts of our unconceptualized sensory input. I think the response concedes too much: as an externalist about justification, I reject McDowell's insistence that it be possible to scrutinize all the stages of a rationalizing or justificatory link (more on McDowell in Section 8.2 below).

Various other objections to non-conceptual content, which focus on the difficulty of understanding what content *is* if it is not conceptual, are not relevant to my proposal, however, since I do not claim that unconceptualized sensory input has content. (Some of these are described by Stalnaker at the beginning of his 1998.) Another objection from McDowell is based on the thought that all experience *must* be conceptual, because the contents of our experiences must also be capable of appearing in judgements (see McDowell 1994: lect. III). This, however, is once again a specific objection to the notion of experience with non-conceptual *content*, and does not seem applicable to non-conceptual *input*. I can allow (for the sake of argument) that experience only has content when that content is capable of appearing in judgement. I can also concede, if desired, that the term 'experience' is not applicable to unconceptualized sensory input because experience must have content and thus must be conceptualized.

This terminological point is unimportant. All that really matters is that sensory input is sensory and that it is a source of grounding for concepts in the sense I have outlined.

It is worth considering whether I might nonetheless fall prey to a more fundamental objection to the notion of non-conceptual experience. Unconceptualized sensory input, as I conceive of it, is supposed to have something like *correctness conditions*. It is envisaged as a differential response to environmental impacts, but not *just* a differential response: I assume that it makes sense to think of some kinds of unconceptualized sensory input as structured in ways which accurately reflect the world's structure, in the sense that they are structured in ways that are in some ways *like* the way the world is structured, and hence guide one towards concepts which accurately represent that mind-independent structure.

Maybe this is not enough for representation.[6] But still it could be argued that only concept-based responses can have correctness conditions of the kind envisaged. For how could some input be said to be structured the way the world is, unless both the input and the relevant aspects of the world are understood as conceptually structured? If we cannot apply our concepts to the input, we must regard it as totally formless—for to regard it as structured is to apply one's concepts to it. If we remove all structure and form from an experience, how can we point to any structural analogy?

This argument involves a mistake regarding first- and third-person perspectives. The argument rhetorically asks: How could some input *be said* to be structured in the way the world is, unless both the input and the relevant aspects of the world are understood as conceptually structured? It neglects to flag the fact that the person who must *say* that this correlation obtains is not the subject who receives the input, but the theorist who describes him. The argument conflates the two perspectives. It continues: If we cannot apply our concepts to the input, *we must regard* it as totally formless. But it is not *we* who are prevented from applying our concepts to the subject's unconceptualized input and to the world. It is

---

[6] Some think that it is sufficient for representation if an experience has *accuracy* conditions; see e.g. Siegel (2005). But I do not think the kind of correctness condition described here amounts to an accuracy condition of this kind. Correctness of sensory input is just structural similarity to the world. An accuracy condition is a condition under which a representation is accurate. Similarity does not suffice for representation, still less for accurate representation.

the subject himself whose concepts are not applied to the input (at least, not initially). Therefore, when the argument asks how *we* can point to any structural analogy between the input and the world, we can answer: By applying our concepts to both. This does not undermine the claim that the input is non-conceptual for its subject. In just the same way, when I see my cat stretched out purring on the hearthrug, I can describe her experience as a veridical experience of (not *as* of) the warmth of the fire, without implying that my cat shares my concept *fire*. I can use my concepts to indicate features of another's experience without implying that the subject of that experience is applying those same concepts to the experience in question.

Even where the subject and the theorist are the same person, there is no objection, provided that the theorizing is done a little later than the experience is undergone. For then the person in question can, in the role of theorist, look back at an earlier experience and appreciate that it was non-conceptual for him when he was the subject of the experience, although he can now apply concepts to it. In fact, not even temporal distance is really required; our descriptions of our own present sensory input may employ concepts, but such descriptions are not the same thing as the input itself.

One more objection of interest here is due to Brewer. In chapter 5 of his (1999), Brewer argues that all perception is conceptual. His argument proceeds from the assumption that perception rationally underwrites judgements, by giving us reasons for making those judgements. Brewer thinks reasons must be accessible to the subject for whom they are reasons, so that if R is a reason for me to believe p, I must be able to see that it is such a reason. It follows, Brewer thinks, that reasons must be conceptualized, for nothing can be understood *as* a reason to believe p if it is not conceptualized. Any experience which constitutes a reason for a belief must, then, be conceptualized. Since Brewer assumes that *all* perception generates reasons for belief, it follows that all perception is conceptualized.

It seems that Brewer only intends conscious experiences to count as instances of 'perception', in which case we need only point out that unconceptualized sensory input need not be supposed to be a kind of experience that is accessible to conscious awareness. (He is, of course, welcome to withhold the terms 'perception' and 'experience' from sensory input on these grounds.) In any case, Brewer's argument can be resisted here owing to its assumption of an internalist conception of reasons as always accessible to the subject for whom they are reasons. If we allow that an experience could give one a reason to believe p (or, indeed, to possess a concept C) without one's being (even potentially) aware of that reason, then we do not have Brewer's motivation for regarding the relevant experience as conceptual.

Another reply to Brewer is to say that, even if reasons must be *accessible*, they might not always be *accessed*. Conceptualization may only be needed at the point of seeing an experience *as* a reason; it might *be* one even in the absence of such conceptualization.

5.6 Ungrounded and inaccurate concepts

Concept grounding and accurateness are novel ideas that I have introduced, and readers may be finding them perplexing. I hope I may be able to elucidate the notions a little further in this section by discussing what *un*grounded and/or *in*accurate concepts would be like. I shall consider four issues: first, what one should do if one came to believe that some of one's concepts were ungrounded and hence possibly[7] inaccurate; second, how the use of inaccurate concepts would affect logic and reasoning; third, what examples we can give of ungrounded concepts; and fourth, how it is that I can talk about inaccurate concepts.

First, let me suggest that if I had reason to believe that one of my concepts C was ungrounded, then I ought to revise or replace it if I knew how to do so. If I did not know how to revise or replace it appropriately, if I had reason to believe that any inaccuracy was not substantial enough to interfere with reference by the concept (or its ultimate constituents) to features of the world, then it might be permissible to keep using it, but be somewhat cautious in trusting it as a basis for learning truths through conceptual examination. However, if I had no such reason, or (worse) positive reason to believe the inaccuracy was very substantial, then I should stop believing *any* proposition involving C. For, upon realizing this, I would realize that I had no reason to trust that C was suited to express truths about the world.

---

[7] This is epistemic possibility.

Let me explain. There are various things we might say about what would happen if one used a seriously inaccurate (and hence unfitting) concept to try to express a proposition: that it would result in the expression of a non-proposition, that it would result in the expression of a meaningless proposition, that it would result in the expression of a meaningful proposition with no truth-value, that it would result in the expression of a meaningful proposition which is false ... No doubt there are other options besides. I cannot go into the merits of each of these options in detail here. Instead I shall simply state, and briefly explain, my own preferred view.

I think that, if we use a seriously inaccurate concept to try to express some claim, we may (but will not necessarily) succeed in expressing a proposition, but that even if we do so succeed it will be a proposition which has no truth-value.[8] I take it that the utterance will be meaningful iff a proposition gets expressed. My reason for saying that sometimes a meaningful utterance can be made despite the involvement of (terms for) seriously inaccurate concepts is that I find an updated verificationist criterion for meaningfulness plausible. According to this criterion, we succeed in expressing a proposition—saying something meaningful—just in case we employ only concepts whose possession could be justified or disjustified by sensory input (and we obey the appropriate syntactical rules, and/or any other constraints generated by the sense of the concepts involved).

It seems to me that any utterance meeting this criterion will be meaningful because the concepts involved will be, in an important sense, *within the scope of our sensory capacities*. That is, our senses will be able to give us some purchase on the relationship between those concepts and the world (i.e. indicate to us whether or not they are accurate). The original verificationist criterion for meaningfulness, which stated that a proposition is meaningful just in case it can be confirmed or disconfirmed by experience, attempted to link propositional meaningfulness to the potential extent of

---

[8] Admitting this possibility of truth-value gaps will mean that some non-classical logic is required whenever we are dealing with propositions that might contain such concepts. But this shouldn't necessarily worry us too much: I take it that all propositions used for any serious purpose (be it practical, scientific, mathematical, philosophical, or whatever) contain only such concepts as we should take to be grounded. So there is no argument here for the use of a non-classical logic in any of these spheres, at least until we acquire reasons to doubt that the relevant concepts are grounded.

our sensory capacities in a somewhat analogous way. Once we appreciate that concepts as well as propositions are capable of receiving empirical justification, we can relax this old-style verificationist criterion without losing what is attractive about it. An utterance can be meaningful by my lights without meeting the old-style verificationist criterion. For an utterance might involve only concepts that can be empirically justified or disjustified even though the proposition expressed is not itself empirically testable.

My preference for the view that the propositions thus expressed have no truth-value is due to the fact that it would seem very odd to say they are true: the concepts involved when we express a true proposition surely must represent aspects of the world, or at least be composed of concepts which represent aspects of the world, if the whole proposition is to succeed in representing the world correctly (truly). But if we say propositions expressed using seriously inaccurate concepts are false, we seem to be forced to say that their negations, which are also expressed using such concepts, are true. Hence we should say that they are neither true nor false; they are not suitable for truth or falsity because the concepts involved do not connect up to the world in the right way.[9]

One might wonder whether it should be such a problem if some kinds of negated propositions involving inaccurate concepts come out true.[10] Perhaps an operator 'Neg' can be introduced into our language which, when placed at the front of a sentence, results in a new sentence which is true just in case the original sentence does not express a truth (see Evans 1982: 24–5). If such an operator as 'Neg' can be introduced (and it is far from straightforward to resist it), then for any sentence S expressing a proposition that involves an inaccurate concept, 'Neg S' is true.

The best sense I can make of 'Neg', however, makes it a tool for talking about (mentioning) the original sentence S, and attributing a property to it (non-truth). A sentence which merely *mentions* expressions for inaccurate concepts does not amount to an attempt to express something by *using* expressions for inaccurate concepts. Something like 'Neg S' can therefore be counted as true, but no pressure is thereby placed on us to acknowledge

---

[9] I do not wish to imply that every attempt to express a proposition which does *not* involve the use of seriously inaccurate concepts will result in the expression of a proposition which *is* suitable for truth or falsity. Such a proposition might, for all I say, fail to have a truth-value for other reasons.

[10] Thanks to Aidan McGlynn here.

that inaccurate concepts can be *used* to express truths. Any attempt to introduce a non-metalinguistic version of 'Neg' can be resisted, with the intuition that it ought to be possible to introduce one explained away as owing to confusion with the metalinguistic version (more on the use–mention distinction on p. 182).

I have not, of course, said enough here to count as having given a serious argument for the views described in this section. But my primary purpose in this section is to open up a debate by putting a position on the table. I'm aiming to show by demonstration the *kind* of philosophical discussion which is made possible once the notions of concept accuracy, concept justification, and concept grounding are in place. I am trying thereby to elucidate these difficult notions by indicating what sorts of issues and possibilities they raise. I am not (for now) trying to establish my own views on these points in any kind of conclusive fashion.

Another question in the same vein which can usefully detain us for a while is: What happens to *logical reasoning* when we start dealing in concepts that are seriously inaccurate? If I am right that seriously inaccurate concepts induce truth-value gaps, then perhaps some kind of three-valued logic will be appropriate (see e.g. Urquhart 1986 for an overview). But deeper questions remain, answers to which may help to guide our choice of an appropriate logic. What does validity amount to on this sort of view? Suppose a piece of reasoning that would normally be called valid turns out to involve an inaccurate concept. Can we still describe this reasoning as valid? A distinctive question we face is that of what would happen to validity were the *logical* concepts appearing in an argument unfitting. This requires us to do more than merely think about what would happen were the sentences treated as atomic to lack truth-values. (Because of the distinctiveness of the challenges raised, I do not assume that any of the extant three-valued logics will cohere with the views developed in this book. Nor do I make any specific proposals here; I merely gesture at some of the most interesting issues.)

Of course, an argument whose premises are all true but whose conclusion contains a seriously inaccurate concept can still be called *in*valid: since the premises are true and the conclusion is not, the argument is not truth-preserving. The more interesting case is that where both premises and conclusion contain inaccurate concepts but the argument otherwise appears to be valid. When this happens, premises and conclusion are no longer suitable for truth. Nevertheless, various notions of truth-preservation can still be applied. The first is counterfactual. Despite the inaccuracy of the concepts involved, one might still accept that if the premises *were* true, the conclusion of the argument would also be true. The second is modal: one might say that at all possible worlds where the premises are true, the conclusion is true.

Some rather difficult questions might be raised here as to whether it is possible for the premises to be true. Is any proposition involving seriously inaccurate concepts possibly true? Assessing this question requires that we assess whether it is possible for a seriously inaccurate concept to be otherwise, for at any world where a proposition p is true, no concept involved in p is seriously inaccurate. And in order to assess this we will probably need to address questions about trans-world concept identity (which is very difficult; see Jenkins (forthcoming *a*)).

Supposing it *is* impossible for the premises to be true, the modal notion of truth-preservation will make no distinction between various arguments whose premises involve seriously inaccurate concepts. All of them will come out valid. I do not think the impossibility of the relevant antecedents would render the *counterfactuals* of truth-preservation trivial or uninteresting. It may be that, *pace* Lewis (1973), not all counterfactuals with impossible antecedents are trivially true (see Nolan 1997 for one way of developing this view). Or (this is the view to which I myself incline) it may be that they are all trivially true, but some are also true for non-trivial reasons, or non-trivially assertable, or something along those lines.

Although these issues are extremely interesting, ultimately it may not be necessary to settle them. For many (myself included) doubt whether the counterfactual and modal notions of truth-preservation are adequate as a guide to validity. It is pretty clear that in general more is required for validity than the truth of the relevant counterfactual. Not every true counterfactual corresponds to a valid argument; consider: *If I were to leave the house now, I would get rained on.* The same goes, or so it is often thought, for the modal notion. The following argument is often taken to be invalid but truth-preserving in the modal sense: *Foxy is a vixen therefore Foxy is female.*

One way of accommodating this thought is to say that valid arguments, here as elsewhere, are those for which it can be *proved* using particular—logical—resources that at all worlds where the premises are true the conclusion is true. Another is to say that the valid arguments, here as elsewhere, are those which have a valid *form* (where this might be cashed out in terms of truth preservation on all models or interpretations). Either way promises a useful distinction among the arguments whose premises involve words for seriously inaccurate concepts.[11] For example, taking 'F' to express some seriously inaccurate concept, we might take the following argument to be valid because of its logical form, or because we can prove using logical resources alone that all worlds where its premises are true are worlds where its conclusion is true:

> (1) All Fs have three sides.
> (2) Everything with three sides is red.
> Therefore (3) All Fs are red.

The same is not true for this argument:

> (1) All Fs have three sides.
> (2) All triangles have three sides.
> Therefore (3) All Fs are triangles.

There is one consideration that might seem to speak in favour of trusting to provability by certain means rather than to form. If it were a *logical* concept that was inaccurate, it is not clear that we would be able to defend the validity of an argument by appealing to form. For it is hard to know how to evaluate for validity the logical form of an argument involving inaccurate logical concepts. This consideration is not decisive, however, first because it is far from clear that we *want* it to be entirely straightforward to divide arguments involving inaccurate logical concepts into those which are valid and those which are invalid, and second because in the cases where we do seem to be able to make such distinctions, it may well be formal considerations that are guiding us.

To see what I mean, let's consider Prior's *tonk* (see Prior 1960). Assuming that Prior's word 'tonk' expresses something, I think what it expresses may well be an example of a seriously inaccurate logical concept.[12] (Even if

---

[11] A similar point might be made about arguments containing meaningless words, were it not to be taken as read that arguments only count as valid or invalid if they contain no meaningless language.

[12] Thanks to Patricia Blanchette for suggesting that I discuss *tonk* here.

it is a compound of accurate concepts, the construction has gone wrong somewhere.) Some validity decisions about *tonk*-involving arguments are not too difficult. Consider the following argument form:

$$\text{(I)} \quad A$$
$$\text{Therefore} \quad \text{(II)} \quad A \text{ tonk } B$$
$$\text{Therefore} \quad \text{(III)} \quad B$$

This ought to come out invalid: clearly, this is not a truth-preserving argument form. But in this case we have form-related grounds for our decision: we know that no argument form which takes us from a sole premise A to the conclusion B regardless of what A and B are is a valid form. Similarly, when considering the following argument:

$$\text{(I)} \quad A \text{ tonk } B$$
$$\text{Therefore} \quad \text{(II)} \quad A \text{ tonk } B$$

we have form-related reasons for pronouncing the argument valid: for this is an instance of A therefore A. More problematic are cases like:

$$\text{(I)} \quad A$$
$$\text{Therefore} \quad \text{(II)} \quad A \text{ tonk } B$$

Clearly, we cannot regard both *tonk*'s introduction rule and its elimination rule as valid. But symmetry makes it hard to choose between them. Despite this, it is far from clear that we need regard both rules as invalid. So should the introduction rule used in the above argument be counted as invalid or not? This is a hard question, meriting further reflection. At present, I do not know what to say.

I now move to the third task of this section: finding examples of ungrounded concepts. It should not surprise us to learn that examples of ungrounded concepts are hard to find. Having the wrong concepts is a more serious matter than having the wrong beliefs. Mistaken beliefs can be corrected without any change in one's conceptual scheme, but revising a concept will involve changing some beliefs, including some that have up till now seemed to be conceptual truths. To correct a mistaken concept one must do something rather more radical than changing one's mind: one must reconceptualize the world. It is because it is so important to get our concepts right (especially fundamental concepts like those of logic and arithmetic) that we do not often go wrong.

The fact that examples of ungrounded concepts seem hard to come by should not, then, be taken to mean that there is nothing substantial to the grounding of a concept. The case is rather like that of natural selection: it is no trivial matter to be a successful animal, yet the only animals we see today are successful ones. Similarly, it is no trivial matter to have grounded concepts of number, but it would be so disastrous for us if we did not have them that (nearly) everyone does. The sorts of concepts which we might now think of as having been ungrounded (such as, perhaps, the Euclidean concept of space: see Section 9.2 below for more on this) are such that the kinds of experience which bring to light their inaccuracy have little immediate significance for our everyday lives.

Moreover, it is pretty much impossible to make a totally secure diagnosis of ungrounded concepts even in cases where classic symptoms are displayed, because alternative explanations are always available. Take the Euclidean concept of space. Maybe Euclidean geometers had a concept of space that was ungrounded. (I take it such a concept would be at least seriously inaccurate, which is enough for ungroundedness, even if the concept was justified for those who used it.) But maybe they had exactly the same concept of space that we have, but were mistaken as to what followed epistemically from that concept (more on this case in Section 9.2 below). Or take *tonk*. Maybe there isn't an ungrounded concept *tonk*, but merely a word 'tonk' which is somehow indeterminate in meaning between our concepts of disjunction and conjunction.[13]

As I mentioned, arithmetical concepts are so fundamental that it is rare to find symptoms of ungroundedness, but some people who suffer from severe dyscalculia may be displaying such symptoms. For instance, Butterworth (1999: 308−9) discusses a subject called Cathy: an intelligent, educated student in her twenties who was unable to solve simple additions when the sum was greater than 10. She appeared to possess a very strange conception of the number line between one and ten, with two positions for five, and she had made no connections between counting, numerosity, and calculating.

---

[13] Thanks to Daniel Nolan for bringing this suggestion to my attention.

Finally, let me mention one puzzle about ungrounded concepts:[14] Why is it that I think that I can talk meaningfully about them, and even express truths involving them? Just a moment ago, for instance, I suggested that

(U) Cathy's number concepts are seriously inaccurate.

And yet I have also suggested that seriously inaccurate concepts cannot be used to express a true proposition. So surely, by my own lights, U should not be taken as true.

This puzzle is based on a use/mention confusion. Seriously inaccurate concepts cannot be *used* to express a true proposition. It is acceptable to *mention* one, as U does. The situation is exactly analogous to that which arises when we state that true sentences must not contain any nonsense words. What is meant is that they must not attempt to use such words; mentioning them is acceptable. ' "Squirgle" doesn't mean anything' is a true sentence.

Even so, surely sometimes we might want to deliberately *use* seriously inaccurate concepts to express true propositions? While I think propositions so expressed can be meaningful, I have denied that they are suitable for truth. Yet, the reader might wonder, surely some of them are in fact true? For instance, suppose we think that Cathy's number concept, let's call it *C-number*, is seriously inaccurate. Then the following seems to be true: *Nothing is a C-number.*

I think the best way of understanding what is happening here is that we are expressing the true proposition that nothing falls under the concept *C-number*. The problematic concept is here being mentioned rather than used. If someone were to insist that there is a true reading on which the concept is used, my response would be to challenge her to explain how concepts so divorced from representation of the world as seriously inaccurate concepts are can yet express truths about that world. I do not know how such a challenge might be met.

5.7 Summary

In this section I began by showing how my proposal coheres with various kinds of structuralism about arithmetic, in particular with a kind of robustly

---

[14] Thanks to Peter Smith and Daniel Nolan for discussion on these issues.

realist structuralism. I discussed the importance of avoiding a tempting, but oversimplified, view of concept grounding. I then related my discussion of arithmetical knowledge to my theory of knowledge in general. Finally, I offered some thoughts about unconceptualized sensory input and about ungrounded and unfitting concepts.

6

Clarifications

6.1 Introduction

In this chapter, I aim to clarify my approach to arithmetical knowledge by distinguishing it from, and where appropriate discussing some of its advantages over, a range of other philosophical projects with which it might conceivably be confused. These are: a sophisticated form of linguistic conventionalism; a version of success semantics; an account of logical knowledge due to Bostock; Maddy's epistemology for set theory; pragmatism about the a priori; and Locke's empiricism. While the most original element of my discussion, the notion of concept grounding, is found in none of these other projects, we shall see that some of them skirt close to it. Other philosophers have made some similar-sounding claims, even if none have put things together in quite the way envisaged here. To conclude this chapter, I speculate as to *why* there is no discussion in the extant philosophical literature of the approach outlined in Chapter 4.

6.2 Conventionalism

To begin this chapter, I want to make clear in exactly what respects my proposal is different from a certain kind of linguistic conventionalism about the a priori; that is, a particular version of the view that a priori knowledge is underwritten by knowledge of linguistic rules. This is particularly important in the current context because conventionalism, a common enough view in its own right in the recent history of the subject, seems also to underwrite some other contemporary philosophies of arithmetic. The neo-Fregeanism of Hale and Wright, for instance, rests on the claim that Hume's Principle is analytic or implicitly definitive in some significant sense, but there is little discussion of how we should say the principle is known once this is established. Often, the neo-Fregeans seem to be relying on conventionalism to account for this knowledge (as when it is claimed that Hume's Principle is an implicit definition of 'number', e.g. in Hale and Wright 2000. O'Leary-Hawthorne 1996: 196 takes Wright to be openly conventionalist). What I want to do here is show that if conventionalists try to be realists, they open up a serious gap in the conventionalist programme. I also want to explain how my proposal is supposed to fill just this sort of gap.

I described some problems with conventionalism in Section 2.3. What I want to stress here is that if conventionalism is only acceptable to anti-realists, it is not a solution to the problem which occupies us this in work; namely, that of locating a kind of arithmetical epistemology which respects apriorism, realism, and empiricism. But, although conventionalism is often taken to amount to the claim that a priori knowledge is knowledge 'of our conventions' (i.e. knowledge of something which depends upon us), the sophisticated conventionalist might want to say this is misleading. Specifically, she might say it involves a sort of use–mention confusion. It is true that, according to the conventionalist, knowledge of the conventions governing the sentence 'All vixens are female' is what *enables* us to know that all vixens are female. But she need not claim that knowledge of the conventions *is* (or includes) knowledge of the proposition expressed by the sentence. Knowledge of conventions is knowledge of propositions wherein the sentence or its constituent words are *mentioned* (such as knowledge that 'vixen' means the same as 'female fox'), but knowledge that all vixens are female is knowledge of a proposition expressed by *using* the sentence.

If the conventionalist takes this line she might then argue, contra the anti-realist, that the truth of *All vixens are female* is essentially independent of us, although our way of knowing it is through having knowledge of our conventions. It is true that knowing about our conventions cannot be described as knowing about something independent, but knowing that all vixens are female is not the same as knowing about conventions. It is just that the latter makes the former possible.

The most serious difficulty with this approach, however, is to say *how* knowledge of conventions makes knowledge of independent truths possible. How can knowing something about ourselves enable us to know an independent fact? We have some serious philosophical work to do if we propose anything along these lines. This is the advertised gap in the envisaged realist–conventionalist view. It is a gap which I propose we fill by postulating a relationship of empirical grounding between our arithmetical concepts and the arithmetical structure of the world. If this relationship holds, we have a reason to think that, by examining our concepts (or, by proxy, the conventions surrounding the words we use to express them), we can learn something about the independent world.

But, of course, once we fill the gap in this way the account is no longer conventionalist. Linguistic conventions now do no significant epistemological work: they can, at most, be regarded as guides to the nature of our concepts, which are in turn regarded as guides to the structure of the world because of their relationship to sensory input.

What might have made the sophisticated conventionalist's view seem attractive is the fact that both halves of what she claims have intuitive appeal: it is intuitively correct that we know $7 + 5 = 12$ by knowing something about how the concepts involved relate to each other, and that could well be taken to be closely related to (or mistaken for) knowing something about the conventions governing the use of the words we use to express those concepts. And it is intuitively correct that $7 + 5 = 12$ is independently true. The weak spot in the sophisticated conventionalist's armour concerns the connection between these two claims: a lot of work needs to be done to explain how they can both be true together.

In some respects this is the same as a point that was made in the discussion of Peacocke's moderate rationalism in Section 2.4 above. Peacocke asserts that we know a priori truths by examining our concepts, which are so individuated as to ensure that we end up believing truths when we conduct these examinations. This has plausibility because both halves of the claim are true. The trouble is that Peacocke, like the conventionalist considered here, does nothing to explain *how come* they are true together. He does not tell us how it has come about that our concepts are so fortuitously arranged. But this, surely, is the crucial question, just as the crucial question for the sophisticated conventionalist is how it has come about that our linguistic conventions are so fortuitously arranged that we can learn truths about the independent world by examining them. Like Peacocke, our realist conventionalist seems to be crucially lacking an input step into his epistemology.

6.3 Success semantics

Success semantics is the attempt to understand mental representation by thinking about the ways in which representing the world can lead to success in action (variously defined). A contemporary version of one type of success semantics, which makes contact with some of the ideas that inform my thinking about arithmetical knowledge, is found in Blackburn (2005). Blackburn offers the following 'fundamental schema':

FS: Suppose the presence of 'a' is a feature of a vehicle 'a...'. Then 'a' refers to a if and only if actual and possible actions based upon the vehicle 'a...' are typically successful, when they are, because of something about a.

(p. 27)

Other varieties of success semantics exist (see e.g. Ramsey 1927: 40, Millikan 1984, and Papineau 1993). But, unlike many other versions, Blackburn's eschews the appeal to teleology to spell out what is meant by 'success'. His discussion is particularly interesting in the current context for two other reasons. First, it focuses on the fact that the success of an action based on a certain mental representation can be *explained* by appeal to that which the proposition the agent is representing. (Compare e.g. Papineau 1993: sect. 3.6 and Whyte 1990, where the emphasis is on whether the truth of the relevant proposition makes success *inevitable*.) Second, it concentrates on accounting for the representative powers of *sub-propositional* items (where previous accounts have focussed on whole propositions.)

The project pursued in this book also places emphasis on the notion of explanation, and focuses on concepts or sub-propositional representations. Another point of contact is the appeal to success and the thought that this is importantly related to reference: I argue that our arithmetical concepts are indispensably useful and I imagine this is closely related to success in action. I also think that what explains this success is that those concepts probably refer (or are composed of concepts which refer) to corresponding elements of the arithmetical structure of the world which they accurately represent (see Section 4.5 above). I also appeal to the usefulness or success of our concepts in scientific contexts as evidence that they are empirically justified (see Section 4.6).

I am quite sympathetic to Blackburn's proposal (at least qua illuminating biconditional; qua analysis of representation it is more problematic). And I think the similarities between the two accounts might help further our understanding of the connections between knowing and representing in ways I cannot develop here. However that may be, I am not in this book proposing anything that could be said to amount to a success semantics. In fact, my approach involves asserting what is almost the *reverse* of a success semanticist's main claim. I want to explain the fact that possessing arithmetical concepts is advantageous (that it enables us to succeed) in terms of the existence of a mapping relationship between those concepts and the world (this was my scientifically realist assumption of Section 4.5); whereas a success semanticist wants to explain the existence of a mapping relationship between certain mental entities and the world in terms of the fact that tokening those entities typically enables us to succeed in certain circumstances.

Nevertheless, this reversal of explanatory direction does not mean my project is *incompatible* with a success semantics. For one thing, the two kinds of explanation are supposed to be quite different: I am offering something like a *historical explanation* of success in terms of reference, whereas the success semanticist is hoping to offer an *illuminating criterion* for reference in terms of success. For another thing, there is a difference between actual success of the kind I appeal to and typical success of the kind appealed to by FS. Even if the success semanticist were to say that reference could be *reduced* to typical success, or that typical success was somehow *constitutive* of reference, he could appeal to reference as explanatory of—therefore distinct from—our actual success.

6.4 Bostock

In a short paper (1990) Bostock seems to be arguing for a view quite similar to mine. Bostock claims that Quine is right to say that logic and mathematics are subject to the test of experience, like the rest of our best scientific theory, and that they are 'in this sense empirical'. But he goes on to say there is 'another sense in which they are not empirical, but remain just as problematic as ever' (p. 571).

Taking propositional logic as his test case, Bostock notes that the choice of a conceptual scheme is sensitive to input from the senses (p. 577) and that the truths of classical logic flow from the classical conception of truth. He adds that those of quantum and intuitionistic logic flow from a different concept of truth. He then claims that our decision as to which logic is applicable to the world is sensitive to experience, and that logic is thus empirical. But he also says knowledge *that* certain logical principles flow from certain conceptions of truth is a priori; that is, does not depend upon experience at all. For it concerns only 'relations of ideas' (in the Humean sense: Bostock 1990: 581), not 'matters of fact and existence'.

Despite some prima facie similarities, however, Bostock's view is much less radical than mine. It is clear that Bostock is not claiming, as I do, that any single piece of knowledge might be both a priori and empirical. His approach to logical truths is pretty straightforwardly Quinean: he says that they (like the conceptual schemes on which they depend) are selected solely in order to generate an optimal scientific theory. Although he notes that logical truths flow from the corresponding concepts of truth, he does not take the crucial further step of proposing that such concepts can be empirically grounded and that this grounding can flow through to conceptually true propositions. It was only by doing this that I was able to say in Section 4.7 that justification for those truths is a priori, despite the fact that it is empirical. Bostock does not claim that logical truths are a priori; he only says that truths about *which propositions flow from which concepts of truth* are a priori.

Bostock does not improve upon Quine's account of how we have empirical knowledge of logical truths. For Bostock, knowledge that a logical truth is true—that is, applicable to the world (as opposed to merely a consequence of a certain conception of truth)—is a straightforwardly empirical matter: our justification for such a belief is due to the fact that the relevant proposition belongs to our best scientific theory of the world. He is thus open to the objection levelled against Quine, that our knowledge of logical truths ought to be different in kind from our knowledge of (say) physical laws. He can say that there is *something* different about logic, because it consists of conceptual truths. But he does not relate this difference to the epistemology of logic. Although Bostock notes that logical truths are conceptual truths and that the selection of logical concepts is (or should be) sensitive to data from the senses, he does not exploit the potential of these observations to solve some deep philosophical problems.

6.5 Maddy

In Maddy (1990), as in the current work, there is an attempt to defend apriorism, realism, and empiricism in mathematics simultaneously. Maddy there proposes that we can know (some) mind-independent mathematical truths through knowing about sets, and that we can obtain knowledge of sets through experience. She claims that we can perceive sets of physical objects, as well as the objects themselves. She has since abandoned this view, but for the purposes of this section, 'Maddy' will refer to the Maddy who held it.

It seems right to say that we often experience pluralities *as* pluralities, and perhaps we could so develop this claim as to make it equivalent to the claim that we sometimes see a group of things *as* a set of things. But, even if this means we can claim that we see particular sets, this does not yet explain how we know *general* set-theoretic principles. As Maddy notes (pp. 67–8), one way of developing the claim that we perceive sets into a full-blown set-theoretic epistemology would be to say that general propositions about sets are known through inductive or abductive inference from the particular propositions known through perception. But this would not respect the special a priori status of (at least some aspects of) our justification for believing in set theory. (Maddy acknowledges the difference between general mathematical beliefs and inductive beliefs on p. 68, and explicitly states that some of the support for our mathematical beliefs is a priori on p. 74.)

So she proposes instead that certain neural developments which allow for perception of sets also give rise to high-level general beliefs about them. She claims that at some stage in our neural development we acquire a set detector, and possession of this goes along with the acquisition of some very general beliefs about sets (e.g. that they have subsets, that the members of any two sets are the members of a further set, etc.). Maddy describes these beliefs as 'intuitive'.

In some respects this looks quite close to what I have said about arithmetic: Maddy is at least proposing that some knowledge about sets is closely related to possession of set-theoretic concepts, and, in some important way, to experience. And at one stage in her thinking on this subject Maddy makes other claims that sound similar to some of the things

I have proposed: she says that 'set theoretic truths... are true by virtue of facts about independently existing sets', and that the general beliefs just described are a priori in the sense that 'once the concepts are in place, no further experience is needed to support [those beliefs]' (1980: 190 n. 52). She is also, like me, an epistemological externalist (1990: 73).

We differ, however, in two ways. First, I make fewer neurological assumptions than Maddy. I do not, for instance, assume that arithmetical concepts, or any concepts at all, are acquired (see Sections 4.5 and 8.3), nor do I make Maddy's assumptions (see her pp. 68 ff.) about what concepts and the corresponding cognitive abilities are like from a psychological perspective. Second, and more importantly, we differ in that Maddy does not offer an account of epistemological grounding for concepts. What Maddy's account, as I have described it so far, lacks is an explanation of how the 'intuitive' beliefs which flow from our set-theoretic concepts can count as knowledgeable or even justified. Particular beliefs about small sets whose members are concrete are supposed to be perceptually grounded, but what about the rest of our set-theoretic beliefs? According to Maddy (some) such beliefs are *acquired*, along with the concept of *set*, through sensory exposure to sets. But this is merely to tell a causal-historical story, not an epistemological one.

Maddy seems to agree that there is a gap: she says that '[w]ithout the corroboration of suitable theoretical supports, no intuitive belief can count as more than mere conjecture' (p. 74). She claims that 'our set theoretic principles demand theoretical or extrinsic support, that is, support, as in natural science, in terms of verifiable consequences, lack of disconfirmation, breadth and explanatory power, intertheoretic connections, simplicity, elegance, and so on' (p. 75). For this reason, she says that, although 'intuitive' support for a proposition is 'impurely' a priori, 'it doesn't follow that even ... primitive mathematical beliefs are a priori' (p. 74), and that 'in scientific contexts, intuitive beliefs must be tested like any other hypothesis' (p. 71).

This makes Maddy sound very close to Quine (and, of course, incurs the familiar objection to Quine's view: that it does not account for the special status of arithmetic). But it sits uncomfortably with Maddy's claim to be a reliabilist, who allows that it is enough for one's intuitive beliefs to be justified if the intuitive method reliably leads to true beliefs (p. 73). How can she square this with the claim that intuition by itself supplies only 'conjectures'?

Later (p. 107) Maddy clarifies the situation a little, saying that in her view intuition supplies 'some preliminary level of justification'. Presumably, this means it is not enough for knowledge but it is better than nothing.

Maddy comes *close* to the view that set-theoretical beliefs are justified through an examination of concepts which are themselves justified, but she does not quite formulate it. She thinks of set-theoretical concepts as acquired in response to experience of an independently structured world, and as accurately reflecting the structure of the world when things go well (see e.g. p. 71, where she describes how we could go wrong and form concepts which do *not* do this). And she thinks of belief in certain propositions as very closely related to possession of these set-theoretical concepts. But at the crucial point she discusses the acquisition of concepts (and the corresponding beliefs) only in *causal* terms; there is no consideration of how intuitive beliefs could be grounded through being appropriately related to concepts which are appropriately related to the world. She does not consider the possibility that full-blown epistemic justification or grounding can be transmitted, from experience, through our concepts, to the beliefs which she calls 'intuitive'. Thus she feels the need to supplement 'intuition' with 'theoretical support' in the way described. And yet, she thinks, if intuition is a reliable source of true beliefs it must provide *some* kind of justificatory support for beliefs. She therefore settles for an uneasy compromise whereby it provides very limited justification.

The compromise is uneasy because it is hard to see a principled reason why if intuition works at all, it cannot work well enough to deliver knowledge. Maddy rightly feels that the mere reliability of intuition is not a satisfactory ground for saying it is a source of knowledge—we need to know *why* it is reliable to understand whether it can be a source of knowledge—but she does not succeed in squaring this with the thought that intuition can nonetheless supply some kind of justification. I think the correct course of action in this situation is not to settle for the uneasy compromise, but rather to explore further the source of the reliability of Maddy's intuition. Once we know *why* it is reliable, we can decide whether it is (potentially) a source of knowledge, or whether it is only reliable by chance, in which case it will not even be a source of limited justification. (An explanation of the reliability of beliefs we hold because of the nature of our concepts is what I sketched in Chapter 4, and I proposed that if something like this was correct then the beliefs in question would be knowledgeable.)

Perhaps, though, Maddy has good reasons for not taking intuition to be a source of knowledge? The only thing she says that might count as a reason for not doing so is that intuition is fallible, so that its deliverances must be supported by other means (p. 71). But the fallibility of a source of beliefs does not mean it cannot by itself supply knowledge. Perception is fallible, as indeed is Maddy's proposed knowledge-generating reinforcement for intuitive beliefs; namely, scientific hypothesis testing.

It is worth noting, incidentally, that Maddy does not need the controversial claim that we see sets to support her claim that the concept of *set* is acquired in response to experience. In Section 5.3 above, I resisted the simplistic view of concept grounding whereby a concept can only be grounded if we have actually seen or bumped into instances of that concept. A similar point might be made about acquisition. It does not seem that we need the claim that we perceive sets in order to argue that our concept of *set* is acquired in response to sensory input.

What seems right about Maddy's position is that there is *some* crucial link between sensory input, our mathematical concepts, and our knowledge of mathematics. But to understand it aright we need to focus not on the perception of sets, nor on the neurological processes through which sensory stimulation may lead to the acquisition of 'intuitive' beliefs, but rather on the epistemic grounding relationship between our sensory input and our mathematical concepts.

6.6 Pragmatism

There are (at least) three ways in which one might appeal to notions of *usefulness* when discussing epistemic justification. What I have proposed is that the usefulness (or more strictly, indispensability) of certain concepts is *evidence* that they are justified (see Section 4.6 above). An analogous claim could be made about belief in propositions. A stronger kind of claim could be made by indispensability theorists, who might want to assert that the indispensability of a proposition constitutes justification (and not because it evinces some other kind of justification).

Pragmatists, in the sense I'm interested in here, make a more radical claim, asserting that usefulness either replaces or constitutes justification *and that nothing more can be said about justification than this*. In particular, it cannot be said that usefulness evinces *truth*. Pragmatism so characterized is at risk of stopping too soon in the search for sources of arithmetical knowledge and/or justification. Once we acknowledge the usefulness of arithmetical concepts and/or propositions, it seems that we can legitimately ask *why* they are so useful. It would take a substantial argument to show that this question was somehow illegitimate or unanswerable, as some forms of pragmatism seem to suggest. But certain answers to that question (such as answers which explain usefulness in terms of fit with the world) will make it seem that there *is* more to be said about justification than the pragmatist suggests. Until these answers are discredited, pragmatism is at an explanatory disadvantage with respect to competing views.

Nonetheless, there are some similarities between my approach to arithmetical knowledge and a pragmatist approach. An interesting philosopher for purposes of comparison is Carnap, who describes arithmetical truths as 'analytic'. Carnap (see e.g. 1950) maintains that the question of whether we should accept arithmetic ('the system of numbers') is a 'practical' question. That is to say, he thinks it depends upon whether that system is useful; it depends, as he puts it, upon the 'efficiency, fruitfulness and simplicity' (1950: 587) of the 'linguistic framework' which constitutes that system. But once we have accepted the number framework, along with its rules and methods, it is 'analytic' that (e.g.) there is a prime number greater than a million. That is to say, it 'drops out of' the adoption of that framework.

This line of thought bears some resemblance to the view I proposed in Chapter 4. I have argued that our basic concepts earn their keep through being useful to us, and that arithmetical truths are known through an examination of those concepts or their compounds. A scheme of concepts might be thought to be analogous to a Carnapian framework, in which case I will be tempted to agree with Carnap that the most useful frameworks are (and should be) the ones that get adopted, and that our acceptance of certain propositions in some (at least epistemic) sense 'falls out of' our adoption of these frameworks or conceptual schemes.

But Carnap thinks that arithmetical propositions are *made true by* the conventional rules of the number framework, and that they are known because we know the rules of the framework we have adopted. He is a kind of conventionalist. His view goes beyond the most simple kind of conventionalism in that it suggests that there is *some* basis for the selection of conventions or frameworks. But it is significantly different from my own view, in that it offers only a *pragmatic* basis for the selection. Carnap explicitly refuses to say that the usefulness of certain frameworks is evidence for the reality of the objects whose existence is analytic within those frameworks (p. 587). Whereas I believe that the usefulness of our arithmetical concepts *is* evidence for the reality of the structure they capture.

The reason for this difference is that Carnap believes there is no such thing as evidence for the reality of the number world. He says that the question of whether the number world exists is not a factual question, but a practical question as to whether we should adopt the number framework. According to Carnap, the claim that the number framework exists cannot be assessed rationally in the same way as the claim that $7 + 5 = 12$. Rather (the idea seems to be), in order to be in the business of rationally assessing arithmetical claims we must already buy into the number framework. So although we can have pragmatic reasons for accepting or rejecting the number framework, evidence of the reality of the number world is just the wrong sort of thing to look for.

But why accept Carnap's view? Why think that buying into the number framework is necessary for rational assessment of arithmetical claims? And even if it was, why think that means acceptance of the number framework cannot itself be rationally assessed? Do we become incapable of rationally assessing things once we accept them? Surely not. The idea must be, rather, that any assessment would *rely* on the assumption of the number framework. And I don't think this is true; I have tried to offer an alternative explanation of how we arrive at rational belief in the arithmetical principles we believe. Our rational acceptance of the number framework may be due to a correct investigation of empirically grounded arithmetical concepts.

Separating linguistic and conceptual issues is important here. It is true that our choice of which linguistic vehicles we use to express ourselves is determined by pragmatic considerations. And we can grant (at least for the sake of argument) that there is no 'right' way to go about making this sort of choice except in so far as the 'right' way is the most fruitful and/or simple way. But I think it is a mistake to regard the truth of $7 + 5 = 12$ as in any sense created by the conventional rules of our language. We accept the sentence '$7 + 5 = 12$' because we accept that it is a linguistic representation of a proposition we accept. Our acceptance of that proposition underwrites our acceptance of the linguistic item, the sentence, and so cannot be explained as itself due to linguistic convention. (That is the point pressed in BonJour's objection to conventionalism, described on pp. 40–4 above.)

In my view, it is our concepts, not our language, that ultimately underwrite our belief that $7 + 5 = 12$. Both language and concepts earn their keep through being useful. But what the usefulness of a language tells us is that that language is enabling us to express our concepts well. The usefulness of our concepts, on the other hand, is more fundamental and more philosophically interesting; it raises certain questions which cannot be pushed further back, as questions about language can, but are nonetheless genuine questions.[1] I think that the usefulness of arithmetical concepts is evidence for the reality of the structure they capture.

Another advantage of my proposal over Carnap's, besides the fact that mine avoids any kind of conventionalism and hence respects realist intuitions, is that if we approach concepts as I suggest we can explain why we might consider outdated conceptual schemes to be *mistaken*, rather than simply less useful than our current schemes. The pragmatist seems forced to accept that propositions which follow epistemically from the outmoded concepts contained in them have as good a claim as any to be regarded as (conceptual) *truths*, although they do not employ *useful* concepts. (The pragmatist C. I. Lewis does indeed accept something like this; see his 1926: 255–6.) By contrast, we need not ascribe truth to these propositions, since we can say that the concepts they employ are not merely unhelpful in certain cases, but are actually seriously inaccurate, and hence unsuitable to express truths about the world (see Section 5.6 above).

6.7 Locke

Locke (1689) proposes to ground all knowledge in experience (including introspective experience), and what's more he approaches this task by thinking about how the sub-propositions mental items that he calls 'ideas' relate to experience, rather than by concentrating solely on the relationship between experience and whole propositions. In this respect his approach is an important precursor of my own.

---

[1] One feature of Carnap's philosophy which might have led to confusion on this point is the lack of careful distinction between concepts and linguistic items. More on this in Section 6.8.

Kant's purported refutation of the possibility of an empirical basis for fundamental concepts (which will be discussed in Section 7.2 below) has overshadowed this Lockean way of proceeding, to the detriment, I would suggest, of modern accounts of mathematics and the a priori. I think Locke pointed us in a better direction for understanding these things than Kant did. Where Locke draws our attention to the relationship between experience, concepts, and the mind-independent world, Kant directs our attention inwards, claiming that there can be nothing more to arithmetical knowledge than an examination of the structure we ourselves impose upon what we experience.

Locke and I diverge, however, in that while Locke says that experience is the *source* of all *basic* ideas, I claim sensory input can *ground* concepts, including some compound concepts. By a 'source' Locke appears to mean something like a causal origin, rather than anything like what I have in mind when I discuss concept grounding (see Locke 1689: II. i). Locke's view enables him to claim that some ideas (those of secondary qualities), though they are derived from experience, are not such that by using them we can state truths about the world as it exists independently of our perception of it. However, it would have been consistent for Locke to propose that ideas of *primary* qualities are grounded in experience, and that they represent features of the independent world, and that we can therefore learn about the independent world by examining them.

Although Locke does not explicitly consider concept grounding, he does seem to gesture towards the notion when he says (IV. iv. 4) that the reason 'real knowledge' can be obtained through examining our basic ideas is that these ideas are 'the natural and regular productions of things without us, really operating upon us, and so carry with them all the conformity which is intended, or which our state requires'. But Locke does not consider how grounding for a set of concepts might flow through to beliefs in conceptually true propositions involving those concepts (or compounds thereof). His view of how we know mathematical truths therefore bears no resemblance to my proposals concerning arithmetical knowledge.

Cicovacki, on the strength of certain passages, has been lead to suggest that Locke's theory of mathematical knowledge is a theory of maker's knowledge, rather like Kant's (Cicovacki 1990: 518). But Locke's view is not that simple; he believes that, although we create complex mathematical concepts, the parts of which they are composed correspond to 'real Things' (see e.g. II. xxx. 2).

Locke stresses, however, that mathematical knowledge is knowledge 'only of our own ideas' (IV. iv. 6). This doesn't sit comfortably with his view, expressed later in the same section, that mathematical knowledge is still 'true and certain, even of real Things existing'. The apparent tension is supposed to be explained away by the claim that complex mathematical concepts are not (perfectly) instantiated by any real objects, so that although mathematical knowledge is only knowledge of how our ideas relate, it is knowledge 'of real Things' because it *would* be true of anything that *did* instantiate the relevant concepts. The trouble is that this does not explain how it can be that by knowing something about our ideas we can know something about the world, even something counterfactual about the world. In my opinion, we need to think about the grounding relationship between the world and our mathematical concepts in order to understand this properly.[2]

As regards Locke's explicit attempts at the philosophy of arithmetic, philosophers have tended to conclude, with Mackie, that '[w]hat Locke says about ideas of numbers is best forgotten' (Mackie 1976: 121). As Resnik points out, 'Locke confuses a unit with the number one' (1980: 29), fails to distinguish between a number and our idea of it (p. 29), and appears to make arithmetic 'dependent upon human existence and psychology' (p. 37). While these criticisms may be largely justified as regards Locke's specific comments on arithmetical knowledge, they seem to have prevented philosophers noticing that it is possible to apply other aspects of Locke's philosophy to the topic of arithmetical knowledge so as to develop a more satisfying account.

I think that Locke's confusion over the nature of mathematical knowledge (and, to some extent, the ensuing confusion of the empiricist tradition) can be diagnosed as due to his failing to put to best use the theoretical space he had created for himself. He gave us a set of powerful tools by focussing on the relationship between 'ideas' and experience, and by discussing the

---

[2] I should note another difference between my view and Locke's, though it is not particularly relevant to epistemology. Locke is a conceptual atomist: he believes concepts can be broken down into their smallest parts, which then cannot be broken down any further. I, by contrast, make no assumptions as to whether atomism is correct, though I do suppose that some of a concept's ultimate constituents are, as a matter of fact, the most fundamental units of *justification*.

composition of concepts which correspond to 'real Things'. Because the best use has not yet been made of these Lockean tools, philosophers studying mathematics and a priori knowledge in general have tended to become disillusioned with empiricism. I think this is a false step, and I hope that my discussion of arithmetical knowledge will be interpreted as an attempt to develop some of Locke's insights in a more promising way.

6.8 In search of a literature

I have now described several philosophical projects which are *not* concerned with the precise kind of arithmetical epistemology I am advocating. What about the literature which *is* on this topic?

Unfortunately, to the best of my knowledge, none exists. The approach I am advocating does not seem to have been considered before. In this section I shall describe the places in which one might search (and I have searched) for a literature on this topic, and offer tentative explanations of its absence in each case.

Locke, as I have said, was interested in the relationship between experience and concepts (or ideas). We might therefore hope, even though Locke himself did not produce a promising account of the a priori, that the secondary literature on Locke would contain some discussion of the possible epistemological import of Locke's work. In fact, however, secondary work on the relevant aspects of Locke's philosophy tends to focus on the task of explicating his notion of an 'idea', and on relating it to modern philosophical discussions of the mind, perception, and representation (see e.g. Ayers 1991, Chappell 1994, and Woolhouse 1994). While this work is important, and importantly related to my project, it seems not to have included any consideration of the possibility that sourcing ideas in experience might affect the *epistemological* status of the propositions known through an examination of those concepts. Thus Ayers, who acknowledges that Locke's 'principle that all our ideas come from experience served ... as a secure basis of our knowledge'(1991: 68), points out later on that Locke believed we knew conceptual truths through the exercise of 'a priori intuition', and goes on to defend *that* view against objections (sect. 29).

If not in the secondary literature on Locke, perhaps some discussion of the epistemological importance of concepts might be expected in the context of contemporary philosophical accounts of concepts. However, the received wisdom is that 'the topic of concepts lies at the intersection of *semantics* and philosophy of *mind*' (Rey 1998; emphases added). Its relevance to epistemology tends to be overlooked by those seriously interested in determining what concepts are and how they work. In the encyclopaedia entry just cited Rey only raises one epistemological issue: that of saying how we know when some object falls under some concept. Contemporary philosophical discussions of concepts simply do not provide the right sort of philosophical background for a theory of a priori knowledge as knowledge obtained through an examination of empirically grounded concepts. 'Empiricism' about concepts has been defined as the view that all concepts are *acquired* in response to experience, not that concepts are empirically grounded (see p. 232 below).

Another obstacle that may have been operative here is that during the twentieth century talk of concepts was mixed up with talk of linguistic items, such as words, word meanings, or rules for the use of words. (For a few classics see Tarski 1935: 152; Ayer 1936: ch. 6, esp. p. 107; Quine 1950: 79; Grice and Strawson 1956: 157.) The project of finding definitions for terms has come to be known as 'conceptual analysis', and the study of language has often been regarded as fundamental to philosophy in ways conducive to the conflation of the conceptual and the linguistic. An investigation of our linguistic practices is explicitly an investigation of something we have created, however, and so one danger of this trend is that it can lead to the assumption that knowledge gained through conceptual examination is knowledge of something we have created through our linguistic practices, rather than of facts about the independent world.

One might expect to find discussion of some theory like mine in the contemporary philosophy of mathematics. However, discussion of the epistemological significance of conceptual truth in this field has clustered around faculty rationalism of the kind alluded to by Gödel (1947), logicism (like that of Russell 1903) and more recently neo-Fregeanism (for discussion of which see Section 4.3 above), and to some extent the notion of proof (see e.g. the essays collected in Detlefsen 1992).

Naturally, we also look to contemporary work on a priori knowledge. In this field, there are many advocates of the view that concept examination somehow underwrites our a priori knowledge (e.g. Peacocke and Bealer, whose views are discussed in Section 2.5 above, and the 'moderate' empiricists, discussed in Sections 2.3 and 2.4). However, they have in the main failed to appreciate that much more must be done to explain a priori knowledge than establishing that it is knowledge of conceptual truths. Even Peacocke, who expands upon that claim by saying that the possession conditions for relevant concepts are tied to those concepts' semantic values, does not do enough to explain how this correlation comes about. In addition, the entrenched idea that a priori knowledge cannot be in any way empirical has been a serious barrier to the development of a theory along the lines proposed here.

One final point to note is that in order to develop a theory along the lines of that of Chapter 4, we have to dispense with the seemingly universal assumption that empirical justification and grounding accrue only to propositional beliefs, and not to concepts. At the beginning of Part III, I shall look in some detail at how this assumption has appeared to rule out of court my approach to arithmetical knowledge. This in itself, I tentatively offer as a further explanatory factor regarding the absence of any literature concerning my proposal.

6.9 Summary

In this section I have aimed to clarify the views presented in Chapter 4 by distinguishing my thoughts about arithmetical epistemology from a range of other philosophical projects. I have also made some guesses as to why a proposal along the lines of that presented in Chapter 4 has not been made before.

PART III

Objections

7

On The Very Idea of Concept Grounding: Thinking Too Big

7.1 Introduction

In this chapter, I discuss a habit of thought which seems to have been one of the main things stopping philosophers taking empirical concept grounding seriously as the basis for an account of a priori knowledge. 'Thinking too big' is my name for this habit: it is the habit of thinking of sensory input solely as a source of justification and grounding for belief in whole propositions, rather than as also a potential source of justification and grounding for concepts; that is, sub-propositional representations. This habit tends to induce forms of anti-realism, though we shall see that it does not always do so. It does, however, always make an account along the lines I have proposed seem impossible.

The habit of thinking too big has an illustrious history, going back (at least) to Kant's *Critique of Pure Reason*. I shall be able to discuss only a few highlights. Readers should note that not all the philosophers to be discussed in this chapter think too big in the context of objecting to the idea that our concepts have a sensory basis of some kind. Some are included merely to show how widespread the habit of thinking too big is, and what some of the benefits of kicking this habit might be.

7.2 Kant

In the *Critique of Pure Reason*, Kant's arguments for his transcendental idealism often rely on the assumption that experience cannot be the 'source' of certain fundamental concepts (like those of space, time, and hence—for Kant—arithmetic[1]), because the relevant kinds of experience are possible only if one already employs the concepts in question. This is most evident in the Transcendental Aesthetic, and is summed up in the slogan: 'intuitions without concepts are blind' (A51/B75). Passages of particular relevance to the points to be made in this section include A23/B38:

Space is not an empirical concept which has been derived from outer experiences. For in order that certain sensations be referred to something outside me (that is, to something in another region of space from that in which I find myself), and similarly in order that I may be able to represent them as outside and alongside one another, and accordingly as not only different but in different places, the representation of space must be presupposed. The representation of space cannot, therefore, be empirically obtained from the relations of outer appearance. On the contrary, this outer experience is itself possible at all only through that representation.

and this passage from A30/B46:

Time is not an empirical concept that has been derived from any experience. For neither coexistence nor succession would ever come within our perception, if the representation of time were not presupposed as underlying them *a priori*. Only on the presupposition of time can we represent to ourselves a number of things as existing at one and the same time (simultaneously) or at different times (successively).

Kant appears to be making a claim about concept acquisition rather than concept grounding in these passages, but the point might well be taken to carry across. At least, I am happy to grant for the sake of argument that if we must employ a concept in order to have the kinds of experience which could *generate* that concept, then we will also need to employ the concept in order to have the kinds of experience which could *ground* that concept. And, more specifically, I grant that if we cannot experience time and space without employing our concepts of time and space, it is hard to see how it could be argued that such experience could ground those concepts. (For all that concessiveness, however, I maintain that 'filter brain' hypotheses

---

[1] In different works Kant appears to have held different views as to whether arithmetical structure was derived from temporal structure alone or from both spatial and temporal structure. See Potter (2000; sect. 1. 11) for discussion.

about the nature of concept grounding are untouched by anything Kant says: see Section 4.5 above.)

If we are to accept that experiences as of space and time are impossible unless they involve the application of pre-existing concepts of space and time, 'experiences' must be construed so as to include only conceptualized experiences, and to exclude the kind of unconceptualized sensory input which I have suggested can ground fundamental concepts. And, indeed, for Kant, 'experience' is conscious (B67) sensory knowledge of objects (B218–19; see also B147). That is, it is a source of sensory confirmation for conceptualized beliefs about objects.[2] It may well be right to say that *this* cannot be had without employing fundamental concepts such as concepts of space and time: we may well need to use those concepts to structure our sensory input so as to regard it as confirming a correspondingly conceptualized belief.

But if 'experience' is construed so narrowly, the conclusions of the Transcendental Aesthetic concerning the nature and source of our concepts of space and time (and hence of mathematical concepts) are evidently non sequiturs. For it simply does not follow from the fact that our concept of space is not supplied by conscious sensory knowledge of propositions about objects that the concept 'does not represent any property of things in themselves' (A26/B42), or that space is merely 'the subjective condition of sensibility' (ibid). The concept may be instead supplied by (and grounded in) preconscious and/or unconceptualized sensory input.[3] As such, it may well be a non-accidentally accurate representation of some real feature of the mind-independent world (or else composed of such representations).

It is important to be clear that I am not simply taking issue with Kant's use of the term 'experience' here. Kant's drawing the conclusions he does from his claim that experience is not the source of our concepts is

---

[2] For the Kantian definition of 'knowledge' which I am drawing on here see A822/B850:

The holding of a thing to be true ... has the following three degrees: *opining, believing* and *knowing.* *Opining* is such holding of a judgment as is consciously insufficient, not only objectively, but also subjectively. If our holding of the judgment be only subjectively sufficient, we have what is termed *believing.* Lastly, when the holding of a thing to be true is sufficient both subjectively and objectively, it is *knowledge.*

[3] Kant in fact acknowledges the existence of raw sensory material which is later 'worked up' into what he calls experience (see A1/B1).

impermissible unless he intends 'experience' to include any kind of sensory input which might connect us epistemically with a mind–independent world. His intending this whilst simultaneously taking experience to consist in propositional knowledge (ignoring its possible role as a source of grounding for concepts) is a genuine mistake, rather than the upshot of terminological preference.

When Kant thinks of experience solely as a source of knowledge of propositions, he is thinking too big. Key arguments for his anti-realist conclusions (that space is nothing but 'the subjective condition of sensibility', for instance) depend on his doing so, and can be resisted if we refuse to join him.

7.3 C. I. Lewis

As I noted in Section 6.6 above, pragmatist accounts of the a priori bear some resemblance to the proposal I have outlined, although there are also significant differences. Here I want to point out another difference: pragmatists have a tendency to think too big. C. I. Lewis is a good example.

Lewis accepts that our conceptual scheme is determined by our need to make sense of the world we experience in order to survive and succeed (see e.g. 1926: 251). But, like Carnap, he does not ask *why* some conceptual schemes enable us to be successful. What is clear is that he would not accept my answer to this question, which trades upon the claim that our concepts (or their ultimate constituents) are accurate representations of real features of the world. Lewis believes that 'we confront what is presented by the senses with certain *ready-made* distinctions, relations, and ways of classifying' (1926: 250; emphasis added), and that 'the naming, classifying, defining activity is essentially prior to investigation' (1923: 234). He assumes, that is, that sensory input can have no role in the grounding of our concepts; that the only justificatory role for the senses is that of confirming or disconfirming propositions employing previously fixed concepts. In other words he thinks too big.

Lewis allows that '[e]xperience has *instigated* our attitudes of interpretation' (1926: 250; my emphasis added), since he thinks it is the need to make sense of the confused array of raw experience which forces us to create concepts. But he does not take the further step of saying the concepts we create may be ones which are *appropriate to* differences in that raw experience. In acquiring a conceptual scheme, he says, 'I am coerced only by my own need to understand' (1923: 237). He does not consider the possibility that the world also coerces us, by dictating what sorts of concepts will satisfy that very need.

Lewis does not take this further step because he thinks we cannot respond to differences in experience before our concepts are in place. Like Kant, he does not consider the possibility that there are differences in our sensory input to which our brains and psychological mechanisms can respond in ways independent of our conceptualization of them. So he reaches a similarly anti-realist conclusion, that concepts are the mind's 'own intellectual instruments' (1930: 15). Truth in general is taken to be a joint product of the given and our mind's conceptual structuring thereof; we 'can and must prescribe the nature of reality' (1930: 16). The responsibility for a priori truth, it then follows, is ours alone: '[m]ind makes classifications and determines meanings; in so doing *it creates* the a priori truth of analytic judgments' (1923: 233; emphasis added). The a priori concerns 'the uncompelled initiative of mind' (1923: 231).

Confusingly, Lewis sometimes seems to admit that there are pre-existing distinctions, in the world or at least in experience, to which definitions or concepts can be more or less appropriate; he says that 'if definition is unsuccessful ... it is because the classification thus set up corresponds with no natural cleavage' (1930: 19). It is hard to see how to reconcile this insight with the passage, later on the same page, where he claims that unsuccessful definitions 'cannot be said to be false; they are merely useless'. Perhaps he has in mind a kind of naturalness for classifications which is a mere naturalness-for-us, rather than indicating correspondence with a mind-independent category.

Lewis also believes that if concepts were 'produced' by experience, 'knowledge would be pure feeling, and thought would be superfluous' (1926: 254). But my approach to arithmetical knowledge does not threaten the distinction between, on the one hand, the empirical input which grounds our conceptual schemes and, on the other, our *use* of those schemes in belief and reasoning. In saying that sensory input grounds our concepts we do not deny that knowing and thinking are different from the mere receiving of sensory input.

7.4 Ayer

Ayer continues the tradition of thinking too big. This habit, maintained alongside Ayer's radically empiricist approach to meaning, generates a view beset with well-known problems: traditional verificationism. Apart from 'tautologies' (which are true solely in virtue of meaning and do not 'describe any facts at all': pp. 16–17), only sentences expressing *whole propositions* which can be confirmed (or disconfirmed) by experience are meaningful, according to Ayer:

> The criterion which we use to test the genuineness of apparent statements of fact is the criterion of verifiability. We say that a sentence is factually significant to any given person, if, and only if, he knows how to verify the proposition which it purports to express—that is, if he knows what observations would lead him, under certain conditions, to accept the proposition as being true, or reject it as being false.
>
> (1936: 35)

One issue which this raises is due to the fact that the meaningfulness of sentences is importantly connected with the way in which they are built up out of sub-propositionally meaningful parts. Ayer does not consider how, or even whether, the meaningfulness of sub-propositional representations might depend directly upon *their* relationship to experience, or how their meaningfulness might be related to that of sentences. There is no argument that only the relationship between experience and propositional representations, rather than (also) that between experience and concepts, is relevant to meaningfulness.

Ayer does consider the possibility of a concept's being a mere 'pseudo-concept' (see his ch. 6). For instance, he says that ethical concepts are pseudo-concepts, meaning that '[t]he presence of an ethical symbol in a proposition adds nothing to its factual content' (p. 107). His argument for this view, however, is that pure ethical sentences (such as 'Stealing is wrong') express nothing which can be confirmed or disconfirmed by experience, and that complex sentences involving ethical and other vocabulary (such as 'You acted wrongly in stealing that money') have verifiable content only in so far as they have verifiable non-ethical content. That is to say, for Ayer, it appears that the meaningfulness (verifiability) of certain whole sentences is what is relevant to the meaningfulness of ethical terms and the authenticity of ethical concepts. Sentence meaning seems to be construed as primary, which potentially creates a tension with compositionality (more on this in Section 7.5 below).

I am reasonably sympathetic to the idea of placing empiricist restrictions of some kind or other on what should count as meaningful; this has its attractions from a naturalistic point of view. It may well be right to think that we cannot accept any notion of meaning which allows meaning to be totally disconnected from the kinds of things that the senses can put us in touch with. But the senses, I have suggested, are not merely a source of confirmation for whole propositions. Once we think small, that is once we accept that sensory input can justify concepts, we can envisage a more subtle connection between meaningfulness and empirical input. We can demand that, for a proposition to be meaningful, it should involve only concepts which can be justified or disjustified by empirical input (as suggested in Section 5.6 above). This obviously does not entail traditional verificationism or share its undesirable consequences, but it preserves what is attractive about it, in that it insists that meaningfulness be restricted to that with which our senses can put us in touch. Besides its other benefits, therefore, thinking small enables us to offer a new and more plausible empirical constraint on meaningfulness.

Ayer's epistemological line concerning the true sentences of mathematics and logic is one of the now-traditional 'moderate empiricist' lines: he claims that these sentences are analytic and have no factual content (see Ayer 1936: 74–85). They can be known a priori, by thinking about the meanings of the words they contain, because they serve only to illustrate 'the way in which we use certain symbols' (p. 79). He says that:

We see, then, that there is nothing mysterious about our apodeictic certainty of logic and mathematics. Our knowledge that no observation can ever confute the proposition '7 + 5 = 12' depends simply on the fact that the symbolic expression '7 + 5' is synonymous with '12', just as our knowledge that every oculist is an eye-doctor depends on the fact that the symbol 'eye-doctor' is synonymous with 'oculist.' And the same explanation holds good for every other *a priori* truth.

(p. 85)

Ayer does not consider the possibility that the way we use certain symbols—and, correspondingly, the nature of the concepts those symbols are used to express—might itself be a guide to matters of fact about the mind-

and language-independent world. Correlatively, he does not consider the role that experience might play in shaping our concepts so that they can serve as such a guide.

7.5 Quine

Quine (1960 and elsewhere) attempts to defend mathematical realism against epistemological objections by thinking even bigger than anyone I've considered so far. He takes the smallest units of empirical confirmation to be not individual propositions, but total theories (i.e. large collections of propositions). And the issue of what to take as a unit of empirical confirmation is, for Quine as for Ayer, intimately bound up with the question of what to count as a unit of meaning. He writes:

> The totality of our so-called knowledge or beliefs … is a man-made fabric which impinges on experience only along the edges … A conflict with experience at the periphery occasions readjustments in the interior of the field … But the total field is so undetermined by its boundary conditions, experience, that there is much latitude of choice as to what statements to re-evaluate in the light of any single contrary experience … If this view is right, *it is misleading to speak of the empirical content of an individual statement…*
>
> (1951: 39–40; emphasis added)

And, again, in a similar vein:

> The idea of defining a symbol in use was … an advance over the impossible term-by-term empiricism of Locke and Hume. The statement, rather than the term, came with Frege to be recognized as the unit accountable to an empiricist critique. But what I am now urging is that even in taking the statement as unit we have drawn our grid too finely. The unit of empirical significance is the whole of science.
>
> (1951: 42)

In other words, Quine wants not only to reject 'term-by-term empiricism' (of roughly the kind I am interested in resurrecting), but also the kind of 'sentence-by-sentence empiricism' which Ayer dealt in. Like Ayer, Quine wants the units of confirmation and (at least the primary) units of meaningfulness or content to be the same. And, by analogy with one of the issues facing Ayer, we can note that Quine's view is in tension with the (relatively uncontroversial) fact that the content of a total theory or web of belief depends crucially on the content of its sentence-sized (and sub-sentence-sized) parts.

My suggestion is that on this issue Quine moved us in exactly the wrong direction (although I hope it is obvious from the preceding sections that I also believe he provided many crucial building blocks for an improved view to work with). Certain potential issues raised by 'sentence-by-sentence' empiricism are exacerbated rather than resolved by Quine's 'theory-by-theory' proposal.

Also, it would be dangerous to claim (and Ayer does not do so) that *only* sentences have meaning, because only they can be tested. The intimate relationship between sentence meaning and word meaning would be unjustifiably ignored if one were to claim this. Yet Quine does precisely this sort of thing at the next level up, claiming that *only* theories, and not the individual sentences or statements that make them up, have 'empirical content'. It is pretty uncontroversial that the meaning of a total theory is intimately related to the meanings of the sentences that make it up (together, perhaps, with facts about how those sentences are arranged), just as the meaning of a sentence is intimately related to the meaning of its sub-sentential parts.

Even a weaker quasi-Quinean or (quasi?-)Ayerian claim, to the effect that theory meaning or sentence meaning is *prior to* (as opposed to: precludes) meaningfulness for smaller units, is problematic. Features like compositionality suggest that it is in fact the meanings of sub-sentential parts that (together with facts about syntax) determine the meanings of sentence-sized representations, not the other way around.[4]

My view is that we should proceed in the opposite direction to that indicated by Quine. Thinking small—thinking about experience as a source of justification and grounding for concepts rather than merely sentences (or theories)—is compatible with thinking that the smallest (primary, non-derivative) units of meaning should also be the smallest units of empirical justification. Taking concept-sized representations to play both roles is a plausible option, and it genuinely alleviates the compositionality problems I have been discussing for 'sentence-by-sentence' and 'theory-by-theory' empiricism.

---

[4] This is, in essence, the 'First Problem' described by Pagin (1997: sect. 1) for combining compositionality with holism. Note that Pagin's ways of arguing that there is no tension between compositionality and *some* kinds of holism do not apply to the holistic views under discussion here.

Thinking super-big does not in Quine's case engender anti-realism concerning the subject matters traditionally thought of as a priori (as it does for Kant, Lewis, and Ayer), but it does leave him unable to defend his empiricist realism adequately. It is because he thinks super-big that he feels pressure to reject the category of the a priori, and that of the analytic, with which he tends to identify it. The analytic is rejected on the grounds that it assumes a smaller unit of meaning (and sameness-of-meaning) than a total theory, and Quine does not think it makes sense to talk about such smaller units of meaning because there are no smaller units of empirical confirmation.[5]

That Quine cannot deal with the intuition that there is a difference in kind between our knowledge of arithmetic and our knowledge of physics has been one of the significant sources of philosophical resistance to his view (and rightly so, in my opinion). If, unlike Quine, we take *concepts* to be empirically justifiable, we can remove the appearance of incompatibility between empiricism and a priori knowledge, in the manner I have outlined. Moreover, we do this without denying that the units of meaningfulness and the units of empirical justification should be the same. So it may well be that a priori knowledge in my sense is to be had in virtue of what Quine would think of as a kind of analyticity. But his objection to analyticity, resting as it does on a *different* view as to what are the smallest units of empirical confirmation, need not concern us.

Note that one can, if one wishes, retain a kind of confirmational holism while rejecting the practice of thinking too big. Thinking small only

---

[5] He emphasizes concerns about the adequacy of attempts to say what analyticity amounts to, and in so far as these concerns are supposed to stand on their own two feet as an argument against the analytic, they are vulnerable to the responses made by Grice and Strawson (1956), who stress that inadequacy of explication would not be sufficient reason to reject the notion, and that in any case Quine sets too high a standard for such adequacy in this case. However, as Grice and Strawson rightly note (p. 142), the positive views outlined late in Quine (1951) are doing much of the heavy lifting in his case against analyticity. I do not think that either of the aspects of Quine's view which Grice and Strawson take to be playing this role—i.e. his rejection of the idea that some statements are immune from revision and his confirmational holism—is quite the one that Quine's case actually rests on. Or rather, more cautiously (since Quine exegesis is hard), it *might* well be that Quine intends his case to rest, at least in part, upon the assimilation of units of meaning with units of confirmation. He might be intending us to join him in thinking that this assimilation, *together* with his confirmational holism, enforces the rejection of a notion of sameness of meaning for sentence-sized representations. The envisaged lack of immunity to revision is, on this exegetical hypothesis, appealed to in order to make vivid the claim that confirmational holism means we cannot associate any individual statement too closely with any particular sets of experiences which would confirm or disconfirm it, and therefore that we cannot associate any individual statement too closely with any particular empirical import, or meaning.

requires that we acknowledge the possibility of concept grounding; it has no implications for the nature of grounding for propositions (except in the case of conceptual truths). It is thus compatible with believing that empirical grounding accrues to propositions *directly* (as opposed to in virtue of their being conceptual truths involving only grounded concepts) only qua parts of total theories which are empirically grounded. In other words, we could allow that as far as *direct* empirical confirmation for things other than concepts goes, Quine is right to say that sentence-sized beliefs do not get confirmed individually, but only whole theories at once.

Those who deal in concept grounding might also be holists in another way: that is, we might take whole conceptual schemes, rather than individual concepts, to be units of empirical justification. I'll call this view *justificatory concept holism.*[6] This might be motivated by sympathy with Quine's reasons for adopting justificatory holism for belief justification, or independently. (For instance, one might think that holism is inappropriate for belief confirmation but appropriate for concept justification, because it is possible to identify experiences which justify individual beliefs but impossible to identify experiences which justify individual concepts.)

I make no assumptions here as to whether one, both, or neither of these forms of holism should be adopted. Although I appeal to the indispensability of arithmetical concepts, and indispensability arguments are traditionally associated with holism, I do not assume the kind of justificatory concept holism just described. A concept's appearing indispensably in our best theories is only construed as *evidence* of its empirical justification. Not much follows, as I see it, about what that justification is like in itself. Thus even if confirmational holism must be assumed by all indispensability arguments that directly concern arithmetical propositions rather than concepts—and for some versions of the argument this is far from clear—justificatory concept holism is not being assumed in this book. (Which is not, of course, to deny that it might be *argued for* on the basis of things I *do* assume here.) Some versions of the ordinary indispensability argument that do not appear to require holism include Resnik's 'pragmatic' version

[6] A cautionary note: Quine talks about justification for selecting a conceptual scheme (1951: 43), and suggests that holistic considerations should be employed. But for him there is no difference between adopting or revising a conceptual scheme and adopting or revising certain beliefs (as he stresses in this very passage). For me, there is an important difference (see pp. 132–4). So the kind of holism I am describing here is not to be confused with anything that Quine adopts.

(1997: 46–8), and indeed any version which claims only that our best theory, *however confirmed*, includes quantification over mathematical objects. Confirmational molecularism is pretty clearly enough of a basis for the latter kind of argument. Confirmational molecularism for propositions holds that propositions get confirmed in clusters, rather than individually (confirmational atomism) or as total theories (confirmational holism).

It might be asked whether justificatory concept holism would undercut the claim that by thinking of concepts as units of justification we can alleviate the problem of accounting for compositionality that I discussed above. But I don't think so, for two reasons. First, recall that this is only a problem for those who maintain that the smallest primary units of meaning should also be the smallest units of empirical justification. It might be felt preferable to adopt justificatory concept holism and drop this assumption.

A second option is to conclude that conceptual schemes, rather than individual concepts, are indeed the primary units of meaning, that is, accept what I'll call *semantic concept holism*, but deny that this is in tension with compositionality. One way to argue this would be to point out that the relations of dependence invoked by compositionalists who are also semantic concept holists are not supposed to hold in both directions between the same two things. According to a semantic concept holist who accepts compositionality, theories depend for their meanings on the meanings of their constituent sentence-sized representations, sentence-sized represent-ations depend for their meanings on the meanings of their constituent concept-sized representations, and concept-sized representations depend for their meanings on the nature of our whole conceptual scheme, which is where the chain of dependence ends.[7]

It may also be helpful to notice that a midway position between holism and atomism is available, with regard to both justification and meaning. A *justificatory concept molecularist* holds that concepts are justified in groups rather than individually, but that these groups are smaller than whole conceptual schemes. A *semantic concept molecularist* holds that the primary units of meaning are groups of concepts rather than individual concepts, but that these groups are smaller than whole conceptual schemes. (For the record, I am inclined towards molecularism of both kinds.)

---

[7] This option has similarities to Pagin's preferred resolution to his 'First Problem' for combining compositionality with holism, in his (1997: sect. 1). The rest of what he says in this section and the previous section (headed 'Preliminaries') is also germane to the present discussion.

7.6 Fodor

The later chapters of Fodor (1998) include a discussion of whether we can rationally base our concepts on our experience. Fodor concludes that (in the cases he considers) we cannot, and this leads him to think that these concepts are constituted by our responses to the world, rather than being reflections of the world's mind-independent structure. One thing which is interesting about Fodor's discussion, however, is that he does some justice to the contrary view.

Fodor is interested in defending a position which he calls 'informational atomism'. This consists in the following two theses:

(a) Most lexical concepts have no internal structure.
(b) Content is constituted by some nomic mind–world relation.

In his chapter 6, he is concerned to respond to an argument (which he calls the 'standard argument') purporting to show that informational atomism leads to radical nativism about concepts. The premise of the standard argument is that acquiring[8] a concept C must be an inductive process, whereby hypotheses as to which property a thing must have in order to fall under C are formed and empirically tested. From this it is argued that, since to formulate such a hypothesis one needs to possess C, no basic concept can ever be acquired. (Note how similar this is to Kant's argument that concepts of space and time cannot be derived from experience.) Since informational atomism asserts that most concepts are basic, it follows that most concepts cannot be acquired and hence must be innate. (Fodor himself was once sympathetic to nativism—see e.g. his 1975: 82 ff.—but he is opposed to it here.)

This is clearly an argument which belongs to the tradition of thinking too big: it assumes that the senses can only ground a *hypothesis* about the nature of C, and not C itself. Fodor does consider some ways to resist the standard argument: we could, with Ryle (1949), argue that concept possession is know-how rather than know-that. But he says that this would get us nowhere until we could show that know-how can be acquired without our conducting something like the kind of inductive

---

[8] Note that although Fodor is interested in concept acquisition rather than concept grounding, I assume that the relevant points could be taken to carry across.

process described above. He acknowledges that we could question the standard argument's initial premise, which states that empirical concept acquisition must be inductive. But if this premise is denied, we need some other explanation as to why it is experience of doorknobs which gives one the concept *doorknob*, rather than experience of cows. This grounds what Fodor calls a 'what-else?' argument for the view that concept acquisition is inductive (p. 133).

He considers a 'Darwinian' response to this 'what-else?' argument. Fodor's Darwinian argues that a psychological mechanism which triggers acquisition of the concept X in the presence of Xs is more useful than one which triggers acquisition of the concept Y in the presence of Xs, so we would expect the former kind of mechanism to be selected for over the course of our evolution. Thus, according to this Darwinian, it is probable that we possess from birth some such concept-selecting mechanism, and there is no reason to suppose it to be the same as the cognitive process by which we inductively confirm various hypotheses.[9]

Fodor has two objections to this. First, he says, Darwinian hand-waving tells us nothing about the actual mechanism supposedly involved in selecting concepts for us, so we are not yet in a position to say there is some such mechanism and that it is non-inductive. Second, according to Fodor, '[y]ou can only trigger a concept that's there, genetically specified, waiting to be triggered', so this response is really nativism in (a thin) disguise.

However, Fodor's first objection neglects the fact that Darwinian hand-waving is not required to show *which* non-inductive concept-forming mechanisms we might have, but merely to make it plausible that we could have *some*. That is enough to defeat a 'what-else?' argument of the kind under consideration.

His second objection trades on an ambiguity. Fodor appears to have been misled by his own terminology here. He calls our concept-generating mechanisms 'concept-triggering' mechanisms. If we use this term, we are liable to suppose that a concept-triggering mechanism can only trigger concepts which are already there. But Fodor gives us no reason to suppose that the mechanisms which evolution selects to generate concepts which are appropriate to our environment are merely 'triggering' mechanisms in *this* sense.

---

[9] This Darwinian view bears some resemblance to what I have called the 'camera brain' hypothesis (Section 4.5 above), though it leaves out some epistemologically important aspects.

Fodor's own proposal is that many concepts are like the concept *doorknob*, about which he says: 'being a doorknob is having the property to which minds like ours generalize from experiences (as of) [*sic*] the properties by which the doorknob stereotype is constituted' (p. 140). This is supposed to explain why it is experience of doorknobs that gives us the concept of *doorknob*, without recourse to an inductive view of concept acquisition. It is intended as an answer to the 'what–else?' argument. But it isn't the only possible answer, as we have seen. By thinking small we are able to remove the motivation for Fodor's position.

7.7 Summary

The habit of thinking too big, that is, thinking of the senses solely as a source of confirmation for propositions, has perhaps been the most important obstacle to the development of a theory of arithmetical knowledge of the kind discussed in Chapter 4. This habit makes empirical grounding for concepts seem impossible. I have traced the assumption that sensory input grounds only propositions through Kant, C. I. Lewis, Ayer, Quine, and Fodor, but found no convincing argument for it—rather, it appears repeatedly as an unargued assumption or a premise in other arguments.

I shall now move on to consider some other, subtler, objections to the very idea of empirical grounding for arithmetical concepts.

8

More On The Very Idea
of Concept Grounding

8.1 Introduction

In this chapter, I first consider some general objections to empirical concept grounding, derived from McDowell's *Mind and World*. Then I consider whether arithmetical concepts in particular are too rich to be grounded in sensory input. Among other things, I shall argue that certain theories from experimental psychology supply no basis for such objections since the issue of whether arithmetical concepts are innate is tangential to the epistemology of arithmetic.

8.2 McDowell[1]

McDowell has put forward some arguments which ought, if successful, to rule out the kind of proposal I outlined in Chapter 4. McDowell offers these arguments in the context of arguing against a more well-known target than the view I develop here; namely, traditional forms of empirical foundationalism. Nonetheless, he takes himself to have shown that our concepts cannot have any rational empirical basis, so it is important to assess his arguments to that effect.[2]

Among the many philosophers who reject the possibility of a rational empirical basis for our concepts McDowell is unusual, in that he argues against it in ways which do not rely on his thinking too big (see Chapter 7

---

[1] Thanks to Aidan McGlynn for helping me think about this section.

[2] These arguments are also relevant insofar as I am correct in thinking that by developing my proposal we may be able to rescue a kind of empirical foundationalism from certain standard objections (see my Final Remarks).

above). These are to be found in his (1994). The main argument is given in the first lecture, though we shall see that other parts of the book are also relevant in so far as they reveal some of the motivations and assumptions at work in the main argument.

McDowell cannot be accused of thinking too big. It is true that he reserves the word 'experience' for conceptualized experience (see e.g. p. 10). He also seems to think that what it supplies is proposition-sized pieces of information. He says, for instance, that '[i]n experience one takes in, for instance sees, *that things are thus and so*' (p. 9, emphasis in the original). But, as I have stressed, what matters for our purposes is not what one calls 'experience', but rather whether one admits the possibility of sensory grounding for concepts. McDowell is prepared to consider the possibility that what he calls 'observational' concepts are (as he puts it) constitutively related to our sensory justification for applying them, that conceptual capacities are therefore 'acquired from confrontations with suitable bits of the Given' ('the Given' being, I take it, closely related to what I call sensory input), and that in this way 'empirical substance is infused into concepts' (p. 7). If we are allowed to think of empirical concepts as related to sensory input in this way, it will be a relatively easy further step to say that it is sensory input which epistemically *grounds* our possession of them. Since these concepts are constitutively related to the bits of the given which lead to their acquisition, contact with the given results in the concepts' being non-accidentally accurate representations of the relevant bits of the given. McDowell does not accept that any concepts really *are* related to the given in the way described. But at least he does not dismiss it out of hand, by saying that in order to experience something we must already have the concept of that kind of thing.

Not, of course, that this is the only way to understand the empirical grounding of concepts. For one thing, it is too simplistic to think that the only way sensory input can justify a concept of a property is by bringing one into contact with things which have the property (see Section 5.3 above). But perhaps in the case of whatever 'observational' concepts McDowell has in mind this sort of simplicity is acceptable. For another, I do not think a concept needs to be constitutively related to sensory input in order to be empirically grounded. And, third, our story about concept grounding needn't be an acquisition story (see Section 4.3 above). But, still, McDowell is taking seriously *a* view on which empirical concept grounding would make sense.

McDowell's own world-view is basically a Kantian view *manquée*: it differs from Kant's in leaving out the transcendental aspects. He proposes that experience is passive, and yet that it involves an element of 'spontaneity', an element of our own contribution, different from mere 'receptivity' yet not even notionally separable from it (see e.g. p. 9). The element of 'spontaneity' is due to the fact that conceptual capacities are drawn upon in experience, and, necessarily, these same capacities can also be used spontaneously in 'active thought': to make judgements, and to reason.

Why the fact that conceptual capacities are drawn upon in experience means there is always an element of our own contribution in experience is not at all clear. The essential point for McDowell, however, is that the passive element of experience is not even theoretically separable from the spontaneous (or conceptual) element. Attempts to separate out the passive part are misguided. In my terminology, this amounts to saying we should not try to think about mere sensory input as divorced from the concepts we draw upon in conceptualized experience. But, unlike some, McDowell realizes it will take an argument to establish this—it can't just be assumed.

What McDowell aims to do is to undercut any motivation for believing in a distinction between the conceptual and the given by showing that such a distinction cannot do the kind of work its proponents want it to do: that is, that the given cannot provide a rational basis for judgement. This does not amount to a direct argument that there is no such distinction. Nevertheless, it is crucial for our purposes, as I want to make the distinction do just the kind of work McDowell argues it cannot do.

Although he sympathizes with the felt need to postulate the given, in order to have something that rationally constrains our thought 'from outside', McDowell says this craving is impossible to satisfy. The central argument for this claim appears on pages 7–8. McDowell first characterizes belief in the given as belief that 'the space of reasons, the space of justifications or warrants, extends more widely than the conceptual sphere'. What he means is that believers in the given think that justifications may come from unconceptualized sources (such as the mind-independent world, or unconceptualized sensory input). The aim, as he says, is to posit some constraint on our conceptualized thinking from the outside. Such constraint, he explains, must be 'the result of an alien force, the causal impact of the world'. This too seems to me probable (though I might use different imagery if I were making the point). But McDowell also claims that, while such impact would ensure that we 'cannot be blamed' for what happens at the boundary between our conceptualized thought processes and the unconceptualized input to those processes, it cannot constitute a *justification* for what happens there. As he puts it, 'the idea of the Given offers exculpations where we wanted justifications'. On this point I disagree.

McDowell has made an assumption in order to derive the conclusion that sensory input cannot be justificatory from the premise that it is unconceptualized. His argument requires the additional premise that nothing unconceptualized can constitute a justification for anything. Unfortunately, as McDowell himself admits, he '[does] not offer any argument... for the claim that only what is conceptually shaped can justify';[3] this seems to him to 'stand on its own feet' (2002: 293).

Putnam has noted the failure to argue this point (2002: 183−5), and assumes that McDowell's basis for his claim is an assumption to the effect that efficient causes cannot be justifications. But, Putnam argues, McDowell's reasons for saying this rest heavily on the attribution to his opponent of a Davidsonian picture of what experiential impacts are like and how they relate to beliefs. Others, such as functionalists, 'would simply not see why an experience... could not be both a cause and a justification of a belief'. McDowell replies (p. 293) that he doesn't rule out the possibility of X being both a cause and a justification of Y, but rather simply denies that anything *non-conceptual* could be a justification. However, he is forced here to point out that he does not argue for the latter assumption at all. Putnam's misreading is apparently due to a charitable attempt to find some basis for such a crucial premise in McDowell's argument.

Blackburn (2006) shares my uneasiness concerning the way McDowell thinks about justification. Blackburn discusses the case of Mary, who believes that there is butter in the fridge because she went and looked, and she saw it. He says that the causal relationship between the butter and Mary's belief is crucial to our understanding of why she is justified in that belief. McDowell, Blackburn says, does not ignore platitudes like this, but 'it is fair to worry whether causation is entirely central to McDowell's

---

[3] A cautionary note: McDowell cannot simply mean that only what is *shaped in the same way* as our concepts can justify. This is a claim I might accept, since I think sensory input may justify our concepts by being structured in a way that corresponds to the structure of those concepts. But if his argument is to go through, McDowell must mean rather that only what is shaped *by* concepts, i.e. conceptualized, can justify.

thinking. Could the notion of spontaneity take its leading role if it were? There is nothing spontaneous in any ordinary sense about Mary's coming into awareness of the butter, however many conceptual abilities are in play as she does so' (p. 209). The activities of looking and seeing may involve the use of Mary's conceptual capacities, but it is not at all clear that they involve them in the right sort of way for us to deny that Mary's justification comes from 'outside the conceptual sphere'. McDowell's determination to the contrary is supported by nothing more than some rather vivid imagery (particularly evident on page 8 of McDowell 1994).

One possible reason for McDowell's making the assumption that only what is conceptualized can justify is that he is an epistemological internalist. This is not something he discusses in so many words in his (1994), but if he did believe (a certain version of) the claim that all justification must be accessible to the subject, this might be what is causing him to conclude that unconceptualized causal impact is not a source of justification. It is not clear whether such an inference would be reasonable, however. One might become aware of an unconceptualized causal impact on oneself and of its role in justifying one's beliefs. The process of becoming aware of the impact would require conceptualizing the impact, but still it might be the impact itself—unconceptualized—that is and was one's justification.

Although McDowell does not announce his internalism as such in *Mind and World*, he does say that 'we cannot really understand the relations in virtue of which a judgement is warranted except as relations within the space of concepts: relations such as implication or probabilification, which hold between potential exercises of conceptual capacities' (p. 7). Internalist leanings are also suggested by McDowell's repeatedly distinguishing between 'causal' and 'rational' influences on our thought processes (see e.g. p. 34). But it is simply begging the question against the externalist (not to mention certain kinds of internalist) to assume that unconceptualized causal influences cannot play a rationalizing role; at least one prominent externalist has argued that knowledge is in fact *fully analysable* in terms of causation (see Alvin Goldman 1967). I do not make that claim, but I do think the physical effects of the world on the brain explain our possessing the concepts we do, and explain it in the right sort of way for those concepts to count as grounded.

It is unclear whether, or to what extent, any version of internalism is what is actually motivating McDowell. On pages 4–5, he makes some remarks about freedom which may be supposed to suggest another motivation. Here he seems to be endorsing a view he attributes to Kant: that 'rational necessitation' is 'constitutive' of freedom. So no freedom, no reasons. And freedom for McDowell is closely associated with the exercise of conceptual capacities. One hopes this is not his sole motivation, since the existence of any interesting relationship between normativity and freedom is highly controversial in the epistemic case, and certainly ought not be assumed at the outset of an argument against realistic epistemology.[4] The same goes for the association between freedom and the exercise of conceptual capacities.

8.3 'Arithmetical concepts are too rich to be grounded in sensory input'

Arithmetical concepts, if they are to serve as an epistemic basis for (much of) our arithmetical knowledge in the way I envisage, must be extremely rich in content, and unusual in various ways. They have a number of features which might be thought to put pressure on the claim that they are grounded in experience. This section investigates some of them.

One thing that is unusual about our arithmetical concepts is that they (seem to) include concepts of *abstract* objects. A corresponding worry is that it is hard to see how empirical input could ground a concept of an abstract object. Such input could, perhaps, ground concepts closely tied to experience: concepts, say, of objects, like apples, and properties, like shape, which are straightforwardly empirically detectable. But how could a concept of an abstract object be constructed using concepts such as these? We don't seem to get far by disjoining, conjoining, negating, etc. these more obviously empirical concepts.[5] It may be that we can construct abstract number concepts from less abstract concepts in a manner inspired by neo-Fregean abstraction (see Section 4.3 above), but this debate seems to me too unsettled for it to be desirable to rest a response to the present worry on its outcome.

My preferred response is that, on the picture I envisage, concepts of abstract objects need not be grounded purely in virtue of being constructed

---

[4] See e.g. Feldman (2000: sect. C) and Jenkins (2007b: 30).
[5] Thanks to Patricia Blanchette here.

out of other grounded concepts, but may, at least in some cases, be grounded directly, by earning their keep in helping us to make best sense of our sensory input. There is no reason to doubt—and, I think, some reason to believe—that (simple) concepts of abstract objects earn their keep in this sense. I think, for instance, that the indispensability of quantification over numbers in our best scientific theories (in conjunction with the difficulty of seeing how number concepts could be constructed out of other, non-abstract, concepts) is evidence that something like this is going on. It is not only concepts which are closely tied to experience in the sense envisaged in the previous paragraph that are susceptible of empirical grounding in my sense.

Another respect in which arithmetical concepts might seem different in kind from (most, or at least many) ordinary empirical concepts is that arithmetical concepts (or at least most of them) are completely non-vague. While there might be borderline candidate instances of cathood, mountainhood, redness, and so on, there are no borderline candidates for being a number divisible by three without remainder. It might therefore be asked whether sensory input can sensibly be said to ground concepts which are so *determinate* as our arithmetical concepts. One apparent reason to doubt that it can is that it seems that what we learn through the senses can always be made *more* determinate, and hence can never be regarded as *fully* determinate. We could never, for instance, conclusively establish that an object is a perfect circle by looking at it: however powerful a magnifying lens we used, it would always be possible that the circle was imperfect, although we would need an even more powerful lens to detect this.[6] Does this not sit uncomfortably with the claim that sensory input can ground concepts which are fully determinate in the sense described above?

Not unless we adopt the kind of simplistic view of concept grounding rejected in Section 5.3 above whereby we must actually experience instances of a concept in order for sensory input to ground that concept. I have suggested that whenever sensory input renders a concept indispensably useful, we should take that concept to be justified by that input. If the concept of a perfect circle is indispensable to the effort to render our sensory input comprehensible, then it does not matter if we can never actually see perfect circles.

---

[6] Cf. Wright's discussion of limit concepts in his (1986: 14–15).

Moreover, as regards concepts of number, which are more relevant here than concepts of shape, we surely *can* experience things as fully determinate in the required way. Once a sortal is fixed upon, there is no vagueness as to whether the playing cards I see in front of me are 52 in number or not, and nor is there any indeterminacy with respect to *that* question in my experience of the cards. I might make a mistake in counting them, but once a correct visual count has been performed, there is no way for a further, more detailed, visual investigation to tell me to a higher level of determinacy (as opposed to, say, a higher level of certainty) whether or not there are 52 cards.

A more interesting worry, I think, is the following. How can a finite amount of sensory input ever justify a particular concept over various rivals? Surely no finite amount of sensory input could distinguish epistemically between a 'straight' concept like *plus* and all the 'bent' alternatives along the lines of Kripke's *quus* (see Kripke 1982)?[7] In fact, I am inclined to think that if *plus* is grounded then concepts like *quus* are probably grounded too, in virtue of their being composed of other grounded concepts. But the general worry remains that a finite amount of sensory input cannot distinguish between two concepts (or sets of concepts) whose relationship to sensory input is exactly the same as far as the finite amount of actual input goes, but which diverge in content in some way that is not highlighted by this input.

One thing to note about this problem is that it does not threaten to undermine the thought that some account of arithmetical knowledge along the lines of Chapter 4 is the right account of any such knowledge that we may have. It is a threat only to the claim that we *have* some arithmetical knowledge. The bogeyman here is a form of arithmetical scepticism. Those who doubt that epistemology is in the business of defeating scepticism may not yet see any problem here at all.

The problem (if there is one) is no worse than that which arises when we consider the familiar problem of the underdetermination of empirical *beliefs* by empirical data. The worry here is that a finite amount of sensory input cannot distinguish between the target propositions and a number of deviant, but observationally equivalent, alternatives. This is a very close

---

[7] This question must be kept distinct from a well-known issue which arises more directly from Kripke (1982). Kripke's Wittgenstein argues that, by dint of our finite nature, no fact about us determines whether we have up till now been using *plus* or *quus*.

analogue of our worry about the underdetermination of concepts by empirical data.

In the propositional case, many philosophers think that we can—and should—select a theory from among empirically equivalent alternatives by applying other criteria, such as simplicity, explanatory power, unificatory power, or fruitfulness. And many think that theories which are simpler, more explanatory and so on are not merely pragmatically better to believe but epistemically better. (Nolan (unpublished) has a description of some of the dangers of thinking otherwise.)

This type of response can be modified to make it applicable to concepts as well.[8] For instance, we can say that, if two concepts have an equally good fit with our sensory input but one of them is simpler than the other, we should (epistemically, and not merely pragmatically) prefer the simpler concept. It is an interesting question which of the other theoretical virtues that are often cited in defence of our preference for one of many observationally equivalent theories have analogues at the level of concepts. To some extent, it may be possible for conceptual virtues to piggyback on theoretical virtues: so, for instance, it might be a virtue of a concept, or set of concepts, if it enables us to formulate a theory which is more explanatory, unified, fruitful, or whatever than any which can be formulated using other empirically equivalent concepts. There may also be more direct analogues in some cases: perhaps, for instance, certain concepts are themselves 'fruitful' in some relevant sense, or help to 'unify' our conceptual scheme. There might also, for all I have said, be some conceptual virtues which are not analogues of theoretical virtues.

One thing that might seem a bit puzzling about this claim is *how* exactly concepts with more virtues are 'chosen' over others. Take simplicity, for example. It is relatively easy to see how simpler, neater *compounds*

---

[8] It may seem that conceptual virtues in something like my sense are under discussion in Quine (1948: 16–17)—

[W]e adopt, at least insofar as we are reasonable, the simplest conceptual scheme into which the disordered fragments of raw experience can be fitted and arranged. Our ontology is determined once we have fixed upon the over-all conceptual scheme which is to accommodate science in the broadest sense ...

—and in his (1950: 78–9), where the pragmatic usefulness and 'elegance' of conceptual schemes are discussed. However, in Quine (1951) a 'conceptual scheme' is identified as something that includes 'an ontology' (that is, a view or theory about what exists), and in his (1950) our 'conceptual scheme' is identified with 'our philosophy', and 'concepts' with (bits of) our language (p. 79). So it is far from clear that in these passages Quine intends anything akin to what I am interested in here.

of existing concepts might be more or less consciously chosen over less simple compounds. But what about the concepts which are justified directly by experience rather than through being composed of justified concepts? The idea here is that we possess sub-personal or otherwise non-conscious mechanisms which favour the adoption of the simplest or neatest concepts which will serve the purpose of making sense of our sensory input, the workings of which are not necessarily recoverable by conscious introspection. We do not—at least in most cases—do any conscious choosing of our directly grounded concepts.

There are familiar objections to the simplicity response to the under-determination worry for propositional beliefs. Notably, there is the worry that we have no particular reason to think that simplicity is a guide to truth. (The same worry can be raised about explanatory power, fruitfulness, and so on.) This sort of worry might be adapted to the conceptual version of that response: we might worry, for instance, that we have no particular reason to think that simplicity is a guide to fittingness or accuracy. But as far as the current work is concerned I shall be satisfied with establishing that empirical grounding for concepts is shown to be no *more* prone to underdetermination worries than empirical confirmation for our best scientific theories.

One might suspect that concepts *are* more prone to such worries than propositions, however. For, in addition to the foregoing point, there is another issue which seems damaging to the simplicity response in the conceptual case. An objector can admit that our concepts seem simpler to us than any 'deviant' empirically equivalent concepts, but doubt whether they would seem so to a user of the alternative concepts. To them, surely ours would seem to be the less simple, 'bent', concepts (cf. Goodman 1954: ch. 4). On what grounds, then, can we assert that our concepts are *really* simpler?[9]

---

[9] Another point which could lead to confusion if not addressed here concerns Kripke's dismissal of another kind of simplicity response to his own (distinct—see n. 7 above) underdetermination worry. Kripke writes: 'Let no-one—under the influence of too much philosophy of science—suggest that the hypothesis that I meant plus is to be preferred as the *simplest* hypothesis' (1982: 38). This suggestion is rejected because it could only help us to *know* that I meant plus by 'plus', and could not show what fact about me *made it the case* that I meant plus. Kripke's argument here has been diagnosed as question-begging (see Wright 1984). But, in any case, the suggestion Kripke rejects is not analogous to the one I propose here. I do not propose that the hypothesis that experience justifies the concept *plus* is the simplest hypothesis, but rather that *plus* is a simpler concept than *quus* or any other deviant alternative.

In fact, however, this problem is not specific to the relationship between sensory input and concepts either. It has an analogue at the level of propositional justification. Background beliefs will influence one's assessment of the simplicity of a theory. For instance, if my background beliefs were Christian, I might suppose that the simplest theory which accounted for my presence on earth was one invoking God's purposes and creative powers. If they were atheistic, it might seem simpler to suppose that I exist here and now as the product of a massive accidental chain of purely physical causes and effects.[10] Simplicity for beliefs or theories therefore seems as much in danger of depending upon one's epistemic situation as does simplicity for concepts.

Before we leave the topic of underdetermination, one further question worth considering is whether it could turn out that no concept or set of concepts is ever grounded by sensory input, because whichever concepts we happen to light upon, there will always be another equally good set, even taking into account all the conceptual virtues (simplicity, explanatory power, fruitfulness, unificatoriness, and so on).

It would be quite extreme to suppose that this was so (and I'm not sure how one could begin to argue for it). But even if it were true, it might still be possible to identify elements of common structure between the various equally good conceptual schemes, in which case concept constituents or concept compounds corresponding to these elements of common structure might turn out to be indispensable, and we would have something to work with. If one is extreme enough to doubt even this, I do not know how to respond. But, once again, all we have is an analogue of a problem familiar from the propositional case. In just the same way, for any scientific theory, one might suppose that it will always be possible to formulate an alternative theory which fares equally well even when all the theoretical virtues (simplicity, explanatory power, unificatoriness, and so on) are taken into account. I don't yet see any *special* reason to be concerned about the concept-level version of this worry.

---

[10] It might be argued that for this reason only *total belief systems* can be assessed for relative simplicity. But this manoeuvre does not solve any problems. The issue surfaces again at the level of total belief systems, because total belief systems include beliefs as to what counts as a simple belief system. Thus it could happen that belief system A appears simpler from within A than does a rival system B, although from within B, B appears simpler than A.

A different argument that sensory input is not rich enough to underwrite arithmetical concepts could be made along the lines of a point developed by Carruthers (1992: 99 ff.), who (at p. 84) traces the underlying idea back to the *Meno*, and therefore calls it 'Plato's problem'. Plato's problem as applied to concepts is that if our fundamental concepts are acquired, they are acquired in a very short space of time, very early in life, and on the basis of seemingly inadequate empirical data.

One might reply that assistance is provided by others when a child is learning new concepts. But, as Carruthers points out,

very little explicit teaching of concepts takes place. In general, adults simply *use* concept-words in the presence of children, providing them with a sample of applications that is necessarily limited, only occasionally correcting the child's mistakes. Not only this, but much of the data is, from the child's point of view, corrupt. For much adult usage consists of irony, metaphor, jokes and teasing, in none of which are concept words used literally ...

(p. 99)

This point is made quite generally by Carruthers, but it seems that the rich content of arithmetical concepts can only exacerbate the problem in their case. To the extent that we are worried by this, we may be tempted to regard arithmetical concepts as innate. This raises two issues: first, does the fact (if it is a fact) that our arithmetical concepts are too rich to be acquired on the basis of the meagre amount of relevant sensory input we receive early in life mean that they are similarly too rich to be grounded in sensory input? And, second, would the innateness of arithmetical concepts be a reason to doubt that they require empirical grounding in order to be trustworthy epistemic guides to the world?

With regard to the first issue, I hope it is clear that the answer is 'no'. Maybe the amount of input required to ground the concepts is less than would be required to acquire them. Or maybe our concepts are not grounded when we first acquire them, but gradually become grounded as a lot more sensory input comes in.

Let us move, then, to the second issue. Butterworth (1999: esp. ch. 3) has argued that certain arithmetical *skills* are innate; in particular, the ability to distinguish collections of different numerosities (pp. 112 ff.). But note that to be born with arithmetical skills is not necessarily to be born with anything relevant to justification for arithmetical concepts or beliefs. I take it that the bare ability to distinguish colours is innate, since we are born with eyes responsive to light of different wavelengths. Yet I doubt many would think it follows that colour concepts are not grounded in sensory input. Maybe we are born *able* to distinguish colours, but we must get down to the business of *actually distinguishing them* before we can acquire an epistemological basis for our colour concepts. If we never saw anything coloured, the ability would be of no epistemic use to us: by itself, it could not ground any colour concepts. The sensory exposure to lights of different wavelengths is the ground for our colour concepts, not the innate ability to distinguish between lights of different wavelengths. The same should go for arithmetical concepts.

Even if some arithmetical *concepts* (as opposed to mere skills) are innate, this does not mean they are justified before we have had any sensory input. On my empiricist view, until they have been found to help make sense of sensory input, we have no epistemic right to trust any innate concepts we may have as guides to the world. What is relevant to the justification of a concept is not its *source* but whether it earns its keep by helping us make sense of sensory input as it comes in. I shall say a bit more about this in a moment.

Because the epistemic status of concepts has been neglected in philo-sophical debate, the terminology and argumentative structures found in the literature can be confusing on this point. For instance, in the context of a discussion of concepts, the word 'empiricist' is used to mean someone who believes that our concepts are *acquired* in response to experience (see e.g. Carruthers 1992: esp. ch. 4; Cowie 1999: 28–9; Laurence and Margolis 2006 sect. 3), and not, as is more consonant with the notion of empiricism that I am working with in this book, someone who believes that concepts can only be grounded and/or justified through the senses.

I am not suggesting that we ought to believe arithmetical skills and/or concepts *are* innate. There are, at the very least, some reasons to be cautious about adopting such a belief on the grounds usually proffered. For example, the kind of experimental evidence cited in support of the claim that arithmetical abilities are innate—usually their universality (see Butterworth 1999: ch. 2) and babies' ability to display some arithmetical skill (see his ch. 3)—might also be explained by the hypothesis that nearly everybody acquires these abilities before birth. There are not (and there are not likely to be in the near future) any experiments testing the arithmetical competence of babies in the womb. Since babies have (at least auditory) experience in the womb, this means there are (at least to my knowledge) no experiments which suggest that babies have arithmetical skills before they have received any sensory input.

Whether or not these empirical findings justify nativism about arithmetic, Plato's problem remains. But it is far from clear whether Plato's problem by itself represents a sufficient reason for adopting nativism. Underdetermination problems of an essentially similar kind to Plato's problem abound in philosophy. Surely we do not want to retreat to further nativist claims in order to solve Hume's problem of induction, the problem of the underdetermination of scientific theory by data, Kripkenstein's rule-following problem, and so on. Moreover, some doubt has been cast on the supposed paucity of information available to concept learners. (Cowie 1999: ch. 8 describes relevant problems with arguments from the poverty of stimulus; although Cowie focuses on language learning rather than concept acquisition, similar points can be made in the latter case.)

Nativist arguments may seem more plausible than they should if one uncritically adopts a simplistic view of empirical concept generation analogous to the sort I cautioned against in Section 5.3. If it is assumed, for instance, that we have to experience perfect triangles in order for sensory input to bring about the rational acquisition of a concept of a perfect triangle, empirical concept acquisition is obviously impossible in many cases. But it may be that our minds are so configured as to acquire a new concept whenever sensory input renders that concept indispensably useful. If so, then sensory input might well cause us to acquire concepts which are not actually instantiated by objects of our experience and the motivation for nativism is much less obvious.

Be that as it may, accepting that arithmetical concepts are innate does not undermine the claim that it is sensory input that underwrites these concepts *epistemically* (see Section 4.5 above). A concept should not be regarded as being epistemically grounded just because it is innate. Maybe the innateness of arithmetical concepts gives us a *head start* in the process of securing grounded arithmetical concepts, but it does not do all the work. Reliabilists might be impressed by the thought that evolution of innate concepts can be expected to reliably generate ones which are accurate representations of the world. But I am not a reliabilist. (See pp. 97 and 130–1 above and (e.g.) Foley (1985) for some objections to reliabilism.)

My own approach to concept grounding suggests that innate concepts will *not* count as automatically grounded. If we explain A's possession of a concept C to an outsider just by saying C is accurate, the outsider would be lead to expect that A's possession of C was sensitive to the way the world was. And although A's possession of C may be due to the evolutionary sensitivity of A's *species* to the way the world is, epistemic sensitivity to the world is normally thought of as occurring at the level of individuals, not at the level of species. So if A in fact possessed C just because C was innate for A, we would have misled our audience. Hence C would not count as grounded by my lights. This seems to me intuitively correct: by analogy, I do not think innate, reliably true, but otherwise epistemically unsupported beliefs count as knowledgeable.

Be that as it may, others who are more inclined to reliabilism, or who doubt that the outsider would be misled in the above case, may be happy to regard innate concepts as grounded provided they are produced by the right kind of evolutionary process. This opens up the possibility of a non-empiricist version of my concept-grounding epistemology. Since my task in this book is to develop three intuitions, one of which is empiricism, I shall not develop this possibility here, but merely note that the basic idea of concept grounding is amenable to being developed in a variety of interesting ways. I shall say a little more about this in my Final Remarks.

My purpose here has not been to argue for or against concept nativism, but to show why our views on this subject do not affect the claim that arithmetical concepts are empirically grounded.[11] In this respect, results from experimental psychology which are taken to support nativism, even if they succeed in that object, do not undermine my project.

8.4 Summary

I have now discussed a range of objections to the claim that arithmetical concepts are grounded in sensory input, but found none persuasive.

---

[11] See also Moser (1987: 4), where the irrelevance of the innateness of concepts to the question of *belief* justification is raised.

I argued that McDowellian objections to empirical concept grounding are unfounded or else rest on assumptions that I would resist, and considered a variety of reasons for thinking that arithmetical concepts are too rich to be grounded in sensory input, none of which was found to be persuasive.

9

Other Objections

9.1 Introduction

So far I have focused on objections to the claim that sensory input grounds our arithmetical concepts. In this chapter, I consider some other ways of objecting to the kind of arithmetical epistemology described in Chapter 4. First, I address some issues arising from a Quinean perspective. Then, I consider a way in which one might attempt to establish that an account of the kind envisaged would be somehow circular, and relate this to the Wittgensteinian claim that I am talking 'deep nonsense' in attempting to say anything about the relationship between concepts and the world. After this, I raise a few issues concerning the epistemic step between possessing grounded concepts and knowing conceptual truths. Finally, I return to the question of whether empirical knowledge is by definition a posteriori, and offer detailed reasons for saying that it is not.

9.2 Quinean objections

Quine was keen to stress that all knowledge, including what we think of as a priori knowledge, must be sensitive to our ongoing sense experience. I agree with him on this point. However, I want to *relocate* the sensitivity displayed by our knowledge of conceptual truths. Instead of making all propositions directly sensitive to sensory input by making them hostage to the empirical results they must help predict, explain, and so on, I make our concepts sensitive to sensory input by making them hostage to the empirical input they must help us make sense of, and then allow that some propositions are sensitive to sensory input solely because of the sensitivity to sensory input of the relevant concepts. But there are important similarities between the kind of sensitivity which I ascribe to concepts and that which Quine ascribes to propositions. The idea of a proposition or concept *earning its keep* by successfully facing the tribunal of experience is at the root of both notions of sensitivity.

Despite this commonality of aim, a broadly Quinean objection to the proposal of Chapter 4 can be envisaged. A Quinean may want to argue that there are no such things as conceptual truths in my sense, for the same reasons that motivated Quine (1951) to claim that there are no such things as analytic truths. Regarding Quine's main arguments for that claim, I have nothing to add here to my discussion of Section 7.5. But an underlying motivation for being sceptical about conceptual truth, or at least something that has been regarded as such a motivation and is clearly of relevance to Quine, is left untouched by this discussion.

The motivation I have in mind is that some things previously thought to be conceptual truths have consequently come to be regarded as false. For instance, the advent of non-Euclidean geometries has brought with it the rejection of *All triangles have angles which sum to 180°*. If the process of examining one's concepts is fallible in this way, can concepts really be regarded as an epistemic source of truths about the world, in the way suggested by my definition of conceptual truth? Quine is motivated to denounce the analytic partly because he rejects the possibility of infallible a priori knowledge, such as he thinks knowledge of analytic truths would purport to be. For instance, in Quine (1951: 43) we read that once we reject the 'two dogmas' of empiricism

it becomes folly to seek a boundary between synthetic statements, which hold contingently on experience, and analytic statements which hold come what may. Any statement can be held true come what may, if we make drastic enough adjustments elsewhere in the system. Even a statement very close to the periphery [of the web of belief] can be held true in the face of recalcitrant experience by pleading hallucination or by amending certain statements of the kind called logical laws. Conversely, by the same token, no statement is immune to revision. Revision even of the logical law of the excluded middle has been proposed as a means of simplifying quantum mechanics; and what difference is there in principle between such a shift and the shift whereby Kepler superseded Ptolemy, or Einstein Newton, or Darwin Aristotle?

Can the notion of conceptual truth be sensibly maintained if we admit that examining one's concepts is *not* a source of beliefs which are 'immune to revision'? Let me attempt to answer this question by considering what actually might have happened to make us reject *All triangles have angles which sum to 180°*. The issue of fallibility is interesting because it enables me to bring out the fact that, by my lights, there are various different ways to go wrong when attempting to use conceptual examination to find out about the world.

Let's begin by assuming that we are now right to assert that it is not the case that all triangles have angles which sum to 180°. Those who earlier were prepared sincerely to assent to the sentence 'All triangles have angles which add up to 180°' may have been making either of two types of error:

(1) a *step-one* error, whereby their sensory input led them to possess inaccurate geometrical concepts, different from our own geometrical concepts in at least some respects;

or

(2) a *step-two* error, whereby mistaken examinations of their accurate geometrical concepts, which were just the same as the concepts we use now, led them to accept false beliefs.

Note that a step–one error could have been due either to the receipt of misleading data or to an inappropriate response to data which was not in itself misleading. Also, note that if there was a step–one error, there might be enough of a difference between their concept of *triangle* and ours for these to count as numerically different concepts. But this need not be the case; if the differences do not count as sufficiently substantial, perhaps it could be said that we share a single concept, albeit one which has evolved over time. If we do not share a concept, it seems likely that the proposition that used to be expressed by the sentence 'All triangles have angles which add up to 180°' is different from the one we now express by that sentence.

In my opinion, the best—because most charitable—way to make sense of the case is to say that people previously used an inaccurate set of geometrical concepts, different to the one geometers now use, albeit a set that was justified for them at the time. On this diagnosis, the reason people went wrong is simply that they had less data than us—we have data about space over a very large scale which they lacked. Their concepts were adequate to the data they had and they were right about what followed epistemically from those concepts. The other available diagnoses involve attributing a mistake either in the formation of concepts or in the examination thereof. They are thus less charitable.

Supposing this to be correct, do we really disagree with our predecessors? To address this question it will be useful to have some terminology and simplifying assumptions to hand. Let's assume for the sake of simplicity that it is our concept *triangle* (rather than any other geometrical concept) which in some way differs from the closest equivalent concept used by our predecessors. Let's call those predecessors 'Euclidean geometers'. And let's refer to the closest equivalent to our concept *triangle* in their conceptual scheme as 'the Euclidean geometers' concept of triangle'. Note that this should be carefully distinguished from the concept *Euclidean triangle* (that is, the concept of a triangle whose angles do sum to 180°). We can best explain the difference between these two, and explain what has happened to the former concept, by saying that, although we often still *mention* the Euclidean concept of triangle, we no longer *use* it. We do, however, still use the concept of *a Euclidean triangle*. And an examination of *this* concept does not lead one to accept that all triangles must have angles which sum to 180°.

The way of looking at the situation which I am recommending has a strong and a weak version. On the strong version, the Euclidean geometers' concept of triangle is a numerically different concept from *triangle*, and hence our word 'triangle' and theirs do not mean the same. So when we say 'Not all triangles have angles which sum to 180°' we are not contradicting anything they asserted. We are not expressing the negation of the proposition they expressed by saying 'All triangles have angles which sum to 180°'.

Nevertheless, there is an important sense in which we disagree with the Euclidean geometers even on this strong version of the view. The propositions they asserted involved inappropriate concepts, but so did the negations of those propositions, which is why we do not assert the latter. But we do not agree with them, because we do not assent to the propositions they assented to. And this is not just because we haven't thought about the matter—it is a considered rejection. We disagree with them in a more fundamental way than through straightforward contradiction of what they asserted: we reject the very conceptual tools they used to frame their assertions.

On the weaker view, there is more obvious scope for disagreement. The weaker view has it that Euclidean geometers managed to refer to the property of trianglehood (that property expressed by our word 'triangle' and picked out by our concept *triangle*) even though the tool they used to do this—their Euclidean concept of triangle—was flawed in that it misrepresented its subject matter in a way that we can now appreciate with the benefit of our more wide-ranging data.

Where does all this leave the worry with which we started this section? Well, it certainly means that by my lights knowledge of conceptual truths through conceptual examination can make no claim to be an *infallible* source of knowledge about the world. It can go wrong, even when properly conducted, if the concepts under examination are inaccurate. And this could happen through no epistemic fault of our own, since those inaccurate concepts might be amply justified.

But a source of knowledge is not required to be infallible. The fallibility of conceptual examination does not render conceptual truths or our knowledge of them in any way dubious. Any Quine-inspired assimilation of the conceptually true with that which cannot be rationally undermined would be a mistake. Consider again the passage from Quine (1951) quoted on p. 237 above. One thing that is noticeable about this passage is a slip between talking about what is necessarily the case (that which holds 'come what may') and talking about what can be believed whatever empirical input is received (that which can be 'held true come what may'). However plausible it might be that conceptual truths are necessary truths, this has nothing to do with their being impossible to undermine once they are believed or known. To say that there is scope for error when one believes something through conceptual examination is not to say that it is metaphysically possible, of the things we believe in this way, that they be false.

One element in Quine's argument is that there is not such a great difference between the way in which experience can lead us to change our beliefs about contingent matters and the way in which it can lead us to change our beliefs concerning supposed conceptual truths. The proposal defended in Chapter 4 offers us a way to respect that claim without denying that there are conceptual truths and they are interestingly different, epistemologically, from other truths. Beliefs are subject to the tribunal of experience whether or not they are arrived at through conceptual examination, according to that proposal. For the concepts under examination are subject to this very tribunal. We can even allow that conceptual truths can be undermined by straightforward empirical evidence, in the way Quine proposes. None of this forces us to deny that *one* of the ways in which conceptual truths can be known (and undermined) is through empirical grounding (or loss thereof) for certain of our concepts. It is no part of my notion of a priori knowledge that such knowledge cannot be undermined by good old-fashioned empirical evidence.

The case of Euclidean geometry is a useful testing ground for my ideas about conceptual truth and concept grounding. What we find is that, far from supplying a reason for scepticism about the very idea of conceptual truth or about the special epistemic role I assign to it, the case helps to illustrate exactly how, on the envisaged view, our knowledge of conceptual truths is related to our sensory input and hence constrained by the independent world.

9.3 Circularity and deep nonsense

A different objection to my account might be based on the thought that the account involves a certain kind of vicious circularity. I have appealed to the scientific indispensability of arithmetical concepts as evidence that they are justified. But recognizing this indispensability is a process which involves the use of my own concepts (such as *science, theory, concept, indispensable*). Is this not circular?

Dummett (1991: ch. 9) attempts to solve a circularity problem by arguing that certain kinds of justificatory circularity are non-vicious. Dummett's idea is that we can justify a logical rule by means of an argument which employs that rule, providing we are not attempting to convince someone that the rule is acceptable, but merely explaining, to someone who already accepts it, *why* it is acceptable. An explanation of a fact does not have to convince you that the fact obtains; rather, the only reason for believing the explanans might be that you already believe the explanandum (see Dummett 1973a: 295–6). Dummett calls this sort of circularity 'pragmatic circularity'. Perhaps *we* could argue, similarly, that we can employ a concept in citing the grounds on which we take that concept to be justified, provided we are only attempting to explain why it counts as a justified concept, and not trying to persuade anyone who does not already accept it that it is such.

Dummett does show that pragmatic circularity is not the same thing as ordinary argumentative circularity, whereby one simply includes the conclusion one is trying to prove amongst one's premises. For in the latter case success is guaranteed, whereas it is not guaranteed that we can in all conceivable cases prove the acceptability of a logical rule by using that rule (p. 203). But this does not imply, as he seems to think, that 'there is nothing problematic about' such a justification provided it is being used only for these explanatory purposes. The fact is that one is still assuming the acceptability of a rule in explaining why that rule is acceptable, and, *when giving such an explanation amounts to providing a justification*, there is something prima facie unsatisfying about this. Maybe some kinds of explanation of why a rule is acceptable can harmlessly involve applications of the rule. But in so far as such an explanation is supposed to amount to an epistemic justification, certain standards must be met. Non-circularity is usually taken to be among them, and the burden of proof is still on Dummett to show that it is inappropriate for certain kinds of justification. Dummett's argument comes to this:

> Justifications don't have to be non-circular; for some justifications are explanations, and explanations don't have to be non-circular.

The form of this argument is clearly invalid, as the following parody shows:

> Cats don't have to be feline; for some cats are striped animals, and striped animals don't have to be feline.

I would therefore be hesitant to rest the defence of my project against the charge of circularity on an analogy with Dummett's defence of circular justifications.

It is important to note, however, that Dummett is trying to defend a much deeper kind of circularity than that of which my project stands accused. Dummett is proposing that *a justification* can sometimes be permissibly circular. Whereas all that has been claimed about my proposal is that it is somehow circular to use certain concepts in *describing* the justification one has for the claim that one is justified in possessing those very concepts. The justificatory relationship between sensory input and our concepts is not itself accused of being circular.

This may seem a bit quick: surely the problem also arises as regards the justification itself (that is, the relationship for which indispensability is taken as evidence)? For in order to describe one's sensory input as justifying one's concepts, one must apply some concepts to that input (even if these are only very vague ones, such as *having the same structure as*). If one tries to give one's justification for the concepts so applied by appealing again to one's sensory input, don't we raise another circularity worry?

Here again, however, it is the attempt to describe our justification which leads to the appearance of circularity; this is not a feature of the justification itself. This means that the accusation of circularity raised here has a very general application, if it has any at all. The circularity of which I am accused is no worse than the circularity which necessarily arises whenever we try to explain why we are justified in believing propositions about anything. Take, for example, our beliefs about the physical world. I say I have reason to believe I am justified in thinking there is a mug on the table in front of me, because I have reason to believe my eyes are functioning correctly and do not deceive me. But what justifies me in believing that my eyes do not deceive me? Either I appeal to my senses again, in which case there is an apparent circularity, or, if I am a rationalist, I could appeal to some rational source of justification. If I do the latter, though, I may be asked what justifies me in trusting this rational source. If I appeal to my senses, circularity seems to reappear. If I appeal again to rational justification, circularity seems to reappear.

But this does not mean *my justification* for believing there is a mug in front of me is circular. I take it that that justification is generated by the relationship between my belief and the sensory input on which it is based, and need not consist in or rely upon another *belief* to the effect that I seem to see a mug and my senses are reliable (which belief would, of course, itself await justification).

The 'circularity' which threatens whenever one tries to give one's reasons for believing that one is justified in believing some proposition or possessing some concept is essentially the same as the regress which renders internalism unattractive (see Section 2.2 above). In both cases what causes the difficulties is the attempt to *find something to say* about one's justification. Provided we do not insist that our justification consists in what we can find to say, we can avoid the accusation of circularity.

Dummett (1991), incidentally, does not question the assumption that a justification for a logical rule will always consist in an argument for the acceptability of that rule. Thus he is unable to avoid the conclusion that any justification for our basic logical rules will be in some way circular, and must try to argue that in some cases the circularity is not vicious. But once we allow that justification may consist in appropriateness to sensory input, regardless of whether we are aware of that appropriateness or can construct an argument showing that it obtains, we can avoid this predicament (for related comments see my discussion of Field in Section 2.6).

An objection interestingly related to the charge of circularity might arise if one claimed, along the lines of a point originally due to Wittgenstein, that we are talking a deep kind of nonsense in trying to say anything about the process through which our concepts are grounded. We cannot talk or think about this process without employing some of the very concepts that we take to be grounded by it. We should therefore consider an analogue of the Tractarian worry that it is futile to attempt to use our language to say how that very language relates to the world it represents. We should consider the worry that it is futile to try to express, using concepts, how our concepts relate to the world.

Passages in the *Tractatus* which might be taken to support such a concern (about language, at least) include:

Propositions can represent the whole of reality, but they cannot represent what they must have in common with reality in order to be able to represent it—logical form. In order to be able to represent logical form, we should have to be able to station ourselves with propositions somewhere outside logic, that is to say outside the world.

(4.12)

What finds its reflection in language, language cannot represent. What expresses *itself* in language, *we* cannot express by means of language.

(4.121)

It is impossible to *assert* the identity of meaning of two expressions. For in order to assert anything about their meaning, I must know their meaning, and I cannot know their meaning without knowing whether what they mean is the same or different.

(6.2322)

The worry, as is clearest in this last passage, seems to be that talk of the connection between language and the world cannot be *informative*, because we must presuppose that our audience already speaks the language whose links with the world we are describing, and that if it cannot be informative it cannot be meaningful.[1] The conceptual analogue of this worry would be that talk of the connection between *concepts* and the world cannot be informative, because we must presuppose that our audience already possesses the conceptual scheme whose links with the world we are describing, and that if it cannot be informative it cannot be meaningful. This deep-nonsense problem is potentially more serious than one of justification: because of the attempt to make claims, using my concepts, about how those very concepts relate to the world, there is a risk that my proposal is actually incoherent, as opposed to merely circular.

Is it right to say that anything which cannot be informative cannot be meaningful? Much depends on what is meant by 'informative'. Obviously, we could never discuss the relationship between our conceptual scheme and the world with anyone not in possession of at least some parts of this scheme, but surely we need not worry about being 'informative' to such a person. No philosophical theory—nor indeed any other kind of theory—is *that* informative. The worry is, rather, that with regard to those who *do* share our conceptual scheme, we can't be telling them anything new in telling them how their concepts relate to the world. They must already know this in order to grasp what we are saying. For we should be using some of the relevant concepts in communicating with them. Thus anyone who could understand us would have to be *already competent* in the use of those concepts, and hence would *already be able to see* how they relate to the world.

But this is confused. For one thing, we can mention *particular* words and concepts without using them, and hence make ourselves understood even by those not competent with the words or concepts mentioned. (That there is a difference between use and mention is one reason why the above-quoted passage 6.2322 is way off-beam.) This fact alone explains how we can talk about some of the meanings of our concepts without using those very concepts. However, this may not be enough to enable us to make general claims about our whole conceptual scheme, since we will have to use some of our concepts in doing so.

Another important point which is ignored by Wittgenstein is that one can understand a language or possess some concepts *unreflectively*. Maybe—and this is almost certainly too concessive—anyone who shares my concepts is

---

[1] My understanding of these passages has benefited from discussion with Michael Potter.

(at least in some suitably broad sense) *capable* of knowing everything there is to know about how they relate to the world. But there is no reason why she should ever have thought about it. One can be a competent user of a language and a conceptual scheme without having any detailed knowledge, or even beliefs, about how that language or conceptual scheme works. We *can* hope to inform such unreflective people on these matters by talking with them philosophically.

And even if we are impressed by the thought that telling someone how their concepts relate to the world cannot count as telling them something 'new' in a certain strong sense, we can certainly query the idea that a proposition can only be meaningful if it could be used to inform someone of something 'new' in this sense. While there does seem to be some link between being meaningful and being capable of carrying information, it is not at all clear that a proposition is only capable of carrying information if it can be used to give someone information that they were not previously in a position to know. Certainly no argument for any assumption of this sort is offered by Wittgenstein, who merely asserts that

It belongs to the essence of a proposition that it should be able to communicate a *new* sense to us.

(4.027)

without saying what counts as a 'new' sense or offering any reasons to accept his claim.

9.4 How do we get from concepts to conceptually true propositions?

I have assumed that examining our concepts of 7, +, 5, =, and *12* is (sometimes) what guides us to the belief that $7 + 5 = 12$. I have tried to explain how such a process as examination of one's concepts could lead to knowledge of independent arithmetical truths, by considering the relationship between these concepts, our sensory data, and the independent world. But I have not said anything substantial about the *way* in which examining the concepts leads to possession of the belief. I have not said how we go about conducting an 'examination' of our concepts, nor how and why the examination process leads us to adopt certain beliefs and not others. I have not said how it is that we can tell by examining our concepts of 7, $+$, 5, $=$, and 12 that they stand in a certain relation, or our noticing this leads to our believing that $7 + 5 = 12$.

This is not because I think there is nothing interesting to be said on these points. Rather, it is because I take it to be common ground among a large number of philosophers that there is some such process as conceptual examination, and that noticing that certain relations hold between our concepts can lead us to adopt arithmetical beliefs. (That is not to say that this is the only way of arriving at arithmetical beliefs, just that it is one of the ways.) The development of a precise account of this process I therefore take to be a less pressing matter than the development of some epistemic theory accounting for the fact that examining one's concepts can lead to knowledge of the independent world. It is also something that ought to proceed in tandem with empirical psychology, not something to be pursued entirely a priori by philosophers.

Although I am not offering a worked-out account of this process, however, there are some questions about the process of examining one's concepts which could cause concern about the current project if not addressed. First, what are the prospects for an account of conceptual examination which will fit well with the account of concept grounding that I am proposing?

I think the prospects are good. I have said that grounded concepts (or at least their ultimate constituents) are importantly correlated with features of the world. And that the *relations* between these concepts or their ultimate constituents will also be importantly correlated with relations between features of the world. It need not be that every relation between two things will necessarily be captured in some relation between two representations of them, but such relations as *are* present between the representations can be relied upon as capturing relations between the things represented.

Whatever account we eventually develop of conceptual examination and consequent belief formation, it will surely depend heavily on the fact that examining our concepts makes us aware of relations between them (and/or their ultimate constituents), and this is what leads us to accept certain propositions. If my views on concept grounding are correct, this process will lead to knowledge of truths about the world because these relations between our concepts and/or their constituents will, non-accidentally, be correlated with relations between the corresponding features of the world.

The analogy with vision mentioned in Section 2.5 may be helpful here. The method of acquiring knowledge through visual perception, as I explained there, has a clear input step: a stage at which there is input from the world into our mental processes. What I'm trying to do in this work is explain how the method of concept examination can also involve an input step. Attempting to describe the processing stages of concept examination in detail would be akin to attempting to describe the processing stages involved in visual perception: not immediately relevant to the epistemological issues we're focussing on, and not the sort of thing that should be done a priori by a philosopher without input from empirical psychology.

That said, some suggestive ideas as to how conceptual examination may lead to belief formation may be found in Laurence and Margolis (2003: sect. 5). Laurence and Margolis suggest that what they call 'intuitions' (which might be likened to the upshots of what I'm calling conceptual examination) can be evidence[2] of conceptual content. If, as I suspect, the representational content of our concepts is correlated in important ways with what's out there in the world, this will be a way of finding out about the world through conceptual examination which is conducive to my perspective. The Laurence and Margolis position suggests that the psychological mechanism which we call intuition is (perhaps among other things) a way of recovering information about the content of our concepts and hence (if I am right) a way of recovering the information about the world that those concepts encode in virtue of representing what they do. Much needs to be done to understand the envisaged intuitive mechanism, but this is at least a step on the road.

A related issue (or rather collection of issues), also concerning the cognitive step from concepts to propositions, needs to be addressed here. Suppose an examination of our concepts leads us to believe that $7 + 5 = 12$. Surely there is something like an *inferential move* involved in this process. At some stage, we *infer* (or do something akin to inferring) from the nature of our concepts to the truth of $7 + 5 = 12$. But what grounds our use of this

---

[2] Not empirical evidence; no empirical input is required when one introspectively checks one's intuitions.

method? We must surely be tacitly employing our knowledge of some proposition of the form of

   I Inference of this kind is likely to lead to truths.

The trouble is that we cannot ground principle *I* through examination of some of our (empirically grounded) concepts *I*: this would be hopelessly circular. But to say that *I* is known a posteriori is likewise unacceptable; in addition to its intrinsic implausibility and the worry that it would make the resultant arithmetical knowledge a posteriori too, we would then need to explain how we know the principles by which we can draw an a posteriori inference from certain experiences to the truth of *I*. Here we cannot appeal to examination of concepts, since this would restore the circularity, or to a posteriori confirmation again, as this would launch an infinite regress. We seem forced to accept that justification either for principle *I* or for something on which our knowledge of *I* depends is secured through 'rational intuition'.

This is not a special problem for my form of empiricism. In his (1998: sect. 1.1), BonJour presents an argument for the existence of propositions known by rational insight alone which resembles that of the foregoing paragraph, though it is not targeted on my particular form of empiricism and it focuses on justification rather than grounding (and, of course, it does not mention justification for concepts but only for propositions). BonJour's argument here is crucial to many of the anti-empiricist moves later in his book, and seems to constitute his major reason for thinking there must be justified beliefs which are not justified by appeal to sense experience. Here is his own statement of it:

Could an argument of any sort be entirely justified on empirical grounds? It seems clear on reflection that the answer is 'no'. Any purely empirical ingredient can, after all, always be formulated as an additional empirical premise. When all such premises have been explicitly formulated, either the intended conclusion will be included among them or it will not. In the former case, no argument or inference is necessary, while in the latter case, the needed inference clearly goes beyond what can be derived entirely from experience.

(1998: 5)

The idea is that in order to justify any proposition p not directly observed to be true, we must appeal to some kind of argument for p. But then seeing that the argument is cogent requires an a priori 'insight'. In BonJour's words, '[e]ven to apply as straightforward and seemingly unproblematic a rule as *modus ponens*, I must see or grasp in an immediate, not further reducible way that the three propositions comprising the premises and conclusion are of the right forms and are related in the right way'.[3]

Let us note first that the problem BonJour has raised cannot, as he seems to think, be solved just by appealing to our being able to 'grasp' in an 'immediate' way whatever a priori principles or truths are supposedly needed to enable one to reason beyond the facts of direct experience. Suppose we are trying to justify p, a proposition not directly experienced, by appeal to an argument *If q then p, q, therefore p*. To be justified (by BonJour's lights) in believing p on this basis, we must be able to see that MPP is justified and that it applies in this case. Suppose both these propositions are 'grasped' by some 'immediate' insight. We still, by the same token, need also to see *that* the truth of these propositions enables us to reason from *If q then p, and q* to p. Maybe some proposition capturing the correctness of this transition is also grasped by an 'immediate' insight. But, again, we will need to see *that* this proposition, together with the original premises plus the acceptability of MPP and its applicability in this case, implies p. And so on.

The difficulty with BonJour's proposed solution to his problem is that, just like any empirical 'ingredient', any rational 'ingredient' can be added to the argument as a premise, and another insight will be needed to see that the conclusion follows from the new set of premises. (This is also noted by Casullo, in his 2000.) Clearly, a vicious justificatory regress threatens. What lies at the real heart of BonJour's problem is the same thing that lies at the heart of Lewis Carroll's discussion of Achilles and the tortoise (1895). The *source* of the justification is not what's relevant; what BonJour is describing is rather the regress on which we are launched *whenever* we try to explain the legitimacy of all justification for inferential moves as due to our having justification for some *proposition* capturing the correctness of this transition.

In a later paper BonJour agrees that what really matters is that the insight required to make the transition should not be propositional in form (2005: 100). But this seems to undercut the use of this argument as

---

[3] Peacocke (2004: 31) seems to have a similar argument in mind when he says: 'Not all warrants can be empirical, on pain of regress'.

motivation for believing in rational intuition, since nothing is said to suggest that such non-propositional insights must always be rationally, as opposed to empirically, grounded.

Moreover, the whole argument can be sidestepped if we simply refuse to make the problematic assumptions about justification. Epistemic internalism is renowned for launching justificatory regresses (see Section 2.2 above), and this is one of them. If we suppose that S's justification for an inferential move is always accessible to S, then it is not (excessively) unreasonable to assume that such justification will always amount to, or at least be accompanied by, justification for some 'insight' concerning the correctness of this transition—perhaps, some such 'insight' will be needed to serve as S's internally accessible justification. This sort of assumption is needed to get BonJour's argument off the ground. An externalist, however, can simply reject it.

In the original argument against my own view the claim is that in order to be justified in moving from concepts to propositions, one must know I (or, perhaps, have some equivalent but non-propositional insight). But we can sidestep this worry in the same way: an *externalist* need not accept the assumption that any such thing is needed in order for the inferential move to be justified.

A more radical response may also be available. This would be to say that the move from concepts to propositions must *preserve* justification, but that is not the same as saying *we must have some justification for making it*, even when the latter claim is construed in an externalist fashion. (By analogy, a good inferential move needs to preserve truth, but it would be a category mistake to describe the move itself as being true.) Provided the move from the concepts involved in $7 + 5 = 12$ to belief in the proposition $7 + 5 = 12$ is a justification-*preserving* move, we can use it to get justified beliefs from an examination of justified concepts. Perhaps it is a mistake to demand anything more than this.

9.5 'By definition, arithmetical knowledge cannot be a priori if it is empirical'

As I said in Section 4.7, it does not really matter whether we decide to continue using the term 'a priori' to describe arithmetical knowledge, given that we respect the special status of that knowledge—the status which has been *called* aprioricity. Nevertheless, I myself think that the term 'a priori' is worth maintaining, as it marks an important characteristic of arithmetical knowledge (its independence of confirmation by empirical *evidence*) for which we will otherwise require some other marker.

Moreover, I hope that qualms about my decision to retain the term 'a priori' may be dispelled when we recall that modern usage of the term 'a priori' was largely determined by Kant, and that Kant allowed that some a priori knowledge—the 'impure' sort—depends upon experience in so far as the *concepts* involved are 'derived from' experience (see the introduction to the *Critique of Pure Reason*, esp. sect. 1). I have proposed that the only way in which arithmetical knowledge depends on sensory input is in so far as the concepts involved must be appropriately related to that input in order for us to count as knowing arithmetical propositions.

In fact, I think this concession of Kant's (endorsed by many later writers) is very significant. Although the notion of 'derivation' Kant had in mind here was no doubt closer to being causal-historical than epistemological, what is being acknowledged here is that the relationship between experience and concepts may be important for our ability to represent the world—to understand or entertain propositions about it. What I am contending is that the existence of precisely this sort of representation relation, together with a proper understanding of how experience is involved in setting it up and ensuring its accuracy, is all that is needed to get a certain kind of *epistemology* of the a priori off the ground.

In post-Kantian philosophy, wherever the a priori is not defined simply as the non-empirical, it is usually defined in ways which imply that arithmetical knowledge is a priori on the kind of view I am defending. For instance, Chisholm writes:

Speaking very roughly, we might say that one mark of an a priori proposition is this: once you understand it, you see that it is true. We might call this the traditional conception of the a priori. Thus Leibniz remarks: 'You will find in a hundred places that the Scholastics have said that these propositions are evident, *ex terminis*, as soon as the terms are understood'

(1977: 119)

If this characterization is even 'very roughly' correct, then it looks as though arithmetical knowledge as I envisage it has as good a claim as any to count as a priori. With grounded arithmetical concepts in place, we are in a position to see that $7 + 5 = 12$ is true. We do not need to conduct any tests or acquire any evidence: we just need to examine our understanding of what addition, sevenness, fiveness, and twelveness are. (Of course it is unlikely that everyone who understands an a priori proposition immediately sees that it is true; it is more plausible that such a person is *in a position to see* that it is true. Charitably, we might suppose that this is one of the respects in which Chisholm's characterization is meant to be 'very rough'.[4])

One might understand a proposition without the concepts involved in it being grounded, and one could not gain knowledge of it as soon as one understood it in that case. But Chisholm's characterization is not (in my opinion) best interpreted as implying that concepts don't need to be grounded in order to be a source of knowledge. Rather, its import is that our grasp of concepts or meanings is what's doing all the work when we come to accept some proposition in an a priori way, and *when things go well* this is sufficient for knowledge. Sometimes things don't go well, and in more conventional ways than through concepts failing to be grounded. For instance, one could come to believe a true proposition on the basis of an incorrectly conducted examination of (grounded) concepts (a variety of step-two error, in the terminology of Section 9.2 above). Chisholm shouldn't be taken as suggesting that *this* sort of belief would be knowledgeable. This sort of possibility is simply not thought worth mentioning, just as when one says that visually based knowledge is acquired by seeing that things are thus and so, one does not bother to mention (e.g.) the fact that in some cases we see that things are thus and so but do not thereby come to know that things are thus and so because we have other evidence which defeats our visual justification.

Chisholm also emphasizes that dependence on inductive evidence characterizes the a posteriori: 'If [a] truth were known a posteriori, then it would be justified by some induction or inductions' (p. 114). I allow that arithmetical knowledge is secured without epistemic reliance on inductive evidence, so by Chisholm's lights it does not count as a posteriori.

Other characterizations which support the claim that arithmetic is a priori on my account abound. Moser (1987: 1) defines a priori knowledge

---

[4] Another concerns the possibility that it may sometimes be necessary to examine concepts not involved in the proposition p itself in order to know p a priori: see above, Chapter 4 n. 7.

as knowledge the 'justification condition' for which 'does not depend on *evidence* from sensory experience' (emphasis added). Elsewhere he has claimed that this is how the a priori is 'ordinarily' characterized (1998). And I have already argued (Section 4.7) that arithmetical knowledge, as I conceive of it, is a priori by this definition. The same goes for Boghossian's characterization (1997), according to which a proposition is known a priori iff one's belief in it is 'justified, with a strength sufficient for knowledge, without appeal to empirical *evidence*' (p. 333; emphasis added); and for one of Field's (2000; p. 117), according to which a proposition is *weakly a priori* just in case 'it can be reasonably believed without empirical evidence'.

Chisholm says that his definition, whereby a priori knowledge is knowledge available as soon as the target proposition is understood, is 'in the spirit of several familiar dicta concerning the a priori' (p. 125). So far so good. But another claim which is 'in the spirit of several familiar dicta' is that a priori knowledge is simply any knowledge which is non-empirical. How, then, can Chisholm's definition turn out to be compatible with my claim that some a priori knowledge is empirical? How, for that matter, can any of the foregoing definitions, which are clearly intended to capture the accepted core of the notion of aprioricity, be compatible with that claim?

In my view, the reason so many philosophers often define the a priori as the non-empirical is that it is generally assumed that, if a proposition is such that we are in a position to know it as soon as we understand it, without the need for inductive evidence, then it *must* be that we can know it in some non-empirical way. This, I am arguing, is a false assumption, because there exist empirical ways of knowing which are non-evidential and non-inductive. But when we define the a priori as the non-empirical, maintaining all the while that aprioricity is simply independence of empirical evidence, the assumption that the only way of securing empirical knowledge is through the acquisition of empirical evidence gets *disguised* as a matter of definition. If the a priori is to be so defined, it should also be allowed that some a posteriori knowledge can be had without reliance on empirical evidence, and can be had merely through an examination of concepts. (Arithmetical knowledge, by my lights, would be of this kind.) But such a situation is not acknowledged as possible.

In short, what we are seeing is that there is a deep instability in the classic collection of platitudes about a priori knowledge, since they include all of the following:

(A) All a posteriori knowledge is knowledge that depends on empirical evidence.
(B) Only knowledge which is independent of experience is a priori.
(C) All knowledge is either a priori or a posteriori and none is both.[5]

In my view, what is brought to light by the kind of epistemology discussed in Chapter 4 is that something has to be dropped from this triad. For, if that kind of account is right, there is some knowledge which depends on experience (and hence, by B, is not a priori) but not on empirical evidence (and hence, by A, is not a posteriori), and so is neither a priori nor a posteriori, contradicting C. I am proposing that we reject B, which may sound radical. But since something has to go, *all* our options here are radical—rejecting A or C would hardly be conservative.

A similar pattern of unstable assumptions can be found in Kripke, who says: 'I guess the traditional characterization [of the a priori] from Kant goes something like: a priori truths are those which can be known independently of any experience' (1980: 34), and also goes on to say the following:

What then, is the *epistemological* status of the statement 'Stick S is one metre long at t_0', for someone who has fixed the metric system by reference to stick S? It would seem that he knows it a priori. For if he used stick S to fix the reference of the term 'one metre', then as a result of this 'definition' ... he knows automatically, without further investigation, that S is one metre long.

(p. 56)

Clearly, for Kripke, anything which can be known 'automatically', as a result of a 'definition', and without 'further investigation', is something which can be known a priori. And by his lights, its being knowable a priori means it can be known independently of experience. But I have been trying to make room for the possibility that something could be known by thinking about one's concepts and without 'further investigation', *and yet be empirically grounded.* Such knowledge would meet what Kripke clearly takes to be a sufficient condition for aprioricity on p. 56, and yet be a

---

[5] This is not to deny that some propositions are knowable both a priori and a posteriori.

posteriori by his definition on p. 34. So something must be wrong with these assumptions about the a priori and the a posteriori.

Kripke, like the others, does not consider the kind of epistemic grounding I have proposed for arithmetic. This is what allows him to treat the a priori and a posteriori as he does without the inconsistency coming to light. But if what I am arguing for *is* possible, his views cannot all be correct. I would propose that these definitions should be revised so as to respect the (widely shared) intuition that knowledge which can be had through conceptual examination, without reliance on empirical evidence, is a priori, and thus brought into line with other characterizations (like Chisholm's).

Whether or not this particular resolution to the problem is accepted, however, it must be acknowledged that there is an instability in the standard conceptions of apriority and aposteriority, which is brought to light by the possibility of the kind of knowledge described in Chapter 4. If knowledge of the proposed kind is genuinely possible, then we cannot respect all the traditional platitudes about apriority and aposteriority.

Williamson (2007: sect. 3) seems to be making a somewhat similar point when he argues that in some situations 'the question "*A priori* or *a posteriori*?" is too crude to be of much epistemological use'. He discusses our knowledge of:

(26) It is necessary that whoever knows something believes it.

and says that:

the experiences through which we have learned to distinguish in practice between belief and non-belief and between knowledge and ignorance play no strictly evidential role in our knowledge of (26) ... Nevertheless, their role may be more than purely enabling. Many philosophers, native speakers of English, have denied (26) ... They are not usually or plausibly accused of failing to understand the words 'know' and 'believe'.

What Williamson has in mind here is that experience can hone our 'offline' (counterfactual) reasoning capacities—those we use when thinking about non-actual scenarios—and that by so doing it guides our judgements concerning the truth-values of modal propositions like (26) in a way which differs from the provision of evidence for or against these propositions, so that our knowledge of (26) is not paradigmatically a posteriori. But he thinks that, despite being non-evidential, the role experience plays here does not amount merely to its enabling us to grasp the relevant concepts or understand the relevant terms so that we are capable of entertaining (26); so our knowledge of (26) is not paradigmatically a priori either.

The idea that experience can play a role which is neither evidential nor merely enabling is one of the key ideas I am pressing for in this book (and elsewhere, e.g. Jenkins 2005*b* and Jenkins 2008*b*). However, it is an idea which can be developed in a number of different ways. One of these is Williamson's way: we can claim that what experience is doing is honing the counterfactual reasoning skills which ground our knowledge of certain (in this case, modal) propositions. Another is to suggest that what experience does is (not merely supply but) epistemically ground the relevant concepts which permits the recovery of information from those concepts through conceptual examination. In my view it is a false step to take a detour via knowledge of counterfactuals or counterfactual reasoning processes in accounting for most of what Williamson would call our 'armchair knowledge'. But we seem to be in agreement on some important points.

9.6 Summary

In this section I have considered various objections to the proposal outlined in Part II. First, I discussed a Quinean point about the revisability of conceptual truths, then some issues concerning circularity and 'deep nonsense'. Then I considered some objections concerning the epistemic link between the possession of grounded concepts and knowledge of conceptual truths. Finally, I returned to the question of whether any of our knowledge can really be said to be both empirical and a priori, using examples from various authors to demonstrate that arithmetical knowledge as I conceive of it meets many of the standard criteria for aprioricity, and that my claim is no more radical than the alternatives available for those who believe in the kind of knowledge postulated in Chapter 4.

Final Remarks

Summing up

In this book, I have aimed to sketch a new answer to the question of how we know arithmetical truths. I have looked for an answer which preserves realist intuitions and respects empiricism, while also preserving the special a priori status of arithmetical knowledge and cohering with a promising conception of what knowledge is in general.

In order to do this, I first had to describe and defend my conception of arithmetical realism. This I undertook at the beginning of Part I. I defined realism in terms of essential independence: the claim that it is no part of *what it is* for an arithmetical proposition to be true that it is in any way related to our mental lives. I distinguished this from modal independence, and argued that essential independence claims cannot be appropriated by the quasi-realist.

Next I discussed my commitments to externalism and empiricism, before proceeding to develop a theory of knowledge. I proposed that knowledge is true belief which can be well explained to an outsider just by citing the proposition believed. I showed how this account is immune to Gettier-type counter-examples and that it makes sense of other prominent accounts and intuitions.

Then, in Part II, I set out to show how arithmetical propositions can explain our arithmetical beliefs in the requisite way. I argued that arithmetical propositions explain the nature of our sensory input, which explains our possession of arithmetical concepts, which in turn explains why we believe arithmetical propositions. According to this view, arithmetical knowledge is a priori, because it is knowledge of conceptual truths and does not depend on evidence from empirical testing. But it does ultimately depend on the sensory input which grounds our arithmetical concepts.

So it is also empirical. In the remaining chapters of Part II, I developed and clarified this proposal, and in Part III I defended it against various objections.

I now want to consider briefly some ways in which one might accept the central parts of my proposal while rejecting other aspects of it. This is of interest in so far as it may broaden the appeal of the central thesis of this work and suggest alternative lines along which it could be developed.

First, it is clear that one could accept the main elements of my epistemology for arithmetic without accepting my theory of knowledge. The thesis that arithmetic is known through an examination of grounded concepts is compatible with other well-known accounts of, and approaches to, knowledge. For instance, we can say to a reliabilist that examining grounded concepts is a reliable method of forming true beliefs. Or we could say to Craig that someone whose beliefs are based on examinations of grounded concepts is likely to be a good informant (see Craig 1990). Alternatives to my account of concept grounding are also available to those whose background epistemology makes them desirable. (We saw some examples on pp. 130–1.)

Second, one might accept some aspects of my arithmetical epistemology while rejecting empiricism. It could be held, for instance, that arithmetical concepts are grounded through the use of some rational faculty. (However, it is not altogether clear what advantages this would have over the ordinary rationalist view that whole arithmetical sentences are known through the use of some such faculty. Perhaps it would do more to respect the phenomenology of arithmetical knowledge.) Or, to give another example, one could be a reliabilist who holds that arithmetical concepts are innate and produced by a reliable process.

Third, one could even reject realism and yet maintain that concepts need to be have some special grounded status if we are to secure knowledge by examining them. The required status, on this view, would not have to do with correlation with a mind-independent world, but might instead be a matter of coherence with other concepts, or perhaps conduciveness to the formulation of a (maximally) coherent theory of the world. The key point that only concepts meeting certain epistemic conditions can be relied upon as a source of knowledge would still be respected by such a view.

Fourth, one could basically accept my proposal in its entirety, but refuse to call arithmetical knowledge 'a priori', on the grounds that it is empirical.

This is merely a matter of bookkeeping, provided we can still assert that arithmetic has a special epistemic status relative to (say) ordinary scientific knowledge of the physical world.

Finally, one could marry something like the proposal of this book to quite a different view about what concepts and conceptual examination are like. For instance, concepts might be viewed as bundles of abilities of certain special kinds (as in e.g. Dummett 1993: 97–9; Brandom 1994: 87–91), and conceptual examination as a process of examining what these abilities amount to and how they relate to each other. We could then argue that some of these bundles of abilities are related to experience (and/or any other sources of input we might postulate) in the right kind of non-accidental way for the examination process to deliver knowledge of the world. Alternatively, concepts could be thought of as Fregean senses (see e.g. Peacocke 1992). We could then argue that which concepts we use (i.e. which concepts are the senses of things that we think), and hence which concepts we have available to us for examination, depends upon sensory input in the right kind of non-accidental way for conceptual examination to deliver knowledge.

It is important to stress before moving on that I do not by any means claim to have completed the task of providing an epistemology for arithmetic. Several challenging problems remain. I have not attempted to give a full account of grounding for concepts, or even for arithmetical concepts. I have not even given a full account of what a concept *is*, or what arithmetical concepts are like. And I have not given anything like a full account of conceptual examination. I do not imagine that any reader will suppose it will ultimately be sufficient to leave matters there, and no more do I. Besides this, I have not attempted to say which concepts are grounded immediately and which are grounded merely because they are compounds of grounded concepts. In particular, I have not said whether arithmetical concepts are of the first or the second kind or a mixture of the two. I have not asked what sorts of pre-conceptual sensory input could ultimately ground our arithmetical concepts, and I have not attempted to give any details of the relationship between this input and our arithmetical concepts in virtue of which the latter count as grounded in the former.

Moreover, I have made, but not defended, some significant philosophical assumptions over the course of this book. A form of epistemological externalism was accepted with only the briefest discussion in Section 2.2. An analogue of scientific realism was assumed without comment on p. 139 and thereafter. I also assumed, in Section 4.4, that there are conceptual truths, and that arithmetical truths are among them. All these assumptions are crucial to the success of my project, but it is not within the scope of the current work to defend or even fully explicate them.

I hope, then, that the current work will be seen as locating a promising research project, not as purporting to have completed that project. A further respect in which the work is not yet finished is that my claims in this book have potentially interesting consequences in a number of other fields, which there is not space to explore fully in this context. A brief survey of some of them should give the reader some idea of what would be involved in drawing out all of the implications of the central theses of this work.

Branching out

The proposals developed in this book have consequences for a range of issues, some of them much broader in scope than the philosophy of arithmetic. These consequences are, I think, significant enough to generate grounds for interest in the ideas developed here, regardless of how one assesses their success in the particular use to which I have put them.

I shall begin with something fairly close to home: the metaphysics of arithmetic. The views developed in this work might ground an argument for the claim that (at least some) mathematical objects exist. The argument I have in mind is this one:

(1) Certain of our arithmetical concepts are indispensable.
(2) It follows epistemically from these arithmetical concepts (and/or their compounds) that there are numbers: for instance, it follows that there is a natural number between 4 and 6.
(3) So there are numbers.

Because of the indispensability described in (1), we have reason to believe that our arithmetical concepts are justified. We ought to believe things which we can see follow epistemically from justified concepts. Hence, by (2), we ought to believe that there are numbers. There are two obvious ways to resist this conclusion; namely, by rejecting the indispensability claim (1) or by rejecting the claim that it follows from our arithmetical concepts that there are numbers, i.e. (2). I do not find either option appealing, but further discussion must await another occasion.

In metaphysics more generally, issues upon which my discussion might bear include the existence and nature of universals.[1] I have proposed an account whereby the world has real features which our concepts enable us to represent. And some of these are the sorts of features we capture in language using predicates. It might be that (some of) the features of the world corresponding to the grounded concepts we express using predicate words (at least in so far as these concepts are *directly* grounded) will be universals. This suggests an argument for the existence of universals. It could be argued that it would be miraculous that our predicate-like concepts work as well as they do unless they (or some of their ultimate constituents) were mapping real universals.

We do not immediately derive any story about which universals exist, since I have not offered any way of telling the difference between a referring concept and a merely fitting one. Nonetheless, it may be possible to make some moves in that direction by developing some of the ideas sketched in this book. For instance, suppose we had a concept that was indispensably useful but which could be decomposed into various different sets of other concepts, such that none of the concepts in any of the constituent sets was indispensable. One might take that as suggesting that all the decompositions together 'chunk matters up' in a finer-grained way than reality itself: that there was a real universal out there corresponding to the compound concept, but none corresponding to the various constituent concepts.

In addition, my definition of realism in terms of essential independence might help to clear up some of the muddles existing in various other areas of realist/anti-realist debate, where confusion with modal dependence might be creating unnecessary difficulties. It has already been applied in aesthetics (see Cooke 2007), meta-ethics (see Sinclair forthcoming) and other areas of metaphysics (see Cameron 2008 and forthcoming).

Moving on to epistemology, it is of interest to note that my proposal suggests a new way to defend a kind of empirical foundationalism. Traditionally,

---

[1] Thanks to Hugh Mellor for a helpful discussion on this topic.

empirical foundationalism is taken to be the view that certain 'observational' propositions are known immediately through experience, and all other (empirical) knowledge rests on these: they are the foundation for all the rest. But we might now aim to develop a foundationalism which is a variation on the extant varieties: one whereby the foundation is not simply a set of observational beliefs but may include a set of directly grounded concepts.

We can then reply to a standard objection to empirical foundationalism: namely, that the truth of the supposedly foundational propositions cannot be 'given' because these propositions can only be known once we impose our concepts upon our sensory input. As Blackburn puts it (1984: 198), the question for the foundationalist is: 'We have to see our concepts as the product of our own intellectual stances: how then are they suitable means for framing objectively correct, true, judgement, describing the mind–independent world as it in fact is?'. This objection is commonly used by those with coherentist leanings to demolish prima facie more plausible alternatives; see, for example, Sellars's famous attack on the 'Myth of the Given' (1956). It is described as 'the well-known trouble with [the] "foundationalist" approach' by Larmore (2002; emphasis added). But a sophisticated foundationalism along the lines I propose has the resources to avoid it. Let us see how, by spelling out the objection in a little more detail.

Larmore puts the problem particularly clearly: 'the Given cannot serve as a justification for a belief, if it lacks conceptual articulation; yet to the extent that it is shaped by an understanding of the world we already possess, it cannot count as simply "given"' (p. 196). It may be right to say that in order to justify one in believing a proposition, one's sensory input must be processed in various ways involving conceptualization. (At least, I am prepared to grant this for the sake of argument to the anti-foundationalist.) But what I propose is that unconceptualized sensory input can justify one in the epistemically more basic matter of possessing a concept. Once this possibility is acknowledged, Larmore's dilemma dissolves: we accept the truth of the first horn, the claim that conceptual articulation is required in order for sensory input to justify a belief, but we do not thereby impale ourselves upon the second horn. For provided that conceptualized sensory input is 'shaped' by an 'understanding' which is itself shaped by what is given to us in unconceptualized sensory input, there is no reason to think that this understanding in any way *distorts* our experience of the world. Rather, we can say that the conceptual shape of our sensory input probably reflects the structure of the world. We can continue to regard conceptualized experience as wholly 'given', since the concepts which shape it are themselves shaped in response to what is 'given' in unconceptualized experience.

If this is correct, foundationalism surely finds itself on a new and more secure footing. This could have profound consequences for the way we view our epistemic relationship to the world. Some philosophers (following e.g. Sellars 1956) tend to consider naive the claim that the world can be coherently thought of as independent of ourselves and our ways of interpreting it. If foundationalism can be defended along the lines suggested here, this attitude ought to be reconsidered.

A different kind of attempt to refute the view that the given is a myth has been made by Fales (1996). Fales, however, only argues that we cannot *assume* that concepts are arbitrary impositions upon sensory input (pp. 96−8). He does not attempt to give us any positive reason to think this is *not* how concepts function. He says that 'the objector is [not] in a position to know that an initially undifferentiated input has had imposed upon it an arbitrary grid of concepts'. But this does not seem to be enough to defend the given. We plausibly also need to motivate the claim that *we* are in a position to claim that our concepts are *not* an 'arbitrary grid'. For all Fales says, we should be sceptical about the given (even if we no longer reject it outright), since we have no reason to suppose either that our concepts carve up sensory input in ways that reflect the structure of the independent world, or that they do not.

Fales does not consider the possibility of our possessing justification for our concepts in the sense I have defended. This results not only in a much weaker defence of the given, but also in his resorting to a very traditional account of a priori knowledge (see pp. 155−65), which amounts to little more than the claim that a priori knowable propositions have some special quality in virtue of which they are 'luminous' and 'transparent'. All Fales has to say about this quality is that everyone knows what it is:

The terms 'transparent' and 'luminous' which I have employed in characterizing *a priori* judgements are, even more obviously than Descartes's terms 'clear' and 'distinct', metaphorical. Nevertheless, they point to a feature of our apprehension of propositions and inferences with which we are intimately familiar. I do not see how anyone could complain that it is obscure what that feature is.

(p. 161)

As well as helping defend foundationalism, accounts like mine might help resolve tricky issues surrounding other problematic kinds of knowledge besides arithmetic, especially other kinds of a priori knowledge like knowledge of other parts of mathematics, and of logic. They might even be of use in ethics: we may perhaps gain some insights by thinking about whether we have epistemic justification for our ethical concepts, rather than concentrating solely on whether we have epistemic justification for our ethical beliefs. I hope to pursue this possibility in future work.

Let me now turn to a couple of issues in the philosophy of language. I mentioned in Section 5.6 above that my discussion suggests an empiricist theory of meaningfulness which, unlike the traditional verificationist theory, considers the relation between experience and justification for concepts (not just that between experience and confirmation for propositions) to be of primary importance.

I also think that that my proposal points to a novel kind of defence of the correspondence intuition in the theory of truth: instead of considering only a proposition's 'correspondence to the facts', we should also consider the correspondence between *parts* of the proposition and parts of the world (a 'correspondence-as-congruence' view: see Kirkham 1998). Given that our concepts are grounded, this manoeuvre (not original in itself) will now enable us to do something new; namely, avoid a certain kind of objection. The objection is similar to the above-mentioned objection to empirical foundationalism. Like foundationalism, correspondence theories are accused of committing one to the naive 'myth of the given'. Blackburn (1984: ch. 7, sects. 1, 4) describes this kind of objection, pointing out that correspondence theories of truth, if they are to be anything other than platitudinous, require that we can conceive of 'the facts' as independent of us and our representational schemes, in order that 'the facts' can provide a non-trivial standard of truth for representations within those schemes. But, it is objected, facts cannot be like that, because the facts, at least in so far as we are receptive or responsive to them, are inseparable (in some significant sense) from an element which is provided by our own concepts. Blackburn (pp. 233–4) puts the point this way: 'the correspondence invitation to truth has often seemed tied to a view which emphasizes an element of "the given": some bare unvarnished presentation of fact to a purely receptive mind', and he says that philosophers are 'virtually unanimous' in rejecting the given on the grounds that 'our conceptual powers themselves infuse and condition… experience'. This, he says, gives rise to the question: 'Is it possible to think of our beliefs as *responding* to facts, let alone corresponding to them?'.

It is not clear that this use of 'let alone' is appropriate. The issue of responsiveness seems at most epistemological, while that of correspondence-truth is intended as metaphysical. We might be incapable of responding to bare unvarnished facts, and that would be an epistemic problem for us; yet still it might be that correspondence to those very facts is what truth amounts to. However, it may be that the objection Blackburn has in mind is supposed to be underwritten by some premise to the effect that, given the epistemic difficulties raised by the lack of 'given' information, correspondence to bare unvarnished facts is not a reasonable standard for the evaluation of our beliefs and utterances, while truth *is* such a reasonable standard. It would follow that truth is not correspondence to facts, considered as fully mind-independent.

On my view, it remains true that in representing or experiencing the facts we are employing our own concepts, but this no longer suggests that the facts as described by these means should be regarded as less than fully independent, less than totally 'given'. For we may take our concepts themselves to be a map of the structure of the (independent) world. They are tools enabling us to represent the world *as it really is*. So even if our conceptual powers do infuse and condition experience, this is no threat to the view that the facts as we conceive them are truly independent of us, and hence able to supply the independent standard that the (non-platitudinous) correspondence theorist requires for truth within our representational schemes.

A reflective conclusion

I shall wind up on a speculative note, with a brief reflection on the way in which various philosophical theories of arithmetical knowledge sit with our conceptions of ourselves and our place in the universe.

In tackling the epistemology of arithmetic we are attempting to understand something quite fundamental to our mental lives. It might seem
surprising, given how fundamental it is, and given that is so clear to us
that we know about arithmetic, that it is so difficult to say *how* we know
it and what *kind* of knowledge it is. But perhaps in fact it is precisely
because arithmetic is so fundamental that its epistemology has proved so
difficult. Perhaps it is because it is obvious that $7 + 5 = 12$ that, when we
are asked how we know this, it is difficult to say more than that we *just
see* it. Rationalists have tried to flesh out this sort of instinctive response by
postulating a faculty of rational insight which enables us to 'see' such things.
Empiricists have tried to argue that arithmetical knowledge is analytic, or
conventional, or definitional, in the hope that this will obviate the need for
any substantial account of how we 'see' that $7 + 5 = 12$. Neither strategy
is philosophically satisfying.

I have proposed a new approach to arithmetical knowledge in response
to what seems to me to be the one overriding difficulty facing all extant
discussions on this topic; namely, that of reconciling the independence and
aprioricity of arithmetic with empiricism. The solution I propose is that
arithmetic is known a priori through an examination of our arithmetical
concepts, but that these concepts are empirically *grounded*: they are not
just our artefacts, but rather form a sort of map of the structure of the
world. This means that by examining them we can come to know not
just facts about ourselves, but facts about the arithmetical structure of the
independent world.

In reflective moments we might understand this situation as follows.
Traditional rationalism postulates that we possess a quasi-supernatural
faculty, a sort of divine spark, giving us access to glimpses of arithmetical
creation. We humans are (typically) supposed to be different from other
animals in possessing this divine spark of reason, enabling us to appreciate to
a much higher level the wonders of the universe. The view sits comfortably
with the Christian conception of ourselves as created by God in His image,
to rule over the rest of creation, and possessing, to some degree, elements
of (quasi-)divine intelligence to fit us to this role.

Empiricists reject the claim that we have such supernatural-sounding
powers. In its place, they have traditionally tried to make out that arithmetical truth is created by us through our conventions or stipulations about
meaning, so that knowledge of arithmetic is knowledge of our language,

our own artefact. (Kant, though not an empiricist in any conventional sense, tried to do something similar.) Adopting this sort of position sits well with viewing *ourselves* as (Godlike) creators and manipulators. The move is from a God-centred to a human-centred perspective. (Kant's move to humanocentrism is explicit: he regards it as a 'Copernican' revolution: Bxvi–xvii.)

And what about the view I propose? I argue that arithmetic is *neither* known through supernatural insight *nor* created by us. To learn arithmetic, I say, is to learn something about the natural world, and to learn it in a natural way, through the use of our ordinary information-gathering mechanisms, the senses. I also happen to reject both God-centred and human-centred ways of thinking about the world. This seems to me a natural combination of perspectives: I say that our arithmetical knowledge does not constitute evidence of a Godlike status, but nor is it knowledge of our own creation. We have no divine spark of rational insight, and nor do we have Godlike creative powers. Correspondingly, I happen to believe that neither a God nor we ourselves are of central importance in the universe. The skills on which some have tried to base our claim to special significance are merely the natural skills developed by a certain kind of animal trying to succeed within its environment by understanding it.

My views on arithmetical knowledge, then, sit most comfortably with an attitude of thoroughgoing philosophical humility, whereby we assign to ourselves no greater place in the scheme of things than that of a small and ordinary part of a perfectly natural universe.

Glossary

Several key terms are defined and discussed on pp. 119 ff. and 126 ff.

A posteriori knowledge: Knowledge which is not a priori.

A priori knowledge: Knowledge secured without epistemic reliance on any empirical evidence.

Accurate concept: See *Relevantly accurate concept*.

Analytic: Notions of analyticity are not appealed to in this work, except when discussing others' views.

Basic concept: A *directly grounded concept* (q.v.).

Camera-brain hypothesis: The hypothesis that concepts are grounded because their acquisition is an appropriate response to sensory input.

Concepts: Sub-propositional mental representations, related to propositional mental representations in more or less the way that words and sub-sentential groups of words are related to sentences.

Conceptual truth: A true proposition whose truth *follows epistemically* (q.v.) from certain of our concepts.

Correct composition of concepts: Composition that, non-accidentally, does not smuggle in extra content.

Directly grounded concept: A concept that is grounded, but not (merely) in virtue of being composed of other grounded concepts.

Disjustified concept: A concept which it is rationally respectable for us to treat as not being an accurate guide to the world.

Empirical foundationalism: The view that all knowledge rests on empirical foundations. Typically these foundations are taken to be basic empirically grounded beliefs, but in my view the empirical foundations of knowledge may include directly grounded concepts.

Empirical knowledge: Knowledge secured in a way which involves some epistemic use of the senses (i.e. in which the senses are used not merely to awaken or prepare the mind; they actually supply, or help supply, the knowledge in question).

Empiricism: The view that all our knowledge of the mind-independent world either is, or else ultimately rests upon, *empirical knowledge* (q.v.).

Essential Independence: p is essentially independent of q just in case it is no part of *what it is* for p to be the case that q be the case.

Evidence: Evidence for a proposition is epistemic support for that proposition.

Externalism about knowledge/justification/grounding: The rejection of the constraints on knowledge/justification/grounding imposed by *internalism* (q.v.).

Filter-brain hypothesis: The hypothesis that concepts are grounded because their retention is an appropriate response to sensory input.

Fitting concept: A concept which either refers, or else is a correct compound (see *Correct composition of concepts*) of referring concepts, or else is a correct compound of correct compounds of referring concepts, etc.

Follows epistemically: A true proposition p follows epistemically from certain concepts iff a correctly conducted examination of those concepts would suffice to ground a belief in p which, assuming there is nothing wrong with the concepts, will amount to knowledge. I also say that a proposition p which is not true follows epistemically from certain concepts iff someone who used those concepts could, after and on the basis of a correctly conducted examination of them, form a belief that p which would have counted as knowledge had there not been something wrong with the concepts.

Grounded concept: A non-accidentally *accurate* (q.v.) concept.

Internalism about knowledge/justification/grounding: The view that in order to have knowledge/be justified/have a grounded concept one must be aware (or at least capable of becoming aware) of what one's grounds are or what one's justification is.

Justificatory concept holism/molecularism: The view that concepts are justified either all at once (holism) or in smaller bundles (molecularism), rather than individually.

Justified concept: A concept which it is rationally respectable for us to rely on as an *accurate* (q.v.) concept.

Rationalism: A view which at minimum rejects *empiricism* (q.v.), and may additionally posit some particular 'rational' (non-experiential) source of knowledge of the mind-independent world.

Realism: Mind-independence realism; the view that how things stand with regard to a subject matter is essentially independent (see *Essential independence*) of our mental lives.

Referring concept: A concept which is a representation of some real feature of the world.

Relevantly accurate concept: A concept C is relevantly accurate (or, sometimes, just accurate) iff C is fitting and neither C, nor any concept from which C is composed, misrepresents its referent in any respect relevant to our current purposes.

Semantic concept holism/molecularism: The view that (among concepts) the primary units of meaning are whole conceptual schemes (holism) or smaller bundles of concepts (molecularism), rather than individual concepts.

Seriously inaccurate concept: A concept which is too inaccurate to count as *fitting* (q.v.).

Ultimate constituents of a concept: A grammatically useful turn of phrase which does not imply conceptual atomism. Something is true of a concept's ultimate constituents iff this thing is true either of its constituents, or of the constituents of its constituents, or of their constituents, etc.

References

Armstrong, D. (1973), *Belief, Truth and Knowledge* (Cambridge: Cambridge University Press).

Ayer, A. J. (1936), *Language, Truth, and Logic*; 2nd ed. [1946] (London: Gollantz).

Ayers, M. (1991), *Locke, i. Epistemology* (London: Routledge).

Baker, A. (2005), 'Are There Genuine Mathematical Explanations of Physical Phenomena?', in *Mind*, 114: 223–38.

Bealer, G. (1992), 'The Incoherence of Empiricism', in *Proceedings of the Aristotelian Society*, suppl. vol. 66: 99–138.

——— (2000), 'A Theory of the A Priori', in *Pacific Philosophical Quarterly*, 81: 1–30.

Benacerraf, P. (1973), 'Mathematical Truth', in *Journal of Philosophy*, 70: 661–79.

Berkeley, G. (1710), *Treatise Concerning the Principles of Human Knowledge*, ed. R. Woolhouse, in *Principles of Human Knowledge and Three Dialogues Between Hylas and Philonous* (London: Penguin, 1988).

——— (1713), *Three Dialogues Between Hylas and Philonous*, ed. R. Woolhouse, in *Principles of Human Knowledge and Three Dialogues Between Hylas and Philonous* (London: Penguin, 1988).

Blackburn, S. (1980), 'Truth, Realism and the Regulation of Theory', in *Midwest Studies in Philosophy*, 5; repr. in his *Essays in Quasi-realism* (Oxford: Oxford University Press, 1993), 15–34.

——— (1981), 'Rule-following and Moral Realism', in S. Holtzman and C. Leich (eds.), *Wittgenstein: To Follow a Rule* (London: Routledge & Kegan Paul), 163–87.

——— (1984), *Spreading the Word* (Oxford: Clarendon).

——— (1988), 'How To Be an Ethical Anti-realist', in *Midwest Studies in Philosophy*, 22; repr. in his *Essays in Quasi-realism* (Oxford: Oxford University Press, 1993), 166–81.

——— (2005), 'Success Semantics', in H. Lillehammer and D. H. Mellor (eds.), *Ramsey's Legacy* (Oxford: Oxford University Press), 22–36.

——— (2006), 'George Berkeley and Julius Caesar Play Leapfrog', in C. MacDonald and G. MacDonald (eds.), *McDowell and his Critics*, (Oxford: Blackwell), 203–17.

Blanchette, P. (1998), 'Realism in the Philosophy of Mathematics', in E. Craig (ed.), *Routledge Encyclopaedia of Philosophy* (London: Routledge). Available at <http://www.rep.routledge.com/article/Y066>.

Boghossian, P. (1996), 'Analyticity Reconsidered', in *Noûs*, 30: 360–91.

Boghossian, P. (1997), 'Analyticity', in B. Hale and C. Wright (eds.), *The Blackwell Companion to the Philosophy of Language* (Oxford: Blackwell), 331–68.

—— (2003), 'Epistemic Analyticity: A Defense', in H.-J. Glock, K. Glüer, and G. Keil (eds.), *Fifty Years of Quine's 'Two Dogmas'* (*Grazer Philosophische Studien*, 66) (Amsterdam: Rodopi), 15–35.

BonJour, L. (1998), *In Defence of Pure Reason: A Rationalist Account of A Priori Justification* (Cambridge: Cambridge University Press).

—— (2005), 'In Defense of the *A Priori*', in M. Steup and E. Sosa (eds.), *Contemporary Debates in Epistemology* (Oxford: Blackwell), 98–105.

BonJour, L., and Sosa, E. (2003), *Epistemic Justification: Internalism vs. Externalism, Foundations vs. Virtues* (Oxford: Blackwell).

Boolos, G. (1997), 'Is Hume's Principle Analytic?', in R. Heck (ed.), *Language, Thought and Logic* (Oxford: Oxford University Press, 1997); repr. in G. Boolos, *Logic, Logic and Logic* (Cambridge, Mass.: Harvard University Press, 1998), 301–14.

Bostock, D. (1990), 'Logic and Empiricism', in *Mind*, 99: 571–82.

Boyd, R. (1981), 'Scientific Realism and Naturalistic Epistemology', in P. Asquith and R. Giere (eds.), *PSA 1980*, ii (East Lansing: Philosophy of Science Association), 613–62.

—— (1984), 'The Current Status of the Realism Debate', in J. Leplin (ed.), *Scientific Realism* (Berkeley Calif.: University of California Press), 41–82.

Brandom, R. (1994), *Making It Explicit: Reasoning, Representing and Discursive Commitment* (Cambridge, Mass.: Harvard University Press).

Brewer, B. (1999), *Perception and Reason* (Oxford: Oxford University Press).

Butcharov, P. (1970), *The Concept of Knowledge* (Evanston, Ill.: Northwestern University Press).

Butterworth, B. (1999), *The Mathematical Brain* (London: Macmillan).

Cameron, R. (2008), 'Turtles All the Way Down: Regress, Priority and Fundamentality in Metaphysics', *Philosophical Quarterly*, 58: 1–14.

—— (forthcoming *b*), 'Truthmakers, Realism and Ontology', in R. LePoidevin and A. McGonigal (eds.), *Being: Contemporary Developments in Metaphysics* (Cambridge: Cambridge University Press).

Carnap, R. (1950), 'Empiricism, Semantics and Ontology', in *Revue Internationale de Philosophie*, 4; repr. in H. Feigl, W. Sellars, and K. Lehrer (eds.), *New Readings in Philosophical Analysis* (New York: Appleton-Century-Crofts, 1972), 585–96.

Carroll, L. (1895), 'What the Tortoise Said to Achilles', in *Mind*, 4: 278–80.

Carruthers, P. (1992), *Human Knowledge and Human Nature* (Oxford: Oxford University Press).

Casullo, A. (2000), 'The Coherence of Empiricism', in *Pacific Philosophical Quarterly*, 81: 31–48.

——(2003), *A Priori Justification* (Oxford: Oxford University Press).

Chappell, V. (1994), 'Locke's Theory of Ideas', in V. Chappell (ed.), *The Cambridge Companion to Locke* (Cambridge: Cambridge University Press), 26–55.

Chisholm, R. (1977), 'The Truths of Reason', in his *Theory of Knowledge*, 2nd edn.; repr. in P. Moser (ed.), *A Priori Knowledge* (Oxford: Oxford University Press, 1987), 112–44.

Cicovacki, P. (1990), 'Locke on Mathematical Knowledge', in *Journal of the History of Philosophy*, 28: 511–24.

Colyvan, M. (2001), *The Indispensability of Mathematics* (Oxford: Oxford University Press).

Cook, R. (2001), 'The State of the Economy: Neo-logicism and Inflation', in *Philosophia Mathematica*, 10: 43–66.

Cooke, B. (2007), 'Imagining Art', in *British Journal of Aesthetics*, 47: 29–45.

Cowie, F. (1999), *What's Within? Nativism Reconsidered* (Oxford: Oxford University Press).

Craig, E. (1975), 'The Problem of Necessary Truth', in S. Blackburn (ed.), *Meaning, Reference and Necessity* (Cambridge: Cambridge University Press, 1975), 1–31.

——(1990), *Knowledge and the State of Nature* (Oxford: Clarendon).

——(1998), 'Realism and Antirealism', in E. Craig (ed.), *Routledge Encyclopaedia of Philosophy* (London: Routledge). Available at <http://www.rep.routledge.com/article/N049>.

Dancy, J. (1985), *Introduction to Contemporary Epistemology* (Oxford: Blackwell).

Davies, M. (2000), 'Externalism and Armchair Knowledge', in P. Boghossian and C. Peacocke (eds.), *New Essays on the A Priori* (Oxford: Clarendon).

Detlefsen, M. (1992) (ed.), *Proof and Knowledge in Mathematics* (London: Routledge).

Donnellan, K. (1966), 'Reference and Definite Descriptions', in *Philosophical Review*, 75: 281–304.

Dretske, F. (1970), 'Epistemic Operators', in *Journal of Philosophy*, 67: 1007–23.

Dummett, M. (1959), 'Wittgenstein's Philosophy of Mathematics', in *Philosophical Review*, 68: repr. in his *Truth and Other Enigmas* (London: Duckworth 1978), 166–85.

——(1963), 'Realism', in his *Truth and Other Enigmas* (London: Duckworth, 1978), 145–65.

——(1973a), 'The Justification of Deduction', British Academy lecture; repr. in his *Truth and Other Enigmas* (London: Duckworth, 1978), 290–318.

——(1973b), *Frege: Philosophy of Language* (London: Duckworth).

Dummett, M. (1975), 'The Philosophical Basis of Intuitionistic Logic', in H. Rose and J. Shepherdson (eds.), *Logic Colloquium '73* (Amsterdam: North Holland); repr. in his *Truth and Other Enigmas* (London: Duckworth, 1978), 215–47.

—— (1982), 'Realism', in *Synthese*, 52; repr. in Dummett (1993), 230–76.

—— (1991), *The Logical Basis of Metaphysics* (London: Duckworth).

—— (1993), *The Seas of Language* (Oxford: Oxford University Press).

Ebert, P. (2005), 'Transmission of Warrant-Failure and the Notion of Epistemic Analyticity', in *Australasian Journal of Philosophy*, 83: 505–21.

Eklund, M. (2002), 'Inconsistent Languages', in *Philosophy and Phenomenological Research*, 64: 251–75.

Evans, G. (1982), *Varieties of Reference* (Oxford: Clarendon).

Fales, E. (1996), *A Defence of the Given* (London: Rowman & Littlefield).

Feferman, S. (1993), 'Why a Little Bit Goes a Long Way: Logical Foundations of Scientifically Applicable Mathematics', in *Proceedings of the Philosophy of Science Association*, 2; repr. in his *In The Light of Logic* (Oxford: Oxford University Press, 1998) 284–98.

Feldman, R. (2000), 'The Ethics of Belief', in *Philosophy and Phenomenological Research*, 60: 667–95.

Field, H. (1980), *Science Without Numbers: A Defence of Nominalism* (Oxford: Blackwell).

—— (1988), 'Realism, Mathematics and Modality', in *Philosophical Topics*, 19: 57–107; repr. in Field (1989) 227–81.

—— (1989), *Realism, Mathematics, and Modality* (Oxford: Blackwell).

—— (2000), 'Apriority as an Evaluative Notion', in P. Boghossian and C. Peacocke (eds.) *New Essays on the A Priori* (Oxford: Clarendon) 117–49.

—— (2006), 'Recent Debates About the A Priori', in T. Gendler and J. Hawthorne (eds.), *Oxford Studies in Epistemology* (Oxford: Oxford University Press) 69–88.

Fine, K. (1994), 'Essence and Modality: The Second Philosophical Perspectives Lecture', in *Philosophical Perspectives*, 8: 1–16.

Fisher, J. (2002), 'Revising Logic: Where the A Priori Meets the Empirical', Ph.D. thesis (City University of New York).

Fodor, J. (1975), *The Language of Thought* (New York: Crowell).

—— (1998), *Concepts: Where Cognitive Science Went Wrong* (Oxford: Clarendon).

Fodor, J., and Pylyshyn, Z. (1988), 'Connectionism and Cognitive Architecture: A Critical Analysis', in *Cognition*, 28: 3–71.

Foley, R. (1985), 'What's Wrong with Reliabilism?', in *Monist*, 68; repr. in S. Bernecke and F. Dretske (eds.), *Knowledge: Readings in Contemporary Epistemology* (Oxford: Oxford University Press, 2000), 166–77.

Frege, G. (1884), *Foundations of Arithmetic [Die Grundlagen Der Arithmetik]*, trans. J. L. Austin (Oxford: Blackwell, 1950).

Fricker, E. (2003), 'Understanding and Knowledge of What is Said', in A. Barber (ed.), *Epistemology of Language* (Oxford: Oxford University Press), 325–66.

Garfinkel, A. (1981), *Forms of Explanation* (New Haven: Yale University Press).

Gettier, E. (1963), 'Is Justified True Belief Knowledge?', in *Analysis*, 23: 121–3.

Gibbard, A. (1990), *Wise Choices, Apt Feelings* (Oxford: Clarendon).

Glüer, K. (2003), 'Analyticity and Implicit Definition', in H.-J. Glock, K. Glüer, and G. Keil (eds.), *Fifty Years of Quine's 'Two Dogmas' (Grazer Philosophische Studien, 66)* (Amsterdam: Rodopi), 37–60.

Gödel, K. (1947), 'What is Cantor's Continuum Problem?', *American Mathematical Monthly*, 54: repr. in P. Benacerraf and H. Putnam (eds.), *Philosophy of Mathematics* (Cambridge: Cambridge University Press, 1964), 258–73.

Goldman, Alan (1988), *Empirical Knowledge* (Berkeley, Calif.: University of California Press).

Goldman, Alvin (1967), 'A Causal Theory of Knowing', in *Journal of Philosophy*, 64: 355–72.

Goodman, N. (1954), *Fact, Fiction and Forecast* (London: Athlone).

Grice, H. P., and Strawson, P. (1956), 'In Defence of a Dogma', in *Philosophical Review*, 65: 141–58.

Hale, B. (1994), 'Is Platonism Epistemologically Bankrupt?', in *Philosophical Review*, 103: repr. in Hale and Wright (2001), 169–88.

—— (1997), 'Grundlagen §64', in *Proceedings of the Aristotelian Society*, 97; repr. in Hale and Wright (2001), 91–116.

—— (2000), 'Reals By Abstraction', in *Philosophia Mathematica*, 8; repr. in Hale and Wright (2001), 399–420.

Hale, B., and Wright, C. (2000), 'Implicit Definition and the A Priori', in P. Boghossian and C. Peacocke (eds.), *New Essays on the A Priori* (Oxford: Clarendon), 286–319.

—— (2001), *The Reason's Proper Study* (Oxford: Oxford University Press).

Hawthorne, J. (2004), *Knowledge and Lotteries* (Oxford: Clarendon).

Hellman, G. (1989), *Mathematics Without Numbers* (Oxford: Oxford University Press).

Horwich, P. (1997), 'Implicit Definition, Analytic Truth and A Priori Knowledge', in *Noûs*, 31: 423–40.

Hume, D. (1748), *An Enquiry Concerning Human Understanding*. ed. T. L. Beauchamp (Oxford: Oxford University Press, 1999).

Isaacson, D. (1996), 'Arithmetical Truth and Hidden Higher-Order Concepts', in W. D. Hart (ed.), *The Philosophy of Mathematics*, (Oxford: Oxford University Press). (Reprinted with revisions from Paris Logic Group (eds.), *Logic Colloquium '85: Proceedings of the Colloquium held in Orsay, France, July 1985*, (Amsterdam: North-Holland), 203–24.

Jackson, F. (1998), *From Metaphysics to Ethics: A Defense of Conceptual Analysis* (Oxford: Oxford University Press).

Jenkins, C. (2005*a*), 'Realism and Independence', in *American Philosophical Quarterly*, 42: 199–211.

——(2005*b*), 'Knowledge of Arithmetic', in *British Journal for the Philosophy of Science*, 56: 727–47.

——(2006), 'Knowledge and Explanation', in *Canadian Journal of Philosophy*, 36: 137–63.

——(2007*a*). 'Epistemic Norms and Natural Facts', in *American Philosophical Quarterly*, 44: 259–72.

——(2007*b*). 'Entitlement and Epistemic Rationality', in *Synthese*, 157: 25–45.

——(2008*a*), 'Boghossian and Epistemic Analyticity', in *Croatian Journal of Philosophy*, 8: 113–27.

——(*b*), 'Romeo, René and the Reasons Why: What Explanation Is', in *Proceedings of the Aristotelian Society*.

——(2008*b*), 'A Priori Knowledge', in *Philosophy Compass*.

——(forthcoming *a*), 'Concepts, Experience and Modal Knowledge', in R. Cameron, B. Hale, and A. Hoffman (eds.), *The Logic, Epistemology and Metaphysics of Modality* (Oxford: Oxford University Press).

Jenkins, C., and Nolan, D., (forthcoming), 'Backwards Explanation', *Philosophical Studies*.

Kant, I. (1781), *Critique of Pure Reason*, trans. N. Kemp Smith (Basingstoke: Palgrave, 1929).

Ketland, J. (2002), 'Hume = Small Hume', in *Analysis*, 62: 92–3.

Kirkham, R. (1998), 'Truth, Correspondence Theory of', in E. Craig (ed.), *Routledge Encyclopaedia of Philosophy* (London: Routledge). Available at <http://www.rep.routledge.com/article/N064>.

Kitcher, P. (1989), 'Explanatory Unification and the Causal Structure of the World', in P. Kitcher and W. Salmon (eds.), *Scientific Explanation* (Minnesota, Minn: University of Minnesota Press), 410–505.

Kornblith, H. (2001) (ed.), *Epistemology: Internalism and Externalism* (Oxford: Blackwell).

Kripke, S. (1980), *Naming and Necessity* (Oxford: Blackwell).

——(1982), *Wittgenstein on Rules and Private Language* (Oxford: Blackwell).

Larmore, C. (2002), 'Attending to Reasons', in N. Smith (ed.), *Reading McDowell: On Mind and World* (London: Routledge), 193–208.

Laurence, S., and Margolis, E. (2001), 'Boghossian on Analyticity', in *Analysis*, 61: 293–302.

——(2003), 'Concepts and Conceptual Analysis', in *Philosophy and Phenomenological Research*, 67: 253–82.

—— (2006), 'Concepts', in *Stanford Encyclopedia of Philosophy*. Available at <http://www.seop.leeds.ac.uk/entries/concepts>.

Lewis, C. I. (1923), 'A Pragmatic Conception of the A Priori', in *Journal of Philosophy*, 20: 169–77; repr. in his *Collected Papers*, ed. J. Goheen and J. Mothershead (Stanford, Calif.: Stanford University Press, 1970), 231–9.

—— (1926), 'The Pragmatic Element in Knowledge', in *University of California Publications in Philosophy*, 6; repr. in his *Collected Papers*, ed. J. Goheen and J. Mothershead (Stanford, Calif.: Stanford University Press, 1970), 240–57.

—— (1930), 'Logic and Pragmatism', in his *Collected Papers*, ed. J. Goheen and J. Mothershead (Stanford, Calif.: Stanford University Press, 1970), 3–19.

Lewis, D. (1973), *Counterfactuals* (Oxford: Blackwell).

—— (1979), 'Scorekeeping in a Language Game', in *Journal of Philosophical Logic*; repr. in his *Philosophical Papers*, i (Oxford: Oxford University Press, 1983), 233–49.

—— (1986), 'Causal Explanation' in his *Philosophical Papers*, ii (Oxford: Oxford University Press), 214–40.

—— (1996), 'Elusive Knowledge', in *Australasian Journal of Philosophy*, 74; repr. in his *Papers in Metaphysics and Epistemology* (Cambridge: Cambridge University Press, 1999), 418–45.

Lipton, P. (1990), 'Contrastive Explanation', in D. Knowles (ed.), *Explanation and its Limits* (Cambridge University Press); repr. in D.-H. Ruben (ed.), *Explanation* (Oxford: Oxford University Press, 1993), 207–27.

—— (1991), *Inference to the Best Explanation* (London: Routledge).

Locke, J. (1689), *An Essay Concerning Human Understanding*, ed. P. H. Nidditch (Oxford: Clarendon, 1975).

McDowell, J. (1981), 'Anti-Realism and the Epistemology of Understanding', in H. Parret and J. Bouveresse (eds.), *Meaning and Understanding* (Berlin: de Gruyer); repr. in his *Meaning, Knowledge and Reality* (Cambridge, Mass.: Harvard University Press, 2001), 314–43.

—— (1994), *Mind and World* (Cambridge, Mass.: Harvard University Press).

—— (2002), 'Response to Putnam', in N. Smith (ed.), *Reading McDowell: On Mind and World* (London: Routledge), 292–3.

Mackie, J. (1976), *Problems From Locke* (Oxford: Clarendon).

Maddy, P. (1980), 'Perception and Mathematical Intuition', in *Philosophical Review*, 89: 163–96.

—— (1990), *Realism in Mathematics*, (Oxford: Clarendon).

—— (1992), 'Indispensability and Practice', in *Journal of Philosophy*, 89: 275–89.

Mancosu, P. (1999), 'Bolzano and Cournot on Mathematical Explanation', *Revue d'Histoire des Sciences*, 52: 429–55.

Mancosu, P. (2000), 'On Mathematical Explanation', in E. Grosholz and H. Breger (eds.), *Growth of Mathematical Knowledge* (Dordrecht: Kluwer), 429–55.

——(2001), 'Mathematical Explanation: Problems and Prospects', in *Topoi*, 20: 97–117.

Mill, J. S. (1843), *A System of Logic* (London: Parker).

Millikan, R. (1984), *Language, Thought and Other Biological Categories: New Foundations for Realism* (Cambridge, Mass.: MIT Press).

Moore, G. E. (1903), *Principia Ethica* (Cambridge: Cambridge University Press).

——(1939), 'Proof of an External World', in *Proceedings of the British Academy*, 25; repr. in his *Philosophical Papers* (London: George Allen and Unwin, 1959), 127–50.

Moser, P. (1987), 'Introduction', in P. Moser (ed.) *A Priori Knowledge* (Oxford: Oxford University Press), 1–14.

——(1998), 'A Priori', in E. Craig (ed.), *Routledge Encyclopaedia of Philosophy* (London: Routledge). Available at <http://www.rep.routledge.com/article/P001>.

Nerlich, G. (1979), 'What Can Geometry Explain?', in *British Journal for the Philosophy of Science*, 30: 69–83.

Neta, R. (2002), 'S Knows That P', in *Noûs*, 36: 663–81.

Nolan, D. (1997), 'Impossible Worlds: A Modest Approach', in *Notre Dame Journal of Formal Logic*, 38: 535–72.

——(unpublished), 'The Dangers of Pragmatic Virtue'.

Nozick, R. (1981), *Philosophical Explanations* (Oxford: Clarendon).

O'Leary-Hawthorne, J. (1996), 'The Epistemology of Possible Worlds: A Guided Tour', in *Philosophical Studies*, 84: 183–202.

O'Leary-Hawthorne, J., and Oppy, G. (1997), 'Minimalism and Truth', in *Noûs*, 31: 170–96.

Pagin, P. (1997), 'Is Compositionality Compatible with Holism?', in *Mind and Language*, 12: 11–33.

Papineau, D. (1993), *Philosophical Naturalism* (Oxford: Blackwell).

Parsons, C. (1980), 'Mathematical Intuition', in *Proceedings of the Aristotelian Society*, 80: 145–68.

——(2004), 'Structuralism and Metaphysics', in *Philosophical Quarterly*, 54: 56–77.

Peacocke, C. (1992), *A Study of Concepts* (Cambridge, Mass.: MIT Press).

——(1993), 'How Are A Priori Truths Possible?', in *European Journal of Philosophy*, 1: 175–99.

——(1994), 'The Origins of the A Priori', in P. Parrini (ed.), *Kant and Contemporary Epistemology* (Dordrecht: Kluwer), 47–72.

——(2000), 'Explaining the A Priori: The Programme of Moderate Rationalism', in P. Boghossian and C. Peacocke (eds.), *New Essays on the A Priori* (Oxford: Clarendon), 255–85.

—— (2001), 'Does Perception Have a Nonconceptual Content?', in *Journal of Philosophy*, 98: 239–64.

—— (2004), *The Realm of Reason* (Oxford: Clarendon).

Plantinga, A. (1993), *Warrant: The Current Debate* (Oxford: Oxford University Press).

Potter, M. (1998), 'Philosophical Issues in Arithmetic', in E. Craig (ed.), *Routledge Encyclopaedia of Philosophy* (London: Routledge). Available at <http://www.rep.routledge.com/article/Y067>.

—— (2000), *Reason's Nearest Kin: Philosophies of Arithmetic from Kant to Carnap* (Oxford: Oxford University Press).

Potter, M., and Smiley, T. (2001), 'Abstraction by Recarving', in *Proceedings of the Aristotelian Society*, 101: 327–38.

—— (2002), 'Recarving Content: Hale's Final Proposal', in *Proceedings of the Aristotelian Society*, 102: 301–4.

Prior, A. (1960), 'The Runabout Inference Ticket', in *Analysis*, 21: 38–9.

Putnam, H. (1973), 'Philosophy of Logic', in *Philosophical Quarterly* 23; repr. in his *Mathematics, Matter and Method: Philosophical Papers*, i (Cambridge: Cambridge University Press, 1975), 323–57.

—— (1975), 'What is Mathematical Truth?', in his *Mathematics, Matter and Method: Philosophical Papers*, i (Cambridge: Cambridge University Press), 60–78.

—— (1979), 'Analyticity and Aprioricity: Beyond Wittgenstein and Quine', in *Midwest Studies in Philosophy*, 4; repr. in P. Moser (ed.), *A Priori Knowledge* (Oxford: Oxford University Press, 1987), 85–111.

—— (2002), 'McDowell's Mind and McDowell's World', in N. Smith (ed.), *Reading McDowell: On Mind and World* (London: Routledge), 174–90.

Quine, W. V. O. (1948), 'On What There Is', in *Review of Metaphysics*, 2; repr. in Quine (1953), 1–19.

—— (1950), 'Identity, Ostension, and Hypostasis', in *Journal of Philosophy*, 47; repr. in Quine (1953), 65–79.

—— (1951), 'Two Dogmas of Empiricism', in *Philosophical Review*; repr. in Quine (1953), 20–46.

—— (1953), *From a Logical Point of View: Nine Logico-philosophical Essays* (Cambridge, Mass.: Harvard University Press).

—— (1960), *Word and Object* (Cambridge, Mass.: MIT Press).

—— (1981), *Theories and Things* (Cambridge, Mass.: Harvard University Press).

Ramsey, F. (1927), 'Facts and Propositions', in his *Philosophical Papers*, ed. H. Mellor (Cambridge: Cambridge University Press, 1990), 34–51.

Resnik, M. (1980), *Frege and the Philosophy of Mathematics* (Ithaca, NY: Cornell University Press).

—— (1997), *Mathematics as Science of Patterns* (Oxford: Clarendon).

Resnik, M., and Kushner, D. (1987), 'Explanation, Independence and Realism in Mathematics', in *British Journal for the Philosophy of Science*, 38: 141–58.

Rey, G. (1998), 'Concepts', in E. Craig (ed.), *Routledge Encyclopaedia of Philosophy* (London: Routledge). Available at <http://www.rep.routledge.com/article/W008>.

Rieber, S. (1998), 'Skepticism and Contrastive Explanation', in *Noûs*, 32: 189–204.

Russell, B. (1903), *The Principles of Mathematics*, [1992 edn.] (London: Routledge).

Ryle, G. (1949), *The Concept of Mind* (London: Hutchinson).

Sandborg, D. (1998), 'Mathematical Explanation and the Theory of Why-Questions', in *British Journal for the Philosophy of Science*, 49: 603–24.

Schaffer, J. (2007), 'Knowing the Answer', in *Philosophy and Phenomenological Research*, 75: 383–403.

Sedivy, S. (1996), 'Must Conceptually Informed Perceptual Experience Involve Non-Conceptual Content?', in *Canadian Journal of Philosophy*, 26: 413–31.

Sellars, W. (1956), *Empiricism and the Philosophy of Mind*, [1997 edn.] (Cambridge, Mass.: Harvard University Press).

Shapiro, S. (1997), *Philosophy of Mathematics: Structure and Ontology* (Oxford: Oxford University Press).

_____ (2000), *Thinking About Mathematics: The Philosophy of Mathematics* (Oxford: Oxford University Press).

Siegel, S. (2005), 'The Contents of Perception', in *Stanford Encyclopedia of Philosophy*. Available at <http://www.seop.leeds.ac.uk/entries/perception-contents/>.

Sinclair, N. (forthcoming), 'Free Thinking For Expressivists', in *Philosophical Papers*.

Smart, J. (1963), *Philosophy and Scientific Realism* (London: Routledge and Kegan Paul).

Smith, P. (2007), *An Introduction to Gödel's Theorems* (Cambridge: Cambridge University Press).

Sober, E. (1993), 'Mathematics and Indispensability', in *Philosophical Review*, 102: 35–57.

Stalnaker, R. (1998), 'What Might Nonconceptual Content Be?', in E. Villanueva (ed.), *Philosophical Issues*, 9 (Atascadero, Calif.: Ridgeview); repr. in Y. Gunther (ed.), *Essays on Nonconceptual Content* (Cambridge, Mass.: MIT Press, 2003), 95–106.

Steiner, M. (1978), 'Mathematical Explanation', in *Philosophical Studies*, 34: 135–51.

Tarski, A. (1935), 'The Concept of Truth in Formalized Languages', pub. in Polish in *Studia Philosophica*, 1, trans. J. H. Woodger in his *Logic, Semantics, Metamathematics: Papers from 1923 to 1938* (Oxford: Clarendon, 1956), 152–278.

Tennant, N. (1997), *The Taming of the True* (Oxford: Clarendon).

Urquhart, A. (1986), 'Many-Valued Logic', in D. Gabbay and F. Guenthner (eds.), *Handbook of Philosophical Logic, iii. Alternatives To Classical Logic* (Dordrecht: Reidel; 2nd edn. Kluwer), 71–116.

van Fraassen, B. (1980), *The Scientific Image* (Oxford: Clarendon).

Whyte, J. (1990), 'Success Semantics', in *Analysis*, 50: 149–57.

Williamson, T. (2000), *Knowledge and its Limits* (Oxford: Oxford University Press).

—— (2007), 'Philosophical Knowledge and Knowledge of Counterfactuals', in C. Beyer and A. Burri (eds.), *Philosophical Knowledge: Its Possibility and Scope* (Amsterdam: Rodopi), 89–123.

—— (2008), *The Philosophy of Philosophy* (Oxford: Blackwell).

Wittgenstein, L. (1922), *Tractatus Logico-Philosophicus*, [1961 edn.], trans. D. F. Pears and B. F. McGuinness (London: Routledge and Kegan Paul).

Woolhouse, R. (1994), 'Locke's Theory of Knowledge', in V. Chappell (ed.), *The Cambridge Companion to Locke* (Cambridge: Cambridge University Press), 146–71.

Wright, C. (1984), 'Kripke's Account of the Argument Against Private Language', in *Journal of Philosophy*, 81: 759–78.

—— (1986), *Realism, Meaning, and Truth*, 2nd edn., 1993 (Oxford: Blackwell).

—— (1997), 'On The Philosophical Significance of Frege's Theorem', in R. Heck (ed.), *Language, Thought and Logic: Essays in Honour of Michael Dummett* (Oxford: Clarendon); repr. in Hale and Wright (2001), 272–306.

—— (2004), 'On Epistemic Entitlement: Warrant For Nothing (And Foundations For Free?)', in *Proceedings of the Aristotelian Society*, suppl. vol., 78: 167–212.

Yablo, S. (2002), 'Abstract Objects: A Case Study', in E. Sosa and E. Villanueva (eds.), *Realism and Relativism* (*Philosophical Issues*, 12) (Oxford: Blackwell), 220–40.

Index

Page numbers *in italics* refer to text containing either a definition or a detailed discussion. Page numbers **in bold type** refer to entries in the glossary.